AF322586

Code Name
Delilah

Donald de Brier

Library of Congress Cataloging-in-Publication Data

Name: Donald de Brier
Title: Code Name Delilah | Donald de Brier
Identifiers:
ISBN 979-8-88589-068-7 (hardcover)
ISBN 979-8-88589-050-2 (softcover)
ISBN 979-8-88589-051-9 (eBook)
 ISBN 979-8-88589-052-6 (audiobook)

Printed in the United States of America

First Edition: 2022

Interior design by Michael Grossman
Illustrated cover design by Jack Baker
Photographic cover design by Lynn Andreozzi

Table of Contents

1942 – The US Enters the Fray

Preface

We were taught in our high school history classes that WWII in Europe ended on May 8, 1945, when what was left of the German government surrendered to the Allies. The Soviets commemorate it every year on May 9th. Whichever date you celebrate, it is largely a myth. The echoes, repercussions and shadows of that cataclysmic War continue to reverberate, haunt us, and stalk us to this very day—75 years later. Like all these viral and bacterial epidemics now so familiar to us, that bloody War lives on and on, and refuses to go away.

In the years immediately following the "End of the War," Germany, which "lost the War," was in ruins. Its economy was gone. Most of its major cities were shattered from years of deadly bombings by Allied bombers. Its total population reduced by 20%. (When I first visited Germany in 1960, the extent of the destruction there was astonishing.) Italy, which also "lost the War," was also in ruins. France and the rest of Western Europe were suffering from widespread destruction. England and the USSR, which "won the War," were on the verge of total economic collapse.

Thanks in large part to the visionary 1948 US Marshall Plan, Europe was able to make an economic recovery, but so many of the scars remain. And included in the aftermath were years of anti-colonial wars, the blockade of Berlin, major wars in Korea and Vietnam and elsewhere, and the Cuban Missile Crisis. And now the Russian invasion of Ukraine. And we thought it all ended in 1945? Really?

WWII and its aftermath broadly shaped the Europe we know today, and also shaped the current North Atlantic Alliances so strategic to our mutual defense.

Seventy-five years later, most of the major nation states of Europe have not changed their stripes, in so many fundamental ways. The Third Reich is gone, but a united Germany does now dominate Continental Europe. Germany and France are closely aligned. To a large extent, the other nation states of Europe fall in line with Germany and France. England, having seen its global empire greatly diminished as a result of the War, continues to keep its distance from the continental powers. The US stands in the wings. Hopefully ready, willing, and able to come to their defense. Hopefully. Ironically, NATO continue to preserve this structure. Yet another long shadow of WWII.

Russia, still the Boogie Man of Europe, remains an overwhelming presence and threat to the entire continent. Russian leaders have continued to justify their domination of all Eastern Europe as necessary to protect Russia from invasion by hostile Western countries. Nationalism rages everywhere, just like a pandemic.

And then, too, there is the overwhelming global refugee problem. That did not end in 1945. In fact, it is now even worse. Much worse. There are estimates of 40 million refugees at the end of WWII. Today there are 100 million refugees.

All these never-ending wars and ensuing problems are not being caused by little bugs or tiny proteins (genomes). All wars are started by people. And eventually ended by people. And so, this novel is largely about people. Who they were, how they came together in a very dark hour for humanity, and how they were able to turn the lights back on all over Europe. We should remember them and celebrate them, because we now must find new people to replace them, and then do it all over again. Some of these same lights are being turned off once again.

In that context, it is always worthwhile to revisit the lessons learned in and from that War. These lessons can aid us immensely as we face these same problems and these same issues again and again and again.

- Nation-states that groom and choose people who lack good sense, lack good advisors, lack basic intelligence, and lack integrity, to be their leaders will always get what they have chosen. And will always pay a heavy price for it.
- Leaders of nation-states do by and large reflect the people who put them into their positions of leadership. The people are therefore responsible for the selection and empowerment of leaders who are a reflection of their values, hopes, and aspirations, and for the removal of leaders who do not reflect these attributes. Forcing other nations to ban together to remove such leaders cannot continue to be the answer. It is just too costly and time consuming for all concerned. No Excuses.

- So if we really want to point a finger at the people who are to blame, we should point it at ourselves. If we continue to elect leaders who do not reflect our values, then eventually we must wake up to the fact that they probably do reflect our values. No Excuses.

- Hitler and his circle of misfits never hid their intentions and plans. They were very plain and very vivid for all to see. It was the responsibility of the German people themselves to put an end to it. No Excuses.

- The Russian people today bear the same responsibility. They cannot just sit back and wait for the rest of the world to fix their internal problems. No Excuses.

- As painful as it will be to remove their own failed leaders, and it will be very painful, it will be far more painful to have some other nations do it for them.

- All nations that develop new weapons of mass destruction will eventually see these weapons used against their own people.

- Any nation that bombs civilian populations of their enemies will eventually suffer the same fate at the hands of those enemies.

- WWIII will be 10 times worse than WWII. We have so many more and more effective weapons of mass destruction, much larger populations of civilians, and so much more self-righteous indignation. Ideological tolerance has almost completely disappeared. Intolerance now Rules the Roost. We all deem anyone who disagrees with our views to be not only inherently wrong, but inherently evil. Plus, increasing pandemics, global warming, widespread starvation, and huge number of refugees.

Intelligence gathering and interpretation are vital in both war and peace. That old adage, "What you don't know can't hurt you" is absolute nonsense. All too often when you do finally learn what you did not "know" it can hurt you plenty. But that old adage did seem to be the credo of the US Government on the subject of foreign intelligence gathering and interpretation in 1939. At that time, the US did not have an established over-arching government agency dedicated to the task of gathering and interpreting foreign intelligence. The US Army, the US Navy, the FBI and the US Department of State did have their own separate intelligence units, but their scope was very narrow and there was no coordination among them. Coordination is the key to effective intelligence gathering and interpretation.

In 1939, at the urging of then US Secretary of the Navy, Frank Knox, President Roosevelt began having discussions with his former Columbia Law School classmate William Joseph "Wild Bill" Donovan about starting a broader and more cohesive US intelligence activity. Notwithstanding the "what you don't know" adage, Secretary Knox was convinced that what the US Government did not know about the gathering European storm could hurt the US very badly.

Donovan himself was a fascinating person. Bigger than life in almost every way. Much admired but highly controversial. He was a highly decorated Infantry veteran of the Great War (WWI) and gained wide popularity from the Warner Brothers film The Fighting 69th in which he was portrayed as dashing war hero. Extremely handsome and a sturdy former American football player, Donovan stood out in any crowd for his stature and presence. He served as US Attorney for the Western District of New York, Assistant US Attorney General, where he broke tradition and hired women, and was an unsuccessful candidate for Governor of New York. As a New York attorney, Donovan knew that the New York Bar was a ready source of clever, thoughtful, insightful and patriotic candidates for his intelligence gathering endeavors. Even before the War, he had organized a group of international lawyers and businessmen who would meet regularly to gather and share intelligence and discuss current events. In 1941, President Roosevelt appointed Donovan as the Chief Information Officer (CIO) and empowered him to begin the formation of what became the OSS (Office of Strategic Services), now called the CIA (Central Intelligence Agency). Donovan had predicted WWII back in the mid-1930s when most Americans were not paying attention to global events. As he built the OSS, to the shock of many (including MI6), Donovan hired and trained many women spies.

Although this novel is not dedicated to Bill Donovan, it was certainly guided by his spirit and legacy.

Bill Donovan quickly learned that the British Intelligence Agencies, MI5 and MI6, were far and away the best in the world. Donovan needed these agencies to teach the Americans "the tricks of the trade," but these agencies had an even greater need for Donovan because he held sway at The White House. As events evolved, their cooperation was critical to the success of the Allied War Effort. (In spite of the working relationship, Stewart Menzies, Chief of MI6, was a bitter opponent of Bill Donovan.)

There are no secrets. Someone is always listening. As part of its intelligence gathering activities in the UK, MI6 was managing the murky Ultra Top Secret British code breaking activities in Bletchley Park, a suburb of London which housed the British Government Code and Cypher School, Code Name Ultra. These code breaking activities were carefully hidden during the war years, notwithstanding the fact that they employed over 10,000 people. Some of the employees there were brilliant mathematicians including Alan Turing. Many of them were bright, energetic young women seeking secretarial-type work in a safe environment. This book is not dedicated to the British Code Breaking activities at Bletchley Park, but the incredible successes of that endeavor leave many footprints on the pages of this novel, and on the pages of the History Books of WWII. Those footprints only became evident to the general public when the Bletchley Park secrets were first revealed in 1974 with the publication of "The Ultra Secret." Although now, as we look back on the critical events of WWII, it's hard to understand why more people didn't follow the footprints to their logical conclusion—the British had broken the German Enigma Code.

All the major military battles described in this novel were fought by the Allied soldiers, sailors, airmen and marines from various military branches on the far-flung fabled battlefields of Europe, where so many British Officers made good use of the fighting team spirit lessons they learned on those fabled playing fields of Eton and Harrow. But most of them were unaware that behind the scenes, like the Coaches' Box up above those bleachers in so many football stadiums, signals were being called by military intelligence operatives who had Ultra Secret knowledge of the enemies' game plans.

War and Peace are just two sides of the same coin. The lessons that we learn in War we must also apply to Peace.

You have been warned.

Acknowledgements

The principal purpose of this novel is to acknowledge and honor some of the highly dedicated people and their incredible contributions to the Allied war effort in WWII in Europe from 1939 through 1942. First and foremost, to acknowledge the terrible sacrifice made by men and women of the Allied Military forces, so many of whom died in the effort, and so many of whom returned to their homes with lasting physical and emotional injuries. We must also acknowledge the tens of millions of civilians who died so needlessly as "collateral damage" of the war and the additional millions of refugees who spent the war years, and many years after the War, displaced and searching for homelands. We must all remember those many millions who perished in the Holocaust, and their family members and friends who lived on without them.

Although they are not the focus of this book directly, so much of the credit must be given to Prime Minister Winston Churchill and President Franklin Delano Roosevelt.

We should acknowledge the contributions of many of the actual individuals who are identified or portrayed in the fictional scenes in the book. The following persons are listed with their significant titles as they were in 1942. Some of these titles changed over the ensuing years of the war, and thereafter.

RAF Chief of the Air Staff, Charles Frederick Algernon Portal

- Commander-in-Chief RAF Bomber Command, Arthur "Bomber" Harris
- Field Marshal General Bernard Law Montgomery
- Scientific adviser to Winston Churchill, Frederick Alexander Lindemann
- Chief of MI6 Major General Stewart Graham Menzies
- Director General of MI5, David Petrie
- British Security Coordination (BSC) for MI6, William Samuel Stephenson, Code Name Intrepid
- Director of British Operational Research, Patrick Maynard Stuart Blackett
- US Secretary of the Navy, William Franklin Knox

- US Commanding General European Theatre of Operations, Dwight David "Ike" Eisenhower
- US Chief of the Air Corps, General Henry Harley "Hap" Arnold
- US Commander of Air Force Combat Command, Carl Andrew "Tooey" Spaatz
- US Commander of the Eighth Air Force, Ira Clarence Eaker
- Head of the Office of Strategic Services (OSS), William Joseph "Wild Bill" Donovan
- Physicist J. Robert Oppenheimer, "the father of the atomic bomb" and Head of Los Alamos Laboratory
- Physicist Enrico Fermi, creator of the world's first artificial nuclear reactor
- Physicist Leo Szilard, Chief Physicist at the Chicago Metallurgical Laboratory
- New Zealand plastic surgeon, Dr. Archibald Hector McIndoe

I want to acknowledge my father, USAF Brigadier General Daniel de Brier, whose deep love of his country, the US Military forces, and the US Air Force in particular, have always been an inspiration for me.

In terms of technical and editorial assistance, I want to thank and acknowledge Elle Carling, herself a published author, for providing valued input and advice. Thanks as well to Katherine Cluverius, a highly skilled professional editor and proofreader. And many thanks to my daughter, Lesley, who thoughtfully read and commented upon every page of this novel.

On a very personal note, thanks and gratitude to my immediate family for always providing support, advice, love, and structure to my life and my work. My wife, Nancy, the light of my life, who gives proof to that ancient proverb, Home is where the Heart is. To my three daughters, Lesley, Rachel, and Danielle, now grown into strong, insightful, quick-witted, and very engaging young women. And to the newest additions, my eight energetic grandchildren.

1940

London Struggles Following the Collapse of France

1

Trouble in the London Underground

21 September 1940, London

Robert Johnston was walking back from his central London office after a lunch meeting when he heard the air raid sirens. The weather was clear and slightly crisp. Good visibility for bombing raids, he thought. His office was still several blocks away, and people were already hurrying into the London Underground bomb shelter. He quickened his step to join them there.

The warning siren, a very loud horn, sounded with increasing volume for five or six seconds, then decreased volume for five or six seconds. Repeating and repeating. Very scary. Very urgent. "Take cover!"

Robert slowed his pace as he reached the stairs, joining the crowd. As a tall American in a brown suit, he stuck out among the general British populace.

A lawyer in his mid-forties, Robert was a partner in an international law firm Stilwell & Crandon, headquartered in New York City. After managing the firm's Berlin office for several years, he had moved to London when the Berlin office closed and opened a small one-man office for the firm. His wife, Ellen, and their two young children stayed for a period, but then returned to New York, leaving Robert in London at the urgent request of his contacts in senior positions in the Roosevelt Administration. Robert's prior experience in Berlin and the US Navy, with connections in both London and Washington, made him a uniquely valuable asset as the war was developing in Europe. He could not say "no" to their request that he stay in London.

Living in Berlin during the first two years of The Third Reich, Ellen had been sickened and disgusted by what she saw there. She wanted none of the impending war. When Robert felt he had to stay in London, and stay involved, she had returned to New York and insisted on a formal separation.

Entering the shelter, shoulder to shoulder with nervous Brits of all walks of life, Robert gently pushed his way deeper inside. Although it was still daylight outside, the shelter was fairly dark. There were lights from the tunnels and in the station itself, but the darkness and crowding only added to the general unease. Although the bombing of London had been going on for quite some time, today was the first day that the London Underground, or the "Tube" as it was known, was "officially" open as a bomb shelter. It did have the advantage of being fairly far underground with adequate ventilation, and it was large enough to hold many people, but most importantly it was there. Its effectiveness as a bomb shelter was far from proven. Robert could see that it might be an ongoing impediment to Tube travel if people made a base camp on the platforms.

Robert moved on down the platform trying to escape the continuing influx of people coming down the stairs, and obeying the barking orders of the Shelter Wardens, mostly British Army enlisted men. Stepping around young and old, men and women, large and small, he found a relatively quiet, small spot to stand with his back against the solid looking wall. Then he heard the sound of German bombers overhead with their heavy, steady engines. No bombs yet. Perhaps the targets were some other parts of London. The bombers were probably the *Dornier Do 17*, the *Heinkel HEIII*, the dreaded *Junkers JU87*, and the *Junkers JU88*. Robert knew that the *Dornier Do 17's*, the backbone of the Luftwaffe bomber force, were old and slow, and no match for the RAF fighters. The *Heinkel HEIII* had a bigger bomb load, but also fared poorly against RAF fighters. The *JU87* "*Stuka*" dive bombers were ferocious in combat, but easy targets on their long-range bombing runs. But the *JU88's* were probably the best bombers available in 1940. They were fast and agile, a challenging target for RAF fighters, and would do a lot of damage. Fortunately, the Germans had only a few of them.

Over the noise of the crowded station, Robert could now hear the sound of a train coming. Ironic, he thought. The people on the platform were stuck in this crowded station on a day when German bombers were making them all wish they were somewhere else. Anywhere else. And all the people on the train were arriving from somewhere else and wanting to come into the crowded station. As the train stopped, most passengers, perceiving the plight of the people in the station, stayed on in order to go somewhere else, while those waiting in the station, hoping that the German bombers were heading somewhere else, elected to sit tight. So, the train closed its doors, and left, noisily, to be followed by a gust of air from the tunnel.

As the sound of the train moved on into the darkness and disappeared, so did the sound of the German bombers. There was no "all clear" siren, so most people hunkered down. In one corner, Robert could see some children doing their schoolwork under the tutelage of a middle-aged teacher. He gradually became aware of the British dialects he could hear. Cockney. Plenty of Irish, Scottish, Oxbridge. But he also became aware that there were foreign accents as well. Some French. Some Spanish. Some Colonials. Quite a stew, he thought to himself.

Slowly, he began to realize that he was also hearing German. German? Why would that be? German voices in a London Bomb Shelter, dodging German bombs? Seems a bit incongruous. It must have sounded the same to others, as a hush fell over the assembled masses. The German voices continued for a few minutes, and then fell silent, causing a bit of a stir. Robert could now see a tall British soldier walking his way over to the people speaking German. They were fairly close to Robert, giving him a good vantage point.

"Who are you Krauts? And what the bloody hell are you doing in here?" the soldier asked, directing his question to one of the older men in the German speaking crowd.

The older man, in somewhat of a panic, did the only thing he knew to do under the circumstances. He responded in German. But the British soldier did not speak or understand a word of German, and having it thrown back at him just made the situation worse. A few other German speaking men added further explanations, also not understood.

A number of Brits on the platform were becoming agitated by this confrontation. A group of four men and two women banded together to give vocal support to the British soldiers. "Get those Germans out of here!" one man shouted.

A woman turned to her friends in a very loud voice and said, "Krauts in our bomb shelter! My God! It's like jumping up on a kitchen counter to avoid a large mouse on the kitchen floor, and then finding the large mouse sitting there next to you on the counter!"

Robert took it all in very quietly. He did have a working knowledge of German, and so he understood that the German men were explaining, unfortunately in German, that they were Jewish refugees from Nazi Germany, and had been invited to stay in London. The German bombs undoubtedly being dropped as much on them as on the British. But Robert was still a bit too far from the action to offer an explanation in English. He was also very concerned that as an American, he was actually a foreigner, too.

The British soldier, charged with maintaining order in the bomb shelter, was having none of it. "Off with you!" he shouted. "All of you. Now! You're taking up space that we need for our own people."

The British soldier was seething with anger and so were quite a few other British subjects. The scene was getting pretty ugly, pretty fast. Robert wasn't sure there was much he could do. Mobs, even mini-mobs, are not logical, and a hatred for Germans was fomenting this crowd, further enflamed by the discomfort of a bomb threat.

"Please, sir, let me explain, if I may." A female voice rose above the din. A woman or maybe a girl. It wasn't clear from where Robert was standing. What was clear, she spoke English. No accent, just Oxbridge. She spoke well. Hearing the beautiful speaker of their mother tongue, the crowd fell silent. Listening.

"These are German refugees from Nazi persecution. German Jews. Many of them recently escaped from German cities, where they were to be rounded up and sent off to the internment camps. The British government has offered them asylum, in a humanitarian gesture. They have all suffered greatly at the hands of the brutal Nazis, and they are here as your guests."

Her words were electrifying, and humbling. Most of the crowd understood immediately, these people had suffered enough and did not need more bullying from the one nation that was now firmly resolved to destroy these Nazi bullies.

The corporal was less impressed.

"Miss—Corporal John Hardy here, Regular Army. It is my job to safeguard fellow Brits from German bombs. The fact is *these people* are Germans occupying space in a London bomb shelter intended for *British* subjects."

Being Jewish didn't help. Corporal Hardy regarded every British born Jew as more of a foreigner than a Brit, and he really didn't understand why the British government was importing German Jews, or any other Jews, into the country when resources were stretched very thin. The woman's accent was a bit too plummy for him. Probably a well-born, over-educated bird, who would never give him the time of day.

"I don't have time to sort out who they are, or why they are here, as that's not my concern. I am in charge of this bomb shelter, and who stays, and who goes. They need to go. I've got good countrymen in the stairwells and even outside, and they all get preference over this bunch of Germans. So, tell them all to move out. Now!"

Robert stepped forward. He debated in his own mind. Was it better to take on the corporal or help these people extract themselves quickly? It would be a man-to-man debate, a fairer "fight" than the young woman was having, and Robert was confident that he could prevail. There were plenty of foreigners in the station. But then what? They were all trapped in a pretty hostile environment. If a bomb did hit nearby, more tempers could flare, and people might well turn on these poor refugees.

He turned to the young woman. "Please ask them to follow me, there are other places they can go besides this shelter."

The dull roar of the bombers was coming again, which explained why the "all clear" never sounded. All the more critical that he and the little band of refugees go quickly. Robert instinctively took the young woman by the arm to guide her. She walked with him, while she was giving strict directions in German to the refugees to follow—no talking, no arguing, no looking at anyone, just move out as rapidly as possible. The other people on the platform seemed to understand. They melted out of the path to allow the exodus to proceed down the platform. On the stairs and then out onto the street. Robert realized the young woman was speaking High German. Maybe she was German and not British, as he first thought. Was she somehow part of their group and not just a helpful bystander?

Out on the deserted street, Robert had time to size up the group he was shepherding. About fifteen in all. Mostly older men and women, seemingly in their fifties, and sort of matched up into couples. No children. Had they been sent off somewhere to safety, he wondered. The young women was standing next to him, looking very anxious.

"Do you think there is somewhere else we could go?" she asked. "You said that you had some other places?"

The bombers were now sounding louder, closer.

"Quickly now. Follow me," Robert said.

Robert walked briskly down several streets to his office building. Now well past closing, the building was dark, quiet and deserted. Robert pulled his key out and opened the door. "Hurry in," he said. "Go on down those stairs, into the basement." Robert found a light switch.

The group followed his direction, one by one disappearing down the stairs. The young woman stood by his side, waiting until they had all gotten down into basement storage room. Robert went down last of all, with her just ahead of him.

The basement was now reasonably well lit, but not deeply set under the ground. It was not a real bomb shelter, but certainly better than standing on the street. The many boxes of stored documents had been carefully stacked against the walls, giving further protection from concussions or shrapnel. And there were flashlights, water, and some canned food rations. There were nowhere near enough seats, so Robert suggested that some of the men pull out file storage boxes and sit on them.

After twenty minutes or so, everyone started to relax a bit. The bombers seemed to have flown by, looking for targets farther west. The young woman was talking to some of the refugees, trying to comfort them. They clearly enjoyed the attention she was giving them. Perhaps they all missed their own daughters, wherever they were.

Robert noticed the refugees looked tired. Their clothing looked worn. He wondered if they had been able to take much with them as they departed their homes, probably on short notice. He had seen newspaper photos of the many refugees pouring out of Europe. This group looked better off than many of them, but similar, too. Thin. Nervous, but appreciative of kindness. Hungry. He wondered when they'd last had a meal. Should he offer them the canned rations? The young woman looked thin. It was difficult not to take sympathy on her in view of all the sympathy she had shown to these refugees. Oh, what the hell, he thought. I should be able to replace the rations.

"Could I offer these people a meal? We have enough ration packs down here for each of them, and for you as well."

"Would you really do this for us? You don't even know us, and you're already going out of your way for us."

Robert could tell from the look on her face that she wanted very much to accept the offer, but also knew he was sticking his neck out, and she should decline.

"Please. The ration kits are from the British government, and I know that I can replace them. These refugees look pretty hungry to me." He thought for a moment, then added, "One condition, though."

Her eyes opened, as she looked at him intensely.

"What is it?"

"You must eat one yourself."

"Oh, no, I can't do that. These older people have been through hell and back. I'm just fine."

Robert was a skilled negotiator, and he knew he had the upper hand.

"That's the deal. Take it or leave it."

She smiled and looked down.

"You are very kind. And very perceptive. I accept. Thank you!"

She then turned to the group and explained the offer, which they gladly accepted. Within a very short time there was an active dinner party underway.

The long, steady whining horn of "all clear" sounded, but none of the refugees moved. They finished the little meals, chatting away in German. Their manners were impeccable, Robert thought. The people were clearly from German middle class families. Well-bred and probably well-educated. He only wished that he could offer them better fare, and a few bottles of wine.

The young woman took her ration tin, and then, looking at Robert said, "This would be much more comfortable for me and for all of us, if you would eat with us."

Of course, he thought, where are my manners? So, he opened a tin, and dug in.

"You said 'us.' But surely you must be English. Your accent is so impeccable."

"Perhaps it is," she said, "but I am not English. I am one of them. I am a German Jew, just like them. But my escape was easier, and my life here in England has been more comfortable."

Robert studied her. Her clothes were not expensive, but good quality. Dark brown hair. Brown eyes. Somehow, a warm smile. Her nose was straight, and thin. Bright spirited and thoughtful. A lovely young woman, he thought, but she seemed to radiate an innate goodness and trustworthiness.

She noticed him looking at her, and, with a small smile, seemed to appreciate it.

"May I know your name, sir?"

Robert was taken aback. There had been so much stress and activity and emotion in the past few hours, he had never even thought to introduce himself, or ask her for her name, either.

"Of course, I am Robert Johnston. My office is upstairs. May I know your name?"

"Hannah. Hannah Hanauer. And greatly in your debt. I've never spent any time with an American. You seem different in some ways from the British."

"Yes," Robert laughed. "We began to notice that ourselves about two hundred years ago. So, we very politely asked the Brits to go home and let us be. Reluctantly, after a nasty war that lasted 'eight years, four months, and fifteen days,' they did finally depart. But then, over the ensuing two long centuries, we came to realize that we stubborn Yanks and those Bloody Brits do share a great deal of common history, common form of government, common language, common values, common laws, and, for many of us, common ancestry. So, we tend to stick together, for the most part anyway."

After listening carefully, she laughed. "That does explain things." The smile disappeared from Hannah's face, replaced by intensity. "We did study the Great War from 1914 to 1918. It was never clear why the US joined the war on the side of the UK. Now it seems that Germany should start paying a lot more attention to the US. It has been a blind spot for us

Germans. Or maybe I should now say, for those Germans! Is it likely that the Americans will enter the war?"

Robert became serious. "Yes. I would stake my life on it. That is why I am here in London. It will take time, but that outcome is a foregone conclusion. Finally, the sin, the depravity and the scope of the never-ending Nazis transgressions will inevitably pull the entire world into the effort to put an end to it, and to make the Germans pay for it. Pay dearly for it."

"I hope you are right. That scenario is frightful—a world at war—but it is also hopeful. And thank you for a day which I shall never forget. I can only hope that our paths will cross again."

2

Britain Stands Alone – RAF HQ

22 September 1940, High Wycombe

RAF Bomber Command was having big problems. After losing well over one-hundred-and-fifty bombers in the Battle of France, plus additional losses from crash landings and flak damage, they were now being diverted from bombings of significant German targets to attacks on airfields, barges, shipping, communications, even forests and crops. Bombing accuracy was also a huge problem. Casualties were high. There was little evidence that the bombings were affecting the German war effort. A meeting had been called to address these issues.

Arthur Harris, commander of No. 5 Group, joined the meeting a few minutes late, having just concluded his morning command meeting down the hall.

"Beg pardon, Marshall," he said to Charles Portal, Air Marshall and Commander of Bomber Command, who was chairing the meeting today. "Just pulling together some last bits of information you requested."

"Understood. Please sit down, Harris," said Portal. "We couldn't begin without you, so we didn't." Portal was an Oxford man with an unremarkable physical appearance and small stature. He seemed quiet and self-effacing, out of place in Bomber Command where large personalities tended to dominate. He always looked unhappy. But he had a long and distinguished career in bomber service and was highly regarded by Churchill.

The meeting included the commanders of Groups 2, 3, 4 and now 5, and a number of new junior Bomber Command staff officers. The mood was grim. There was no good news. Weekly staff meetings mostly involved a great many good questions, and very few good answers. Today's meeting was no different.

What was different was the attendance of Professor Frederick Lindemann, a representative and personal friend to Prime Minister Winston

Churchill. Lord Cherwell or "The Prof," as he was known, was a very crusty former physics professor of some renown. Lindemann did not suffer fools lightly. And he thought that most men were fools. The PM wanted answers. And the PM knew that Lindemann was the man who could get them.

Accompanying the professor was a young RAF Lieutenant, Dr. Aaron Solomon, who served as a sort of aide-de-camp to Lindemann when RAF matters were at hand.

Lindemann got right to the point. "Against the Nazis, we have only one effective offensive weapon, RAF Bomber Command. And it seems to be firing blanks. This is not acceptable. A great deal of time, effort and expense has been devoted to Britain's strategic bombing campaign over the past year, but we have very little show for it. The PM and the War Cabinet would like some answers."

Air Marshall Portal took up the challenge. Portal, who always appeared to be too small for his expensive uniform, bristled and stiffened. He sensed this was a personal attack on him.

"No apologies are due from Bomber Command," insisted Portal. "And none will be given. The Germans started this war, and the bombing campaign. When Roosevelt proclaimed the neutrality of the United States a year ago, he asked both sides to avoid bombing of civilian populations. To curry favor with our key ally, we agreed to refrain as long as the Germans did. Then, 14 May the Luftwaffe laid waste to Rotterdam in a massive bombing campaign. On 23 August, a German bomber dropped its load of bombs on a London suburb. These actions provoked our PM and the War Cabinet to launch a bomber strike on Berlin.

"In the ensuing attack on 24th and 25th of August, Bomber Command suffered severe losses, but the psychological impact on Hitler was highly significant. He ordered the Luftwaffe to break off the attacks on the RAF and start bombing London. Ironically, the RAF was given a much-needed chance to regroup, and those commanding officers who had been seeking justification to expand the bombing offense were given a much stronger voice.

"One of the key members of 'Bomb Germany Now' Group is our own Arthur Harris, serving as Commanding Officer of No. 5 Group.

Arthur is a feisty fellow. At age fifty-two, he has already enjoyed a very diverse life, including several years as a fighter pilot in the Great War."

Lindemann could plainly see that Portal had not finished speaking, but he interrupted nevertheless, "I am aware of all this military history, but Bomber Command is now regarded as a standalone strategic force which must make its presence felt in the war."

Portal responded, "As you must know, Professor, Bomber Command is nowhere near large enough to constitute a 'stand-alone strategic force.' We have at best only five hundred and thirty bombers, mostly British *Blenheims* and *Fairey Battles,* which are close to obsolete, and many *Whitleys* and *Hampdens,* which are due for replacement. We can usually fly only one-hundred-and-fifty bombers each night. And most of the bombers we do fly are woefully inadequate to carry heavy payloads to targets deep in Germany, drop their bombs accurately on their assigned targets, and then return safely to fly another mission.

"The *Bristol Blenheims,* the backbone of our fleet, are much too slow for heavy raids over Germany. We can use them to bomb their U-Boats, but at heavy cost in bombers and crews. Candidly, ordering 1,000 *Fairey Battles* was a huge mistake because they are just too damn old and slow, under-powered and poorly armed. They are being shot down in droves, causing heavy losses to our crews, failure to locate targets and a total waste of productive facilities. I can use them for a few more months, but they are a significant liability. Our crews don't even want to be assigned to them.

"We have probably sixty *Armstrong Whitworth Whitleys*. We call them "Flying Barn Doors." They were pretty effective for leaflet dropping, or bombing coastal targets on the North Sea, Genoa and Turin, but they are medium-range bombers and aren't likely to be able to do much damage over interior portions of Germany.

"We do like our seventy *Handley Page Hampdens*. But they are slow, have little defensive armor and are very uncomfortable for crew members. Since we cannot use them in daylight, they have little prospect of being effective in major raids over Germany.

"The best we have at the moment are the one hundred *Vickers Welling-tons. "Wimpeys."* They are faster and more versatile, can take a beating and still make it back home, and can be built very quickly, but their bomb payload is pretty limited.

"There you have it. If you want us to do more, we need better bombers. A hellova lot more and better bombers."

Portal was clearly agitated. *What the hell does Lindemann think we have been trying to do for the past year?*

He stood up now and walked around the room. "We have concerns about the *Manchester* bombers. The aircraft has interesting design improvements in bombing capacity and armaments, but the engines seem to be unreliable. Perhaps it can be improved. From all indications, the *Halifax* bombers look to be versatile and effective. Their larger fuselage enables crews to escape more easily, improving crew survival rates. We are hoping to be able to power them with radial engines from Hercules, but that improvement will take time. Perhaps over a year. We also have concerns about the *Short Sterling* bombers. They have limited bomb load capacity and are heavy, so they must fly at lower ceilings. This will make them easier targets. The *Lancaster* bombers are superb. Great performance. Large bomb load. Popular with air crews. Very popular with Bomber Harris. I predict they will dominate our fleet."

Then Lindemann spoke, "I take your point about the inadequacies of our current bombers. But that is what we have at the moment. I am reliably informed that better and heavier bombers are in the pipeline. *Avro Manchesters* and Handley Page *Halifaxs* are scheduled for delivery to Bomber Command in a few months. The *Avro Lancasters* won't be operationally ready for many months. Of course, these new bombers cost money. A lot of money. And, in case you haven't heard, the Royal Navy wants the money for more and better ships, and the British Army wants the money for more and better tanks and guns."

Lindemann then turned to the young lieutenant accompanying him. "Lt. Solomon," he said, "explain to Marshall Portal some of the input you have been receiving from your RAF pilot patients."

Aaron looked at Lindemann, and then looked around the room. He was surrounded by RAF officers who were all senior to him. Many of the officers were very senior to him, with ranks he would never achieve. They were members of a very elite military caste. Many had served in

The Great War. They had years of combat duty, often together, in life and death situations. Hours together after work, at pubs and officers' clubs. They also had hundreds of hours in bombers. They all knew far more about the subjects under discussion than Aaron knew or would ever know. They didn't know Aaron from the Man in the Moon, and he was probably at least ten-to-fifteen years younger than the next youngest man in the room. Judging by his name, Aaron assumed that all assembled knew that Aaron was a Jew.

To make matters worse, if that were even remotely possible, Aaron knew that the pilot input he would be addressing today would be enormously unpopular, even if these issues were being presented today by King George himself.

But Aaron was no shrinking violet. He respected these men and their significant accomplishments and sacrifices. He particularly liked military people. And the subject of his pilot and air crew input was vital to the long-term interests of every man in the room.

He slowly stood up. "I have been receiving input from your pilots and bomber crews relating to training, morale, discipline, performance, and sustainability. And most urgently, training. As their doctor, treating wounded and sick pilots and crewmen, they talk openly and freely with me. Please understand that their feedback is preliminary and anecdotal, but their concerns suggest urgent problems for Bomber Command."

A number of men nodded in agreement. Others looked perplexed, perhaps somewhat annoyed. Several looked highly agitated. Aaron imagined it was annoying enough for them to hear they were overlooking a key element of their jobs, but measurably more annoying when that message was delivered by someone they didn't know, and who wasn't remotely in the same line of work. If they regarded him as not even entirely English, and in fact as a Jew, Aaron thought, the criticism wouldn't be any easier to digest.

"These crews tell me that training is a problem," Aaron continued, "and there are not enough crews to fly the missions. The combination is deadly. If Bomber Command reduces the training in order to increase the number of crews, and thereby increase the amount of bombing, the net result is to undermine the overall effectiveness of the bombing campaign.

Planes don't get there. If they do, they don't drop their bombs on their targets. We don't defend our bombers. And our bombers don't get back to base."

Everyone sat stunned for a few minutes. This was not really news, but an unspoken nagging suspicion. Now it had been spoken. Whatever may have been the thoughts of the Bomber Command brass, it was very clear to all assembled, given the very severe nature of the allegations, that only the Commander in Chief, Air Marshall Portal, could respond.

Whereas criticism of bombers was annoying because a cost of thousands was involved in bomber development, criticism of pilots and crew training was a Command responsibility. Portal himself was abundantly pleased and intrigued to hear the views of the fight surgeon, which gave him a direct input he had not heard before. He relaxed, thought, and then spoke.

"We do give our men about as much training as we can," said Portal, "in view of the severe shortage of crews at the pressing demands of our strategic campaign. The training is the bare minimum, but we must get our planes in the air or the war will be lost. We are not engaging Germany on any other front at the moment. Like all of us airmen, these young crews will get their principal training on the job. Frankly, we are all pretty overwhelmed by the scope, intensity, ferocity, and speed of the war."

Aaron knew that Portal was right on all counts, but he also knew the training problems were impeding the entire bombing campaign. He sat still for a measured pause. Looking at Portal, Aaron could see that Portal was now looking at him. Waiting, hoping for a response. If he had Portal's attention, the rest of the audience would also tune in. So, Aaron spoke directly to Portal, taking care to make his points as straightforward and matter-of-fact as possible under the circumstances. He took care not to show his nerves.

"Whatever may be the shortcomings of our bombers, and clearly there are many, the campaign, which is enormously expensive and desperately critical to our very survival, will have very little impact whatsoever if the bomber crews lack the skills to navigate to far distance targets, and therefore never get to drop their precious bombs from our precious bombers on our targets. The crews tell me that they might improve their navigation skills incrementally after five or six missions, but not very much. Their new missions typically have different targets, and so entirely new navigational challenges. And frankly, painfully, many of them never do fly future missions because they are shot down over Germany."

Another stunned silence. Then Air Vice Marshal N.H. Bottomly spoke up, "Look here, Solomon, a thorough navigation course probably requires months of concentrated study, and even then, navigation at night, while flying over enemy territory with constant enemy attacks, in very cold temperatures and lack of oxygen is always very tricky business. And our current bomb sights are very outdated. Maybe you should fly with them on a mission or two."

"Getting to the target, of course, is still only part of the challenge," agreed Aaron. "We know only a small percentage of the bombs we drop are anywhere near the targets. Clearly, if we are unable to deliver a critical mass of our bombs and the designated targets, then the bombing campaign will be a costly failure, with even more costly repercussions. Can we institute better training for this?"

"A major problem is the quality of the bomb sights," responded Air Vice Marshal Richard Peirse. "We currently use our Course Setting Bomb Sight from WWI, but our people in Operations Research are developing a new MK XIV computer sight. We call it the Blackett Sight. It uses a gyro stabilized platform. Much more accurate. We should have it operational in a year."

"Gentlemen, these overall navigation difficulties are myriad and profound," added Lindemann. "And ignoring them because of the 'press of battle' cannot be the answer. Everyone is focusing on more and better bombers, but if the bombers very often cannot be guided to the target areas—and if the bombs, once dropped, seldom land even in the general vicinity of the designated targets, but more often miss the target entirely and fall harmlessly on open farmland—then our precious military funds would be better spent elsewhere."

Noting the silence in the room, as Lindemann's words struck home, Aaron pressed his message. "We have been addressing the problem of getting the bombers and the bombs to the targets. But there is yet another disastrous effect of this lack of crew navigation skills. The crews have enormous difficulties bringing themselves and their precious old bombers back home. Any crew that fails to return, then fails 'to fight another day.' One less bomber. Six or eight fewer crewmen. Plummeting morale. I am seeing it in our RAF patients every day."

"We are losing one sixth of our planes and crews on every mission," Lindemann confirmed, looking very annoyed. "These are intolerable statistics, particularly in view of the minimal results that their raids are producing. And here is the ultimate irony. Precisely because our crews are forced to spend more time over enemy territory, facing the grave consequences from anti-aircraft and lethal fighter attacks, their survival chances drop sharply. They are forced to stay over the target longer to increase the odds of hitting the target. Then they face a very hazardous trip home. The resulting morale problems produce the anticipated result: They do not spend more time searching their targets. They do not hang out over targets searching the perfect drops. They head home as soon as they reasonably can. And too many do not make it back home. That is the truth of it."

Aaron's earlier comments had been a stinging rebuke, but of course he knew very well that his observations were statistically provable and fairly obvious, if unspoken, truths to all. And Aaron's observations had been delivered with quiet respect. But Lindemann's final words were harsh and delivered in the manner of an insult to the integrity of Bomber Command, and perhaps even the British national character.

Many of the assembled Bomber Command officers shuffled in their seats to grumble and complain to each other about Lindemann's stern tongue-lashing. Many faces were flushed with anger. But these seasoned officers were no fools. The flight pilots and crews were very much like their own sons. The revelation of this fairly obvious conclusion based on the facts presented struck home. The crews were in a no-win situation, which was not their fault. Nor was it the fault of Aaron Solomon, who wasn't much older than many of the crewmen. And they understood that Solomon's credibility was reinforced by the fact that the young men in the crews confided in him as a contemporary, particularly one who was their doctor. And they could also see that it made Dr. Aaron Solomon very uncomfortable to relate these shared confidences from his RAF patients.

The doctor patient rule of confidentiality is almost as sacred as the husband wife rule of confidentiality. And whereas a wife might sometimes lose her temper and break that confidentiality or hang out with girlfriends where the practice is for every girl to chip in a bit of gossip from hubby, doctors should never fall prey to that failing.

At this point in the meeting, everyone looked at Portal. If they were expecting an eruption at hearing Lindemann's scolding, they were disappointed. Portal sat still, a measured demeanor. This was the nature of Portal. Not combative. Most usually cool, calm, and collected. And he had an enormous talent for handling difficult men like Churchill and Lindemann.

When the agitation settled down, Portal spoke. "Thank you, professor. And thank you, Dr. Solomon. Bomber Command needs to do a better job at doing our job. I for one still believe we should pursue our goal of more accurate and effective precision bombing. You have our attention. We will do our best to expand and improve training. This meeting is adjourned."

As everyone filed out, Lindemann knew that Air Marshall Portal had deftly and elegantly put him back in his box. He had met his match. Lindemann also knew, which Portal did not, that Richard Peirse would be replacing Portal as Commander of Bomber Command in a week or two, and that Portal would be promoted to Chief of Air staff. A position of enormous power and influence, for which Portal was well qualified.

3

The US is Stirring

15 October 1940, London

Although Robert was a staunch Republican, from a long line of Republicans, he was no isolationist. From his posts in Berlin and then London, it was all too clear that the Germans were on their way to making Europe a German Empire.

His private British secretary, Kathleen Scott, poked her head into his office.

"Excuse me, Robert, there is a radio telephone call for you from New York."

"Who is it, Kathleen? I'm in the middle of this contract."

"It is your friend, William Donovan. He said it is somewhat urgent."

"I better take that. Please put him through and close the door."

Kathleen put the call through, and then quietly closed the door. Tall, thin, soft spoken and very British, she dressed modestly and did her work diligently—the perfect secretary. For a woman in her late twenties, this was a choice job, and she was very dedicated to Robert. She always smiled to herself when Robert told her to close the door, because, if she sat quietly, she could overhear his conversation.

"Hello, Bill. Robert here."

"Ah, Robert, good to talk to you. I wanted to pass along news on the developing political situation in the US Some good, some bad, from our point of view. For you and me, I mean. All indications are that FDR will win re-election pretty easily. You know where he stands on the defense of Britain. But Wendell Willkie and the Republicans are pushing Roosevelt deeper into the Anti-War Camp, as a great many Americans, probably a majority, feel strongly that the U.S. should not get involved in another European war. Assuming he does get re-elected, it will take a while for him to back off of his current staunch anti-involvement policies. It's a little hard to know where this all leads."

"Bill, just to be clear, the situation here in London, and in Britain generally, is far from rosy. And it gets worse by the day. As you know, the Germans have bombed a number of cities. London, Southampton, Bristol, Cardiff, Liverpool and Manchester. You may not yet know that there was not a lot of damage. But a really disturbing trend. Everyone here expects the bombing to get much worse. As you know, the crazy Italians invaded Egypt and were quickly defeated by the British. You may not know that Mussolini rejected Hitler's offer to help Italy, because the idiot Mussolini wanted to "showcase" the Italian Army. When Germany, Italy and Japan signed a Tripartite Cooperation Agreement, the view here is that the purpose was to put pressure on the US and Russia to stay out of the war. Now the Germans are occupying Romania, and no one is lifting a finger. The impression here is that America plans to sit out this war. The Germans are actively planning to invade England. Without US help, the Germans are well on their way to winning the war. What can I tell our friends here?"

Hearing all of this, Donovan struggled to say something positive.

"Robert, I have no official position, I am just a confidant of FDR, my good friend. But you can tell them this. Our people here believe that there a significant change underway in the German plans. Less attention directed at Britain, but we can't tell for sure. My good friend is hoping that your friends in London can give us some insight into Hitler's thinking. Have you heard anything? Anything at all? German focus now seems to be toward the East. Is there a new focus on Russia? Or Greece? Is this a continental consolidation?"

Robert listened carefully, looking at pictures of FDR and Churchill hanging on his wall. He had long doubted that Hitler would try to invade Britain. Their cherished Panzer tanks would be at high risk crossing the English Channel.

"Churchill is convinced that there will be no German invasion of the UK. I think he is right. The Brits' air and sea superiority are a major concern if the Germans have to ferry troops and heavy equipment across the Channel. The Royal Navy is an overwhelming force, and the RAF is in much better shape than the Luftwaffe seems to realize. Maybe the Germans' moves to the coast are just a feigning move. I will see what I can find out on this end."

"Good. The reasons you suggest are persuasive. But German objectives to the East have been known for years, and they are not a timid lot, so there might be an entirely different reason for their apparent change in plans. We are suspicious. Please do let me know if you learn anything."

Robert then relaxed a bit. He and Bill Donovan had been good friends for years. Robert was a member of a group of international lawyers and businessmen, established by Bill before the outbreak of hostilities, who met frequently in foreign cities to share intelligence and speculation of possible German and Japanese future war plans. "Hold on a minute, Bill." He stood up, walked to the door, and opened it. Kathleen Scott was sitting quietly at her desk, apparently looking at some correspondence.

"Kathleen, could you please bring me some tea and a few biscuits? I am running on empty."

When he sat back down at his desk, Donovan was also changing gears.

"Tell me, Robert, how are you enduring your 'semi-official' tour of duty in London? My wife bumped into your Ellen having lunch at The Plaza the other day. That fellow, Tolliver Boynton, was with her again. I seem to recall that Tolliver is a high and mighty Yale Man."

"A Yalie. And a poor choice for Ellen. She regards him as a 'Yale Literary Intellectual.' What a joke! He has never written anything. With a name like Tolliver Boynton, Yale was the only major university that would admit him. Yale likes to accept students just for their funny names. I keep telling her she has come down with a very bad case of TB! What's that Yale Motto? 'Urim and Thummin, Lux et Veritas. Light and Truth!' Well, Yale should shed a little *light* on, and tell a little *truth* about, that egghead *phony*. Sorry, Bill. TB annoys me. I never liked him. He actually wears bow ties. But Ellen is on her own these days. I have a secret suspicion that she really prefers Princetonians, and that she is spending time with that Dopey Draft Dodger just to fry my bacon."

"Well, I guess it is working."

"Yes. I guess it is."

4

Robert's First Meeting at MI5

28 October 1940, London

Two weeks later, Robert was ushered into the offices of Brigadier Oswald "Jasper" Allen Harker, Acting Director of MI5, the UK's domestic counter-intelligence and security agency. Harker had just recently replaced the dismissed Major General Sir Vernon Kell. Harker had a reputation for being very serious about his work. On his office walls, there were a few photos of Harker in India, from his long years there with the Indian Police, culminating in his appointment as Deputy Commissioner at Bombay before returning to Great Britain in 1919. By the time he and Robert met, Harker had already spent over twenty years in the Security Service, though Robert had heard that he was probably not the best choice for the top job. Robert didn't really know Harker very well, but he also knew that the government was searching for a permanent director with more clout

After briefly passing the time of day, Robert got straight to the point. "Congratulations on your promotion to Acting Director. It is a challenging position in challenging times."

Harker nodded in agreement, "Yes, I do quite agree. What can we do for you, Mr. Johnston?"

"Washington has the impression that the Germans are losing interest in invading England. Are they turning their attention to some other theatre of this war? More to the East? Are you hearing anything? Please, call me Robert."

Harker looked surprised at the question. Harker knew that Robert was tight with Bill Donovan, and that Donovan was a special advisor to FDR. Harker could not ignore the very sensitive question, but his response was measured.

"East. Yes. East. I suppose all one has to do is to look at the map of Europe to quickly understand that the vast areas east of Berlin are as much juicier targets than those which present themselves to the west, now that most of the countries west of Berlin, except for this island, of course, have already fallen to the Nazis. And, so, we have the news today, you may not have heard, that the Italians just invaded Greece."

"I have not heard the news. Does MI5 have any insight into whether the Greeks can deal with the Italians?"

"Probably, they can. The Italians will need German assistance. I suspect that the Germans see more substantial, immediate gains in Eastern Europe. The pressure on somewhat neutral governments in Hungry and Romania is intense. But MI5 is also very concerned that the more Hitler focuses on Eastern Europe, the less interesting the war will be for you Americans. If America cannot be convinced to defend places like France, the Netherlands and Great Britain, for heaven's sake, then why would America care a fig for Romania and Hungary. Hitler must surely be well aware of that."

Robert stiffened in his chair, and did his best to reflect the stern air of the acting director. He knew that Harker's statement was a question, but the answer was uncomfortable.

"I don't disagree with you. But President Roosevelt has his own concerns. The election is in a week. The opposition, my own Republican Party, ironically is pushing hard for an isolationist policy. And, so the president needs some space and cover to shift the country away from its strong isolationist mood toward involvement. If Britain can stand alone for the next six months, that will give America time to get its act together. So, 'Adolf's' hope of lulling us dumb Yanks into a false sense of security might well work against him in the long run."

Harker nodded, but Robert could plainly see from the look on his face that he was far from convinced that the Americans were anywhere near joining the War Effort. And from Harker's inside perspective, given the current unpleasant course of events, it was even less clear that there would be a Great Britain around to assist by the time the Yankees ever resolved to do so.

A sharp, urgent knock at the office door interrupted them. Harker looked up, and barked, "Come in."

The heavy, wooden door opened, and in walked a very trim and smartly uniformed young WREN officer carrying a message, which she handed to Harker, and then stood by, almost at attention, as he read it.

The young officer did not so much as glance in Robert's direction. She had obviously been well trained in the discipline of military intelligence. "Whatever you see here, whatever you hear here, whatever you say here, stays here."

Robert was not as well-disciplined. He had been away from home for a long time, and so he found it impossible not to take a long look at this firm, attractive young woman now "stationed" in front of him.

She had that hale and healthy look of the British Anglo Saxon women. Maybe an inch or two shorter than many American girls. Not that tall, lanky look of girls brought up in the US after five or six generations of plenty of good food and exercise. But very shapely legs, from what he could see. A very pretty face, with a very intelligent look. What would you expect to find in the headquarters of British Intelligence? Her skin was very fair. Of course, there is limited sunlight in Britain, and the "natives" don't much like be out in it anyway. Blondish-brown hair which she wore in a bob, probably due to her military status. Deep blue eyes. Her uniform was crisp and neat. Her bearing a bit crusty. For obvious reasons, there was no introduction, but Robert did hear Harker address her as "Lieutenant Leach."

After mulling over the contents of the message, which he did not offer to share, Harker muttered to himself, "Sink the Italian Battle Fleet in the harbor of Taranto…Of course! Use our old *Fairey Swordfish* bi-plane torpedo bombers flying off *HMS Illustrious*. Our beloved little *"Stringbags."* Flying off HMS Illustrious. Brilliant!"

Harker turned to the Lieutenant. "Ask your father if our mutual friend Captain Haythornwaite will be in on the action."

"I did, sir. He will be there."

There was a pause. Robert noticed just a very brief hint of a pained look on the face of Lieutenant Leach. Then it was gone. Harker did not look up.

"Thank you, Lieutenant. Tell the Admiralty to let us know what they need from us. It's a great plan!"

She turned, and quietly walked out, but this time with a quick icy look at Robert. He suspected that she was not happy that Robert "overheard" a top-secret conversation about a major impending secret attack on enemy forces. Robert felt a chill. Few things are as chilling for a man as an icy look from an attractive woman!

After the door closed, Harker and Robert continued their discussion.

Harker observed that the German internal supply lines were very short, and very direct, whereas Great Britain had almost impossible supply lines from other parts of the globe.

"For God's sake, everything we get here has to come across vast oceans, swarming with German U-Boats. If you Americans are not prepared to enter this war as a combatant, we do at minimum urgently need help with our shipping lines of supply. Can you put the message in somebody's ear?"

Robert thought for a few moments. "Do you have any hard details that you can give me to support your point? We really do not have enough hard assets in the sea lanes to get a very precise picture of your cumulative losses and the German's total underwater threat."

"I am sorry to say that I am not in a position to give you precise details today. I will look into it. But, believe me, if I did, it would not help us to plead our case. The more desperate we appear, the less likely you Americans will assist."

"Understood. I will try to get your message into the right ears. But Washington is playing the long game. There is no appetite for getting into another war with the Germans. I'm sure you know, there are plenty of German Americans who would like to see America support the Axis Powers, particularly now that they appear to have the winning hand. Please don't take me wrong, I am obviously NOT in this camp, but there is such a camp."

"I am well aware that America is a nation of immigrants, and that many of them have ancestral links to Germany, as well as the ever-increasing number of European countries who have become allies of Germany, starting with our Italian friends. And then too, there are those all-too-horrible Irish." Looking down at his watch. "Say, have you acquired the British taste for a cup of tea in the afternoon? Maybe we can lighten the mood just a bit?"

"Certainly. I need a little sugar in my system for my long walk home this afternoon."

Harker picked up his office phone and dialed an extension.

"I wonder if you could accompany my guest to the 4pm tea trolley? I need to make a few calls before end of day. All of our "very important officials" go home at 4pm. A long standing British tradition."

In a few moments, Lieutenant Leach came back through the door.

"Lieutenant Sarah Leach, allow me to introduce Robert Johnston, an important American friend of our department. Could you please guide him to the tea trolley, for which he and I will be forever in your debt."

The lieutenant turned towards Robert. "Certainly. Mr. Johnston, please follow me."

Robert could not help but notice that Lieutenant Leach did not have even a trace of a smile on her face. He wondered how he might possibly have offended her in some way, as he had not spoken even one word in her presence.

Lt. Leach walked out of Harker's office and down the hall. She did not look back to see if Robert was following. She took that for granted. As they walked, people looked at Leach. No one seemed to notice Robert. He did notice that she walked smoothly and gracefully. As they passed a small empty office, she took his arm and pulled him in.

"What you just heard is top secret, Mr. Johnston. Do you understand? Not a word of this to your American friends."

"Yes, Lt. Leach. I understand. I hope in time you will learn to trust me."

They left the small office and wound their way around to a large mobile tea cart. Lt. Leach poured Robert a large cup of tea, took one for herself, and then stood by him as they both sipped the very hot tea, very carefully. Robert thought for a moment about how to break the considerable ice. Ask a question? Comment on the world scene? Make an astute observation? Comment on the weather?

"From what I have observed so far, I expect the Italian Army, unless aided by the Germans, will encounter a rough time of it in Greece."

Sarah Leach thought for a moment and said, "I agree. But this Italian invasion of Greece will give the Germans an opportunity to show the Italians how much they need their charming and delightful German allies." She then paused and looked directly at Robert. She spoke very quietly.

"I suspect that the British creative use of torpedo bomber strategy at Taranto will also have long term repercussions. As you and I know, there are many naval fleets parked snugly in harbors, thinking they are impervious to enemy aerial attacks."

Robert was impressed. This attractive young woman knew a great deal about the military situation, had keen insight and was a straight shooter.

"Enjoy your tea, Mr. Johnston. Perhaps I will be assigned to get you another cup on your next visit to our department."

"Yes, thank you. I hope so. This is a bracing cup of tea."

Still not a hint of a smile. "Our department," he thought. She must have some seniority. Rare for a woman in British Intelligence in 1940.

"Are you over here for a short visit – staying at a hotel?" she asked.

"No, I have been here for several years. No plans to leave. I am living in a very nice house on Bouverie Street which is actually owned by my New York City law firm."

"I frequent The Old Bell Tavern near there." She paused a moment and again looked straight at Robert. She softened. Eyes a little wider. Her lips slightly open. There was perhaps a hint of warmth. Almost as though she were seeking a response. "Usually on Friday evenings, for some 'unofficial channeling' among the Spooks and Dukes. Comfort food. Good drinks. Quaint."

But she did not await his response. She turned, military-style, and headed on down the hall. Robert watched her as she walked away. Grace in motion. Could she tell that he was watching her? Somehow, women always seem to know when men are watching them walk away. But she never looked back.

As Robert headed out into the dark and chilly fall evening, he reflected on the loneliness of his situation. His very estranged wife was very far away. And the London nights were always long, cold and lonely.

5

The 1938 – 1940 Refugee Problem

14 November 1940, London

Hannah Hanauer pulled her wool coat off the coat rack in the hallway of the Hawkin's home where she was residing. She stopped for a moment at the mirror in the hallway to gaze at her reflection. She had looked very young when she first arrived with the Kindertransport from Germany in December 1938. She was a teenager then. Now, almost two years later, she looked like a woman in her mid-twenties. She lived in the Maida Vale section of London with the middle-age couple who took her in. She had grown several inches and had a tall, thin athletic build although she had not engaged in any sport activities since leaving Germany. It occurred to her that children grow up faster in trying times.

She left the house and walked to the bus. She visited the Central British Fund for World Jewish Relief every other week. The bus ride took an hour, but once there she received up-to-date reports on the Jewish refugee problems, which seemed to only get worse with each passing day and year.

As she entered the building, she was struck as always by the number of people there. Mostly middle-aged intellectuals, their keen interest and the thoughtful discussions in the lectures and meetings engaged her full attention. Very few people her age attended, but a few sat quietly in the back of the room.

Hannah took off her coat, taking care to keep it close. It had been a much-needed farewell gift from her mother. She sat down and turned her attention to the front of the room. Today's lectures would be delivered by professors, lawyers and military experts. The first speaker was a British professor from University of St. Andrews in Scotland.

"Since 1933, Nazi Germany has pursued a policy of forced emigration of German Jews. Many Jewish people were reluctant to leave and stayed. Germany was their home. Many Jewish families had struggled mightily to emigrate to Germany years earlier. Many had been living there for generations. Most of them simply had no place else to go.

"Germany annexed Austria in March of 1938, and the Kristallnacht program was launched in November. The number of Jewish refugees seeking asylum skyrocketed, and the willingness of countries everywhere to take them plummeted.

"I believe you all know the grim story of the nine-hundred Jewish refugees from Hamburg onboard the *St. Louis*. The passengers were seeking entry into the US, but the ship was turned away by US author-ities, returned to Europe and reluctantly taken in by Britain and three other countries. Even then, half of the passengers were still at significant risk, because the countries that took them in then fell under Nazi control.

"We have raised these issues before. Over the past six years, over one-third of the Jews living in Germany, Austria, Bohemia, and Moravia left their countries. In truth, many are unaccounted for. These numbers are frightening enough, but Jews are only a small portion of the total refugee problem. Over 1.5 million Poles have been expelled, and several million more people from other countries."

The lecture went on. The European refugee problem was beyond comprehension, and certainly beyond Hannah's grasp. Despite her personal experience, she was only beginning to understand the gravity and urgency of the situation. Eventually, the professor sat down, to solemn applause.

A British officer was next. Hannah did not have any real familiarity with the British military, but it seemed to her that he was in the British army. It also seemed that he came out of the Jewish culture. Certainly he was addressing an audience that was largely Jewish and he seemed comfortable in doing so.

"Wars produce refugees," he began. "This current World War has been one of the worst. Starting in the 1930s, refugees by the thousands began to emigrate from various countries in Europe. Germany, Poland, Czechoslovakia, and Hungry. Even Russia. They moved generally south and west, hoping to find receptive countries. The numbers continued to grow, but there were no homes for them in other countries. A great many were held in cramped, uncomfortable, unsanitary refugee camps.

"Unlike many refugees from previous ages, these were not largely poor, uneducated peoples with a long history of being on the fringe. They had been successful, often even well-to-do, in their countries of residence. But they found themselves on the wrong side of the political-ethnic-social rifts that have engulfed western countries and were labeled "foreigners" by their countries of residence due to their "foreign" ancestry. As their numbers increased beyond measure, their collective impact on Europe began to have a decisive impact on the countries that rejected them, and those that accepted them. As the world has learned, again and again, there are no easy answers to refugee issues.

"Great Britain took in a number of refugees due to a long-standing British tradition of being a refuge for displaced persons. The policy has been tolerated by the British people, but not broadly popular. There continues to be an undercurrent of suspicion in both Britain and the US that German Jews could be spies for Germany.

"On the plus side of the Great Britain balance sheet, ten-thousand children in the Kindertransport Program, were admitted here from Germany into Britain in 1938 or 1939.

"On the negative side is our internment program. I am not permitted to give out precise details, but I can tell you, based upon published reports, that over twenty thousand Germans, Austrians, and Italians have been interned here in the UK. Most are apparently men, but some are women and even children. Many of the internees are German Jews. Some of the internees are German or Austrian Jewish teenagers who came here in the Kindertransport."

Hannah was completely exasperated. It seemed so hopeless. Even *she* might be interned.

The final speaker was a Jewish-British solicitor.

"The intertwined history of British policies on Jewish refugees and Palestine is, quite frankly, unbelievably complicated. Take, for example, the background on Palestine. Britain assumed responsibility for the government of Palestine after the Great War under a League of Nations Mandate. There was a stated obligation under the Mandate to facilitate the establishment of a National Home for the Jewish People in Palestine. During the ensuing years, thousands of Europeans Jews immigrated to Palestine.

"With the advent of the current war, the earlier position of Britain, in support of a Jewish homeland in Palestine under the Balfour Declaration, grew murky and elusive. Britain is squarely in a dilemma.

"The new policy of the British Government regarding Jewish settlement in Palestine was then set forth in the formal May 1939 'White Paper,' which overruled the Balfour Declaration. Jewish immigration was permitted 'only if the Arabs acquiesce to it.' My best guess is that might happen in one-hundred years."

The speaker continued, "In Germany, from 1934 to 1938, Jews by the thousands were leaving, hoping to escape the increasingly hostile environment under the Nazi regime. Many could see the gathering clouds, but many others dared to remain in Germany. Ironically, at the time, there was no German government opposition to Jews leaving Germany. The German government was very supportive of Jews leaving Germany. The problem was, and is, that they had few places to go. Some wanted to go to Palestine, and some had actually left Germany to go there, but questions remained. Would they be admitted? And if they were admitted, how would they live there in a desert? It all sounded like a fairytale to many of them, who had never even been outside of Germany."

Hannah sat very upright in her chair. Looking intently at the speaker. Taking notes. Her expression had now changed from anger and disbelief to quiet thought and understanding. Her lips, up until now were tightly closed, opened just slightly, and she said, to herself, "Palestine."

The story of Palestine was not new to Hannah, she had heard bits and pieces for years, but on this particular day the beacon of Palestine lit up for her. That beacon would never go out. For better or worse, it would grow brighter and brighter with each passing year of her life.

Now, Palestine was a real place. In real time. With real people.

The lectures had now ended, and the moderator asked for any questions. The audience seemed far too intimidated by what they had just heard. There was a long silence.

Then one arm went up and a young woman stood. She was blonde, well dressed, tall, and impressive.

"Can you please tell us the current attitude of the US Government toward accepting refugees?" She asked her question in impeccable

British. No apparent German, Eastern European, or Jewish dialect. Only British.

The three speakers looked at each other, trying to reach a visual consensus as to who should answer the guests. After a moment or two, the lawyer stood up.

"In 1938, over 100,000 refugees, many from Germany and Austria, and many of them Jews, applied for visas to enter the US. But, the US granted only about 25,000 visas. They were concerned that some applicants were German spies, forced to spy for the Nazis to protect their Jewish family members being held in concentration camps. The US Ambassador to France made an outrageous claim that the precipitous collapse of France was due to the devious work of German refugees in France. And the US Attorney General, Francis Biddle, has issued warnings against accepting any more German refugees for fear that many of them are spies. It is not a pretty picture."

The young woman sat down. No one else had the intestinal fortitude to ask another question. Everyone stood up to leave, and a number of people, headed to the back of the lecture hall, where there was a table of hot tea and biscuits.

Hannah wondered about the implications of these lectures. Was it possible that some of the Jewish people in this audience were German spies? Could they be motivated to betray the country that took them in? Many of the Jewish people in the room owed their very lives to Britain. But many might have close family members held by the Nazis. They could even be hostages. And what of her own family? Her father, her mother, her brother. No word from them in over a year. Would she become a spy for Germany to get some news of her family? What lengths would she go to save her family? They too had experienced the tug of war between ancestral heritage and current nationalistic anti-Semitic fervor. Her family had to make some compromises. Some very uncomfortable compromises. Nobody is perfect.

Hannah stood in line for a cup of tea, and was very soon joined by two seventeen-year-old women named Esther and Evelyn who had also come to Britain in the Kindertransport. Both women looked very young to Hannah. They spoke to each other in German.

All were disappointed to hear about the Jewish refugee situation. They shared with Hannah news of their personal lives in Britain and then raised the depressing question of news from their families. There was none.

"Where does that leave me?" asked Esther. "Absolutely alone in a foreign country. Maybe it would have been better if we had stayed with our families, to share their fate?"

"Have either of you heard news from other families?" Esther asked. "We lived in Vienna. My parents were in a collection area when the refugee people picked me up."

"Nothing of my relatives or friends," Evelyn said. "I was an orphan when the transport people came for me."

"I have heard nothing from my parents in Dresden nor from their friends," Hannah said.

The young, blonde woman who had been brave enough to ask a question joined them.

"I thought that I might be the youngest person at these gloomy lectures, but all three of you seem to have deprived me of that honor."

"Hello," they all said in English.

The arrival of this British stranger into their small group of foreign people living under difficult circumstances broke their veil of despair.

"If I had to venture a guess, I would bet that you three arrived in Britain two years ago in the Kindertransport from Germany. If so, I do hope that we have made you feel at home here. You are very welcome!"

Evelyn spoke first. "You are correct. I am Evelyn, and this is my friend, Esther."

Hannah introduced herself.

"We have felt very welcome here. Thank you," said Esther.

"Good to hear. This entire refugee problem is way beyond my comprehension, but I am determined to help in some way. My name is Amanda Haythornwaite. I am so pleased to meet you all."

As was her style, Hannah had been taking everything in before speaking. She could see instantly that Amanda could be a very welcome friend to these three lost souls.

"Amanda," Hannah said. "I for one was very impressed that you asked that question about the US attitude. I was not aware that the US was taking such a firm stand against refugees, and for such a presumably inconceivable concern. German Jewish spies?"

"I have been hearing bits and pieces of this. Why I was seeking clarity. The US is such a huge country, yet welcomes few refugees. I had thought Americans always welcomed refugees—as stated on the Statue of Liberty. Aren't there a significant number of very successful Jews living in American already? They must have some influence. Jewish spies? What secret matters could they possibly be privy to? It makes very little sense to me."

"It's getting late and we want to catch the 4:00 pm bus home," said Evelyn. "I do hope we can connect again." Evelyn and Esther said goodbye.

As they headed off, Hannah picked up the thread of discussion.

"The concern about Jewish refugees being German spies is difficult to dismiss. I encounter that same suspicion whenever I speak in German. So, I try not to. But Germans are not unknown here in Britain. They live just across the Channel, and have for a thousand years. They do seem like your cousins. I am told that your Royal Family are of German descent. But yet we German-Jews are seen as being foreign. It almost makes us feel even more foreign than the German foreigners, like a double foreigner!"

"But you speak English so beautifully. Did you study English in school in Germany?"

"Not actually in school, but in a small private tutorial. Fortunately, as it turned out."

"Quite amazing. You even learned Oxbridge. Most people here would have a hard time believing that you are not a noble English lady! A real-life Eliza Doolittle!" Amanda laughed. "That alone would make you appear to be a spy. Oops, sorry. Poor choice of humor. Forgive me. But I suppose our deadly serious 'cousins' just across the Channel might find you too young, too feminine, and certainly too Jewish to be a trustworthy agent for their evil purposes. You would be a clever choice for them, but our German cousins never seem all that clever."

Amanda's lighthearted banter made it easier for Hannah to open up, after such a depressing meeting. Smiling, Hannah said, "If you do regard the Germans as 'sort of cousins,' maybe we German Jews could be your half-cousins?" They both laughed.

"Hannah, rather than leave a second encounter to chance, please give me your address, and number if you have one. I'll shall give you mine. Would that be of interest to you? It suddenly occurs to me that I am being a bit pushy."

"Not at all. We both share this common pursuit of finding solutions to the burning refugee problems. By virtue of your birth, you stand on one side of the Looking Glass. By virtue of my birth, I stand on the other side. But, in our different ways, we are both there."

"Oh, Hannah. Please don't tell me that *Through the Looking Glass* is also your favorite book?"

"It always has been. In both English and German!"

"Next Tuesday afternoon, there will be a meeting of the Refugee Section at the Colonial Office. Are you planning to attend? We could meet there. Maybe take lunch across the street at the little pub first?"

"I am not an invitee. I suppose that I'd not be able to attend."

"You shall come as my guest."

They agreed. Shook hands, and after a grand exchange of addresses and phone numbers, headed off in opposite directions.

1941

The Battle of Britain

6

A Second Meeting at MI5

28 January 1941, London

Robert was ushered into Jasper Harker's office by Lt. Sarah Leach. He thought for a moment when she greeted him that there might have been just a slight hint of a smile. If so, it was elusive.

"Robert. Good of you to come," said Harker as he rose from his desk to shake Robert's hand. "Please sit down and join us for some tea. Would you prefer coffee?"

"No, no. Tea is fine. Less taste, but less kick."

Lt. Leach sat down beside Robert, both facing Harker.

"So, my people tell me that you spent the Christmas holidays here in London. That must have been pretty dismal. Short days. Rain. Fog. Cold winds. No family. And, oh yes, the nasty German bombing campaign."

"It would have been much more pleasant back in New York City, but steaming back and forth across the Atlantic during the Nazi blockade is not conducive to long life and good health. I did get lots of work done, enjoyed a few quiet holiday parties, and went to church on several occasions. I suppose most Europeans had a pretty miserable Christmas Holiday this year, so I am not going to let myself feel too bad about it. My family in New York had a quiet Christmas, as well."

As they exchanged pleasantries, Robert noticed that Harker seemed particularly on edge. Jasper Harker was never a relaxed fellow. It was never *fun* to head up an intelligence office in wartime, but it was even worse when most of the *intelligence* was really bad news. Today, though, he was looking very resigned and grumpy.

"Robert we could use a bit of advice, and maybe some assistance, if you are able to provide it."

"Please proceed," said Robert.

"Since you and I last spoke in late October, there have been some very dark days, but also a few rays of sunlight. We are hoping to get your astute assessment of current events in the US. Some information we know, but some we either do not know, or do not entirely understand. Is that an acceptable agenda for our meeting today?"

"Yes, it is. As you probably know already, I have been receiving a good amount of information and insight from the States. I will tell you what I can."

"Good. You are free to relate back to your US people my explanation of the situation, so long as you are very comfortable that your people are trustworthy, and that your means of communication are secure. Lt. Leach is both ready and able to help you better secure your lines of communication. I am at liberty to disclose to you that your current communications are not entirely secure, but we believe that they have not, as yet anyway, fallen into the wrong hands."

"Let me share what I expect you already know. The US Ambassador to the Court of St. James, Joseph Kennedy, is very unpopular here. Worst still, he is telling your president that Britain will soon fall. He is wrong. There is much he does not know. Your friend, William Donovan, is in our corner. We need you and Donovan to help us to convince the Roosevelt Administration to come to our aid. That is the purpose of our urgent meeting here today. We have some very useful facts and intelligence to help you.

"Two themes are increasingly clear. We need help *immediately* from our friends in Washington, and The Game is Worth the Candle. We can and will fight on. We are starting to inflict wounds on the German military production of armaments. And, if God forbid, Britain were to fall, the US would be their next target. Robert, I should also add here, that while you may already know a great deal about what we will discuss today, our discussion is classified 'Secret' or 'Top Secret.'"

Robert nodded for him to continue.

Harker shifted in his seat and settled in for a long explanation.

"Everyone, everywhere, is focusing on land battles. But Churchill believes, as do I and MI5, that the most serious threat to the UK is the Battle of the Atlantic. German U-Boats are a major threat to our vital supply lines. We believe that there are about twenty U-Boats in operation each day. Not that many really, but they are having a devastating effect on our shipping. A problem that has been hidden from the public. We are desperately reliant on Canadian naval and air forces. And we have blundered ourselves. When the Germans took France, they gained airfields, radar stations and sub pens on the French coast, all of which the Allies lost, of course, and we also lost the French fleet. We were not fully prepared for this U-Boat threat at the beginning of the war, and once we did finally recognize the threat, we diverted our most effective anti-submarine weapon—RAF Bomber Command—to dropping bombs on German farms and forests instead of knocking out the U-Boats. But because the British people are so blissfully unaware of the U-Boat threat, there continues to be a *great* public hue and cry to bomb Germany. And 98 percent of the German people are not even aware that Germany is being bombed."

Sara looked at Robert, as if to plead, "Say something!"

Robert glanced at her sideways. "Interesting point," he said. "I frequently hear the opposite argument from our friends at Bomber Command."

"Yes," said Harker. "I'm well aware. But you *must* tell your people that we need American air and naval forces to turn the tide in the Battle of the Atlantic."

"I can tell you this, director. President Roosevelt is in full agreement with your views. He is working on it."

"Good to hear," Harker responded, visibly relieved.

"Now let me tell you the real significance of the German bombings on Coventry in November of last year. Coventry, as you know, is an important military industrial center. Population two hundred and fifty thousand. In the eleven-hour raid, they used their new X-Gerat radio beam navigation system to generate crossing radio beams precisely over their target. Their later streams of heavier bombers used the fires as their targets.

"The German strategy was brilliant. We are well on our way to learning their systems, and copying, as soon as possible. It will change RAF bombing strategy and strengthen the RAF "Bomb German Cities Now" mob, which will increase pressure on the US to defend England. Just *watch*."

Harker's mood was lightening. He continued.

"On the subject of the Battle of Britain—this is highly sensitive. Our Air Ministry Intelligence propaganda pins the success on pilot valor—the key to a 'Lucky Victory.' The true picture is far more complex. RAF Fighter Command was far better equipped and trained and ready than the Luftwaffe ever was. Britain was preparing for the battle back in 1937. Hitler anticipated a negotiated solution with Britain. Our fighter pilot training and aircraft production outmatched the Germans handily. We had severe losses, but we started the battle last July with 1,200 pilots, and by November we had 1,800 pilots. Their total number of trained pilots actually dropped. In the closing days of the battle, we believe they lost over 1,500 aircraft. Half the number of the aircraft they had from the beginning. Except for one day, German losses far exceeded RAF losses in every encounter. They were running out of air crews and aircraft. Ironically, we over-estimated the strength of the Luftwaffe, and so we over prepared. The Luftwaffe greatly underestimated the size and strength of RAF Fighter Command, and greatly underprepared. The outcome was no fluke, or stroke of luck. We whipped them soundly. The first major German defeat in the war. Its outcome does not auger well for the Luftwaffe, nor for Germany."

Harker paused finally. Robert sat forward poised to ask questions, but Harker wasn't done.

"I hope you don't mind, Robert, but I've invited Colonel Burnett, one of our senior intelligence advisors, to join us. He will outline what we know, or what we think we know, about German plans to invade England."

Harker buzzed his secretary. "Colonel Burnett can come in now."

Burnett entered and pulled a free chair from against the wall to sit down. Harker introduced him around and Burnett got down to business.

"This potential German invasion saga is enormously intriguing. Last summer, the British people, and probably most Americans, thought a German invasion of Britain was imminent. Watching the tides, there were key dates noted in August, September, October, and November. Weather in the English Channel was an increasing problem for the Germans in September and October, by which time they had assembled a large number of barges. But during those months there were only two or three short periods when there would be a weather opportunity. By November the seas were too rough.

"The prime minister never believed such an invasion was possible. He approved sending troops abroad for other engagements. Hitler allowed the Luftwaffe to try to cripple the RAF, but that never happened. On the contrary, the Luftwaffe was left depleted, and RAF Fighter Command remained largely intact. Moreover, the German Navy was no match for the Royal Navy. By October 1940, it was very clear that Churchill was correct, the Germans were not pursuing an invasion. They lack both air and sea superiority. They also lack a well-trained and well equipped amphibious landing force. But even if they could have successfully landed here, they would have needed ten divisions and thousands of horses. There is no way they could ever have supplied an army half that size. Nor could they have captured the English ports to facilitate that level of supplies."

Done with his report, Burnett shook hands all around and strode out of the room. Harker closed the door behind him, sat down, and lit his pipe.

Robert and Sarah had been listening intently. They asked questions on U-Boat risks and bombing strategies. Then Harker continued.

"I want to call your attention to an issue that everyone seems to be ignoring. Eastern Europe. Hungry tried to stay out of the war. But, in order to fend off the Soviet Union, was pressured to join the Axis last November. That probably added five-hundred-thousand troops to the Axis forces. Then Romania joined the Axis. Another five-hundred-thousand troops, plus the Ploesti Oil Fields—so critical to the German war effort—as Germany has no oil. Greece has been holding its own against the almost always incompetent Italian army, but Germany cannot remain on the sidelines and see its ally embarrassed by the tiny Greek army. We expect the Germans to invade Greece in the next few months. Britain will weigh in, but ultimately cannot defend Greece from the Germans. With Italy and Greece in the Axis camp, expect enormous pressure on Egypt and the Suez Canal. As you can see, Robert, we do desperately need U.S. supplies, ships, planes, guns and tanks, to take and hold control of the Mediterranean Sea and the North African coast. And we need them *now.*"

"Harker, I'm on the case," Robert said turning toward Lt. Leach.

Sarah nodded her approval and gave Robert a warm smile. Then they walked out together.

7

Bomber Command Continuing Problems

23 February 1941, London

The meeting at the Office of Operational Research in the Admiralty Conference Room was small, but the attendees were intimidating. Professor Frederick Lindemann was there to chair the meeting. His principal invitee was Air Chief Marshal Sir Richard Edmond Charles Peirse, the new Air Officer Commanding-in-Chief of RAF Bomber Command. Peirse, who had just replaced Charles Portal in the job, was the son of an admiral, and himself a former Midshipman in the Royal Navy Reserve. He became a pilot in The Great War, and then a squadron commander. He was deeply committed to precision bombing. He also had considerable background in military intelligence.

Another navy pilot, Captain Spencer Haythornwaite, who was still flying off carriers as a combat aviator, had been invited to join them. Lindemann considered Haythornwaite to be a clear thinker with excellent current aviation and bomber experience.

As the group gathered, Lindemann made a beeline for Jacob Bronowski, the University College Hull Mathematics Professor who was now assigned to Operational Research to increase RAF bomber effectiveness. Lindemann and Bronowski did not always agree, but Lindemann found Bronowski both brilliant and interesting. Lindemann knew, though most people did not, that Bronowski graduated from Jesus College, Cambridge, as Senior Wrangler, "the greatest intellectual achievement attainable in Britain, an honor awarded each year to the top mathematics undergraduate at Cambridge."

"Professor Bronowski. I think you will enjoy our little meeting here today. Right up your alley."

Bronowski chuckled. "I suppose the British Government, in its wisdom, has placed me into the bombing business, and left me up that alley. I actually prefer chess, just as you reportedly prefer tennis." They both laughed.

Because of their last names, both Lindemann and Bronowski were generally assumed to be Jews. Bronowski was. Lindemann was not.

Aaron sat observing the crowd, amused to hear the banter between these two intellectual giants, particularly because he knew Lindemann was an arrogant snob who typically looked down on the common man and Bronowski was a renowned humanist who revered the common man. Aaron muttered, "Bombing strategy discussions make strange bedfellows…"

Lindemann called everyone to attention.

"Gentlemen, I have requested this small meeting to explore operational and organizational issues, and bombing strategy disagreements, arising at Bomber Command. My hope is to keep our 'think tank' small so that creative solutions can be explored without undue criticism. I have also invited Robert Johnston at the suggestion of MI5, because MI5 felt that Johnston was *au courant* on US concerns regarding strategic bombing. As well as Dr. Aaron Solomon, my aide for bomber command issues.

Lindemann began by summarizing the problems laid out at Bomber Command in their last meeting. The British were pursuing a precision bombing campaign resulting in very little effective bombing done at enormous cost, money not being spent on the British Army and Navy, which created enormous problems for those two branches.

Peirse, who like his predecessor, Portal, had to play defense, interrupted. "Please believe me," he started, "no one feels the pain more than I do. But someone has to face reality here. Given our mission, the size of our bomber force is pretty pathetic. And the bombers we do have are not well adapted to the task. We do not have the ability to take this precision bombing campaign to the Germans in any meaningful way."

Lindemann was looking for answers and strategies, not excuses and apologies. He puffed up a bit, as was his usual style, and jumped abruptly.

"It is critical to this conversation that we do not engage in a tit-for-tat. No one here is criticizing Bomber Command. This meeting is an airing of views and insights— ideas and suggestions."

"Our targets do require precision bombing," countered Peirse, who eased his tone from defense to problem solving. "We go for oil installations and aircraft production. But, with only three-to-four-hundred bombers, many mediocre, seeking small targets on a gigantic landscape at night, the results are disappointing. And don't underestimate the Luftwaffe and German anti-aircraft activities. They are imposing. We are suffering heavy losses on every raid. We must be careful not to put Bomber Command out of commission entirely."

"Is that a real probability?" Capt. Haythornwaite inquired.

"We lose on average about one-sixth of our aircraft and our crews on every mission."

Jacob Bronowski spoke up. "Do we have any reliable evidence at all that our bombing is having very serious adverse effect on oil and/or aircraft production in Germany? Are the Germans even aware that we are targeting their oil and aircraft production?"

"We think so," Peirse responded. "It would be hard for them to miss our purpose."

Lindemann broke in. "Bronowski's question is highly pertinent here. If the Germans are not particularly aware of our intended targets, it seems we are spinning our wheels with precision bombing. But if they are aware of our particular targets, then the result is even worse for us. We are missing our targets by so wide a mark, they must see us as incompetent. If Bomber Command is, at present, unable to conduct nighttime precision bombing, then a change in mission is required."

"The stated difficulties that Bomber Command are encountering," Capt. Haythornwaite asserted, "makes us wonder whether it might be more fruitful to switch to entirely different targets. The German U-Boat offense is having a terrible impact on Britain. Our best weapon is our aircraft. We could get a much better payback by switching our precision bombing effort to U-boat destruction."

Lindemann jumped at the idea. "Even acknowledging that the captain has a strong branch of service prejudice to the Royal Navy, his suggestion is very worthy. I will speak to the PM about it."

All heartily agreed.

Lindemann continued, "Mr. Johnston, as our captive 'American Adviser,' would your government have wisdom to shed on this conundrum?"

Robert, always the lawyer, measured his comments. "*First*, the US favors only precision bombing of military and industrial targets. Civilian blanket bombing, even as a result of bombing inaccuracy, is condemned by the US Government. Period. The London Blitz was a major factor in pushing the US toward supporting Britain and its allies.

"*Second*, the German U-Boat Offensive in the battle over the Atlantic is a more immediate threat to Britain than German oil and aircraft production, so the captain's proposal makes good sense.

"*Third*, the cost of the bombing campaign over Germany is enormous, in money, effort, manpower and material. I am told that Bomber Command is now costing about 65% of Britain's total defense budget. In your understandable desire for payback for the London Blitz, don't overlook the cost.

"And *fourth*, it is critical for ultimate victory, that Britain and its allies, and the US, *buy time*. It will take time - a few years probably, for our team to arm and muster our considerable forces. I do suspect strongly that the US will weigh in. But that will take time, too. We can all see the wave coming, but it will take time. *Buy Time.*"

All nodded in agreement.

"There is an entirely different potential scenario here," Bronowski offered. "One worth discussing in an open airing of alternatives. One must wonder now whether Germany really even wants war with Britain. Yes, they are bombing us, and we them. But there are also signs that their attention has turned towards the East.

"Of course, like the good captain, I too have my own background to prejudice my views. I am Polish. So, it seems increasingly evident to me that the German appetite for expanding the border to the East aims not just at Eastern Poland, but beyond. *Way beyond*. Because of my background, I am not made privy to any British intelligence but there is plenty of chatter out there.

"If we were to suppose that German territorial expansion looks to the East, rather than to the West, where does that leave us?

"The current mutual bombing campaign between Germany and Britain is at best a nuisance and a burden to Germany. So, a cease fire on their Western Front would be useful to Germany. And it would give us the precious time that our forces need to regroup and rearm.

"If a timely cease fire holds while Germany fries other fish, that could result in a more permanent *detente* with Germany. Our continued bombing campaign over Germany might diminish the possibility of this happening. This is not clear. If our current bombing campaign is largely ineffective, it might lead the Germans to believe that we are not a threat. If they sense that our bombing will rapidly increase in tempo, and become more effective, it is another story.

"Might it not make more sense for Britain to tone it down for now? Let the Germans vent their spleen on other foes, while we live to fight another day? Give our American friends time to arm themselves?"

"It seems inconceivable that the Germans would cease their U-Boat offensive, even if there were a bombing ceasefire," said Haythornwaite.

"Probably true," Robert replied, "but then Britain has substantially more assets to deploy to the Atlantic Campaign – which is a better war scenario for the US and Britain than it is for Germany. And the Germans are certain to lose the Atlantic war, under almost any conceivable scenario."

"I can understand that your knowledge and visibility of the English Channel, and Western areas of France, give you pretty clear insight into the probability of German invasion efforts into Britain," said Bronowski in his thick Polish accent. "But your ability to be certain as to German intentions to the East are less obvious. Gentlemen, do you have 'reliable evidence' to confirm that the German army might be intending to move East?"

The group fell silent. Captain Haythornwaite and Frederick Lindemann looked at each other. Their hesitation was all too obvious.

Bronowski continued.

"Gentlemen, I duly note your hesitation to answer the question I just posed. I have never claimed to be a clever person, I only claim to be a mediocre mathematician. But it does not require a high level of perception for me to deduce that you are unable to share this intelligence with me because I am deemed a suspicious fellow, and a security risk, by our friends at MI5. I am a Polish Jewish refugee. There are worse combinations, I suppose, but my combination is bad enough. I am also aware that MI5 has been keeping an eye on me. If you have such reliable evidence of German intentions, MI5 would probably not allow you to share it with me. So, I withdraw my question. I trust that time will prove me a worthy ally to Britain. But as Lindemann has explained, we are here today to brainstorm openly current critical issues."

Bronowski paused to collect his thoughts and then smiled. Aaron wondered what was next.

"Let me venture an educated guess, just for the purpose of today's conference," said the professor. "I will assume that 'reliable information' does exist that the German Army is in the process of preparing for an invasion of Russia through Poland. As a mediocre mathematician, let me do some simple math for you enhanced by some knowledge of Russian geography, weather patterns and history.

"Russia itself is huge, almost beyond comprehension, 6000 miles from West to East. The country covers eleven time zones. It is 1,200 miles from Berlin to Moscow. Another 400 miles from Berlin to Stalingrad. Traveling there by train is a very long trip. Transporting a huge army over that distance is a monumental, almost inconceivable task. And armies require enormous amounts of food, petrol, clothing, guns, tanks, ammunition, planes, horses, and on and on, every day. Every single day. Even for the mighty German Army, this is clearly impossible. And the impossible task is made many times worse by seven additional obstacles each having catastrophic proportions: *One*, the enormous length of the supply lines from Germany; *two*, the unbearable heat of the Russian summer; *three*, the unbearable cold of the Russian winter; *four*, the very considerable amount of rainfall in Russia; *five*, the resulting terrible road conditions in Russia; and *six*, the probable complete lack of food supplies in Russian territory – because the Russians will burn everything.

"There is also the minor issue of the Russian Army. You may say it is a pathetic army. At present it is, to be sure. Their war in Finland was a debacle. But Russia always does much better on defense, and in bad weather. It will improve significantly on defense and over the winter. And even if it's mediocre, it is an enormous obstacle to overcome.

"As the war progresses, as it most certainly will, Germany might be able to build an army of eight-to-nine million troops. Russia can eventually, and absolutely will, build an army twice that number and more. Great Britain will at most probably be able to field four-to-five million.

The US will likely be forced to join us – they are already far down the path. They can probably easily assemble an army of ten million men. Italy will be there to aid the Axis, but Italy will be unreliable – it always is. More of a liability for Germany, than an asset. So, as events proceed, Germany's 8 to 9 million troops will be facing combined military forces of probably 40 million or more. And Axis forces are landlocked and finite. Allied forces have far greater geography and population sources on which to draw for additional forces and resources.

"A Russian invasion by Germany is not just unwinnable, it is unthinkable. If Hitler actually proceeds with the madcap plan, the total German war effort is clearly doomed. And, ultimately, Germany itself will be utterly destroyed."

Lindemann sat mesmerized at Bronowski's assessment. Silenced for once by a mind even more keen than his own. Peirse and Haythornwaite mulled over the military repercussions for the immense German army. Aaron sat in awe of Jacob Bronowski. Silence prevailed.

Robert finally broke the silence. "The Germans are now the world masters of surprise and Blitzkreig, using overwhelming force. The Russians are no match for them right now. France was quickly overwhelmed."

"As will be the Russians," Bronowski agreed. "But the Russians can and will *trade land for time*. Large amounts of land for large amounts of time. The Germans might even take Moscow. No big deal. The Russian government will just move elsewhere. Remember 1812?"

Bronowski continued, "Everyone seems to have forgotten the French Invasion of Russia in 1812, but it is highly relevant to events today. Napoleon and his Grande Armée of 500,000 troops crossed the Russian border in June 1812, and headed straight for Moscow. The Russians were greatly outnumbered. At The Battle of Borodino, the French defeated the Russians and then entered Moscow in September 1812. The city had been abandoned, and was burning. Napoleon stayed in Moscow for five weeks, waiting for an expected Russian surrender. But the Russians never surrendered. The French Grande Armée was very soon starving, in bitter cold. The French Army horses were dying in droves. The French Army itself was in tatters. They abandoned Moscow in October 1812 and started a long and disastrous retreat back to Paris. Only 100,000 made it back to France. It was the decisive defeat for the French, effectively ending the twelve-year-long Napoleonic Wars.

"In 1812, the French Grande Armée was heavily reliant upon horses for its cavalry, artillery, and transport. When the horses started to die from lack of fodder, the hungry troopers started to eat the horses. Ironically, the German Armies today are also heavily reliant on horses. I suspect that the German horses will very soon suffer a fate similar to that suffered by the French horses 130 years ago. History so often repeats itself."

"A fascinating and incredible tale indeed. Thank you! What is your expectation of the timeline of the German Invasion?" asked Haythornwaite.

"My guess is that the current German led Russian Campaign will last two years, maybe three."

"If we really have two years, we should be able to develop and build a strategic bombing capability," added Lindemann. "But what do we do for the next two years?"

"We'll only build that expertise with a great deal of practice, trial and error, new equipment and some scientific breakthroughs," said Peirse. "Better and more pilot and crew training and experience. So, we should continue on our present track."

"Time marches on," added Haythornwaite. "Relentlessly. Time is always the best ally. Time never loses."

"But for the Germans, if they want to keep their Great Army," said Bronowski, "they need to use it. Now."

"And, for us Brits, if we want a great Bomber Command, we need to use it. Now," added Lindemann. "Bomb what we can bomb. Just be damn sure they know we are bombing. Dropping half our bombs on farmland is not helpful to our cause. Damn it all, Peirse, if we can't hit their prime targets, let's at least be sure that we get their attention. We will have to bomb cities!"

This was not the outcome of the meeting that Peirse was wanting or expecting. An advocate of precision bombing, he now suspected he was the wrong man for the job of commanding RAF Bomber Command. Aaron looked at Robert. Each of them were subtly shaking their heads. In their view, bombing German cities would not be productive, and could actually be counterproductive. But Lindemann had already expressed his views, and Aaron was not in a position to correct his boss. Haythorn-waite was neither surprised nor bothered by Lindemann's assessment. Bronowski just listened. His own assessment was that this debate was far from over, and would probably rage on for years. He was a wise and patient man.

Looking around the room, Lindemann could see the very mixed reactions. It was his turn to speak, as chairman, to wrap things up. "Many thanks to all of you. It is clear that we do not all agree, but at least we have been open and candid. I will quickly bring these views to the attention of our prime minister and the War Cabinet. And we shall meet again in the near future to revisit our recommendations based upon future events. Meeting adjourned."

8

A Contact from Germany

12-13 March 1941, London

A few weeks later, Robert was working in his office. A quiet day. His secretary, Kathleen Scott, came in.

"Robert, there is an odd call for you. From Madrid. I understood the caller to say that her name is Maria Santiago. She said you won't know her, but she could explain the call if you could speak with her yourself for just a few minutes. She then said that it relates to Gleiss GmbH."

"Gleiss GmbH— that's a name I haven't heard for some time. Please put her through. This might be interesting."

Picking up the receiver, Robert said, "Hello?"

"Forgive me for asking," Maria said in a heavy Spanish accent, "are you Señor Robert Johnston, the American lawyer who performed legal work for Gleiss GmbH in Berlin back in 1937? I do need to confirm."

"I am, and I did. I can confirm that, but I'm afraid that I can't confirm or discuss the nature of the work. It was not a sensitive assignment, but I do not know to whom I am speaking."

"I entirely understand. One more question to verify. Can you name, please, the chairman of Gleiss GmbH?"

"Yes, I can. Doctor Christian von Buckholtz."

"That verification is entirely sufficient for my purpose. I am calling you at the request of Herr Doctor Christian von Buckholtz. He is asking if you would receive a visit from a very close friend of his. A Spanish citizen from Madrid, who has some sensitive information to share with you. Dr. von Buckholtz believes you will find the information of great interest."

"To me? Why?"

"I do not know why Herr Doctor von Buckholtz wishes to share this information with you. But I have known Dr. von Buckholtz for many years, and I trust his word on this."

"I trust his word on this, too. How is he? He was not particularly supportive of the new Nazi Regime, but it also seems that most Germans have now fallen in line with their government."

"I do not know his political views. He has never shared them with me. But he is very wise and perceptive and discreet. Very discreet."

"Very well, Miss Santiago. How am I to meet this friend of his?"

"His name is Juan Frederico. You may have heard of him. He was employed in the Gleiss Office in Madrid for many years. He is currently visiting in London and staying at the Savoy Hotel. He is available to meet with you whenever or wherever is convenient for you."

"Best to meet at the Savoy. I suggest tomorrow at 11 a.m. in a private room, if he has access to one. Miss Santiago, could you relay this information to him?"

"I will call him now, and call you back shortly."

"Please give my regards to Dr. von Buckholtz. Perhaps he and I can talk directly one of these days."

At 10:45 a.m. the next morning, Robert entered the sedate lobby of the Savoy Hotel and asked the doorman to direct him to Room 5 on the Conference Level. When he entered the room, a tall, thin gentleman of a somewhat Iberian appearance rose to greet him.

"Mr. Johnston?"

"Señor Frederico?"

"Please call me Juan. It is so good to meet you. Many people who worked with you at Gleiss in the '30s still speak very highly of you, but most especially Herr Doctor von Buckholtz."

"Kind of him to say. We developed a good working relationship in those days. But now it seems that many old continental friends have become separated by current events. And it gets worse every day."

They both sat down at a small table adorned with a white table-cloth, heavy silverware, a silver coffee urn, and a small plate of neatly trimmed sandwiches, brought by room service at Señor Frederico's request.

"I assume, like most Americans, you probably prefer coffee over tea. I hope so, but I can order tea or perhaps a glass of wine? Living in Madrid, I certainly prefer coffee."

"Please call me Robert. I am curious about the view of the war from Madrid."

"It appears to us that Germany is everywhere. Britain and its allies seem to be withering on the vine. The odds against Britain holding firm are long indeed. May I ask your view from London?

"Britain alone is a long shot. But the U.S. approved Lend Lease just yesterday. Britain plus its global empire plus the U.S. will be a formidable team. If Germany hopes to win the long game, it cannot afford to make many mistakes. They just made a costly mistake taking on the RAF in the Battle of Britain."

"Perhaps so, Robert, but the RAF also paid a high cost. In any event, please allow me to explain the purpose of the meeting. As you may already know from your many contacts in Germany, there are factions there that have divergent views as to which course of action, both military and political, would be in Germany's best interests."

Robert was careful to look interested, but not surprised at this comment.

"Yes. That does seem evident."

"Some military factions believe, for example, that Germany's long-term strategic military objectives could be better accomplished by striking some form of détente with Great Britain."

Both Robert and Juan paused for a moment to let it sink in. This was an unexpected and unwelcome bombshell. Robert realized he had to be careful not to register his discomfort to Juan. He sought a way to defuse the intensity, and quickly. He tried to relax.

"It is difficult to find unanimity in any country today. There are certainly some factions in the U.K. that oppose the war. And, in the U.S., there are many factions that oppose the war. But, I gather that you have something more specific to relate? And some specific reason for relating this to me?"

"I do. The faction I am referring to does not oppose the war. Not at all. But they do believe that Britain is thoroughly defeated and will never pose a serious military threat to a now unified Nazi Europe. Britain will almost certainly seek some sort of alliance with Germany in the near future. Sooner would save a great many British and Common-wealth lives."

Robert tried not to look annoyed. "Living here in London, I don't have the impression that Great Britain senses defeat or is considering withdrawing from the war effort against Germany. On the contrary, the Brits seem to be mobilizing all of their resources and energy to carry the war to its bitter end and destroy Nazi Germany down to its roots."

Juan dug in. "From your viewpoint, and the viewpoint of a typical British citizen, that is the perception. But senior elements in the British Government know it is futile. Entirely futile. Look at the facts. At Dunkirk, Britain suffered the worst military defeat in European history. Over 200,000 British troops left the continent in total disarray. They didn't even inform their French allies that they were deserting the field of battle. Only after pulling out their own troops, after those days on the beach, did they reluctantly rescue a small number of French troops. Over 40,000 French troops— the same French troops that had been defending them—were left behind and captured by the Germans. The Wehrmacht and the Fuhrer claimed it as a major German victory. Tons of British military equipment were abandoned on the beach. Enough equipment for ten German divisions. Almost all of the French soldiers taken off the beach and sent to northern England promptly returned to France where they were killed in the war effort. Now the British seem focused primarily on sending and killing hundreds of British boys to die in a futile bombing campaign where most of the British bombs are dropped on farms."

Midway through this monologue, Robert crossed his arms and sat upright in his chair. He gave Juan a very piercing and penetrating stare. He was now highly annoyed at hearing the painful and one-sided recount of the "German View of Dunkirk." He hoped he wasn't showing it.

"Juan, I guess you have answered my first question, by giving me specifics regarding who sent you here, and why. But I still do not know why you are discussing these specifics with me. Why are you meeting with me today, and why are you giving me all this Nazi propaganda? I'm sure you are not expecting to win me over to the German side."

Juan realized that he had gotten carried away on Dunkirk, and so tried to shift gears. "Certainly not. Here is my point. My friends in Germany need a line of communication to explore whether there might be a possibility for some limited détente between Britain and Germany. I realize this is very awkward for you and for us. But, trust me, it is critical to my message that you understand the view of the war from the Wehrmacht perspective in order for you to understand why they believe so strongly that their position is eminently reasonable for the British. As a lawyer, I'm sure you can appreciate often both sides can hold different and yet reasonable views."

"Am I correct in surmising that this 'message' does not have the Blessing of the Fuhrer?"

"No. Not precisely."

"Doesn't that make our meeting here today a huge waste of time?"

"I urgently hope not. Our group does know with absolute certainty that the Fuhrer would welcome a proposal from Britain along these lines. He has expressed his feelings to close confidants on a number of occasions. There are a good many reasons why he cannot express them directly. For many similar reasons, the British prime minister would never want to pursue and discuss this *directly*. And, in this case, he probably would not be willing to pursue and discuss this even *indirectly*."

"As both you and Dr. von Buckholtz are well aware, I am a private US citizen, living in London with the permission of the U.K. government for the purpose of conducting private business matters between private US persons and businesses and private UK persons and businesses. I have never met the prime minister, and I'm sure that he would throw me out of his office, and out of the country, were I ever to bring this proposal to him."

Juan nodded. "We fully agree that the prime minister would not welcome this overture. We think that it must be brought to the attention of King George VI, personally, or to his inner circle. He is the only leader here in Britain with the scope, vision, and authority to make this happen. Ironically, this is all very reminiscent of World War One when Germany sent out 'feelers' to see if England and France would make a temporary peace, so that Germany could deal with Russia. It never happened, of course."

Both Robert and Juan sat back quietly to think, but Robert knew very well the risk of sitting in silence too long, as silence often conveys acquiescence.

"Juan, I don't know how I could ever convey this information to King George or his inner circle. You surely must know that the king has no authority to enter into a binding agreement or such a detente. The British Government alone has the authority. In any event, I am probably the wrong person to even carry such a message, but I will need some time to digest your proposal. Please convey that message to your group."

Juan looked relieved at having been "deferred" rather than "rejected." He smiled just a little, and said, "I will convey the message to them as you requested. Deal with this proposal as you please. But the US is a neutral in the war, and so are you. You have an affection for the British, that is quite obvious. A great many British lives are at stake here. If the US eventually enters this war, the loss of American lives will also be enormous. Bright young lives. With bright young futures. I'll leave the ball in your court. Thank you for meeting with me. If you want to reach me, you know how to do so."

They shook hands perfunctorily and left the small conference room.

Robert returned to his office, deeply troubled. His legal mind was reeling. Was he committing treason? Probably not. He was just listening. But having heard the "message," there was some obligation to pass it on. And it had a short fuse. If word got back to MI6 or MI5 that this meeting even occurred, and was not reported, it would put Robert in an awkward spot. But take it to whom? Being a lawyer, he pulled out a yellow legal pad and a sharp pencil and began to jot down the names he might contact to report the meeting. Most, if not all, would constitute an "official report through an official channel." But how could he possibly make an official report of such an exploratory meeting. It would make no sense whatsoever to take it to "official channels." What were the "unofficial channels?"

As he sat staring at his list, deep in thought, and wrote the words "unofficial channels." As is often the case, seeing the words in writing triggered his memory.

Unofficial Channeling. Weren't those the words used by that standoffish Lt. Sarah Leach at MI5 last November? He had thought about her from time-to-time. His impression of her that day was still vivid in his memory. Exceedingly attractive, exceedingly bright, excessively "proper," elusive and alluring. What exactly did she say? That pub where she liked to go for drinks on Friday nights for some "unofficial channeling" among the "local spooks and Dukes." What was the name of that place? The Old Bell Tavern on Fleet Street. She was very precise with the details of where and when she had dinners there. *Usually on Friday evenings.* It almost sounded like a standing invitation. And Lt. Leach would be interesting company. Plus a few drinks and a hot dinner. Better than most of his Friday nights. And it was already Thursday!

9

The Old Bell Tavern

14 March 1941, London

At 7 p.m. the next evening, Robert walked into The Old Bell Tavern for the first time. There was quite a crowd. Some talking and drinking. Some snuggling and drinking. Some eating and drinking. Many just drinking.

Mostly a professional crowd. Some in dresses, suits and ties, even some uniforms. Some junior British officers – Army, Navy, and RAF. It was clearly a bit of a pickup scene.

Music played from somewhere behind the long, large bar. A big band sound. A woman singer. Warm mood. Was there a record player back there? A nice touch, Robert thought. All very cozy. Very British. Very convivial. And best of all, very noisy. Good cover for a sensitive conversation.

After ten minutes or so, Robert spotted Sarah in a group of impressive looking young men and women. Five men, three women. Everyone talking at the same time. A beer or ale in every hand. It looked like a movie set.

Sarah was not wearing her uniform, but one of the men was, and so was one of the other women. Probably a safe assumption that they were all military types. They looked pretty professional, but they were letting loose "after hours." Robert paused for a minute – should he be spoiling their fun? Would Lt. Leach be annoyed to see him?

He soon had his answer. Sarah saw him and lit up like a firefly. She actually smiled. Broadly.

"Robert! So nice to see you here. You look like you need a drink or a hot supper, or both after a long day at the office."

She walked over to him but did not offer a handshake. Maybe people don't usually do that in pubs during witching hours?

"Hello Sarah. Nice to see you. Do you recommend the food here? I am actually pretty hungry tonight, and there does appear to be a number of people eating – always a good sign."

"Very good food. Are you alone? I was hoping to get a bite myself. Should we join forces and fight our way to a table?"

Robert nodded and looked around. There didn't appear to be any empty tables.

"It looks like we may have to eat at the bar."

"No, no, no, Robert. That won't do. I will get us a nice quiet table where we can visit."

Robert wondered if she might have read his mind. He recalled a couple of her spot-on insights at the MI5 tea trolley, and he surmised that she surmised his "bumping into her" in the pub was not just a chance encounter.

For her part, Sarah was on the same wavelength. She sensed that Robert had a purpose. And whether the purpose was MI5 business or pleasure (beyond the drink and hot meal), she wanted to hear all about it. Robert was a special fellow on several fronts. A quiet, private table was just the ticket.

Sarah eyed the most secluded table in the pub, back in a dim corner under the stairs. A nice young couple sat there huddled close. Sarah grabbed the arm of one of the waiters—one of her chums—and spoke a few words into his eager ear.

Owen, the waiter, listened very carefully, cast a slightly annoyed look at Robert, and then spoke with the two people at the table. In short order, the couple stood up and moved over to the bar, with Owen carrying their plates behind them. Then Owen ceremoniously uncorked an expensive looking bottle of wine "on the house," poured each a glass, and set the bottle down on the bar between them. The young couple looked very happy. It was a fair trade.

Owen then cleared and reset the table and seated Robert and Sarah. Sarah gently placed her hand on Owen's right upper arm, and gave him a warm smile. As she did, she pointed at the expensive looking bottle of wine between the young couple. Owen smiled broadly, placed his left hand on Sarah's hand, and nodded. Within three minutes flat, Owen was back with a bottle of the very same wine, plus two wine glasses, all of which he carefully placed between Robert and Sarah. Sarah gave Owen a big smile and a wink.

As Owen walked away, Robert said, "You seem to be pretty well-known here. What do you think our waiter told that couple to get them to move?"

"Owen told the couple that one of his "regulars" had booked that particular table to have dinner with a "very dear old friend," who was just back in London from a dangerous mission in the North Atlantic. He offered them a pricey bottle of wine if they would move to the bar. Looks like they were happy to accommodate."

As they drank the wine, Robert and Sarah chatted about London and the war and the weather and such, then ordered some dinner, and poured another glass.

Sarah behaved like a Siamese cat. She kept looking into Robert's eyes. Carefully listening whenever he spoke. Never interrupting him. Smiling just a little, but keeping her distance without seeming distant. He thought, she's a classic British beauty like those lovely young women in Gainsborough portraits. She made Robert feel very comfortable. As they began to dig into their light supper, and drink some red wine, he found it very easy to open up to her.

"It is no coincidence that I came here tonight."

Sarah the Siamese cat opened her eyes just a tiny bit wider.

"I do suspect that you sort of know that," Robert said. "You told me last winter that you like to come here for dinner on Friday nights."

Sarah looked at him with her cat-like eyes. Not smiling. Not talking. Just listening. All big eyes and ears. But she opened her eyes just a bit more, and she moved her chair just a bit closer.

"I was hoping to get your insight, advice maybe, on a particular situation that arose earlier this week."

"Of course," she said. "Please continue."

Robert then told her all about the Juan visit. Sarah spoke not a single word while Robert went through the visit. Did she ever blink? Robert couldn't remember. It was almost like she was casting a spell. This lady is a real pro, he thought. I've come to the right "unofficial channel."

"I realized I had to report this meeting to someone. I don't want the British Government to suspect me of being a foreign agent."

Sarah thought for a minute. "You were wise to share the story with me. With us. If this meeting with Juan Frederico is known in MI5, suspicions might be raised. A number of German agents are working in the country these days. We keep a close eye on their activities. I cannot say that this Frederico is one of them. I just do not know. Several aspects of his conversation do have a familiar sound. We are aware that the Fuhrer has expressed some interest in a separate peace plan with Britain. But his reasons are not immediately evident.

"There is a good amount of logistical evidence that the Germans have sidelined their plan to invade Britain. Maybe wishful thinking on our part. There is also a good amount of logistical evidence that the Germans are positioning their troops either to invade Russia or defend against a Russian attack. Maybe more wishful thinking on our part.

"*First,* a separate temporary stand down with Britain would be useful to the Germans. *Second,* the deep and well-founded fear in the Wehrmacht of waging a two-front war would explain and justify some high-placed Germans pursuing this stand-down of forces, and *third,* using a well-regarded Yank—you of course—to broker a deal makes good sense. Churchill would never consider a deal with Germany if it meant jeopardizing U.S. support. As you well know, Robert, any such deal by Churchill would constitute one of the biggest and most embarrassing turnarounds in history. Not going to happen. Never."

Robert frowned, but then smiled. "I guess you have summarized things very succinctly. I'm beginning to wish that I never met with Frederico. I don't like being the monkey in the middle."

Sarah laughed, maybe for the first time.

"Your meeting with him was very useful, for all of the reasons I've just laid out. Would you be willing to meet with him again? Through his contacts in Germany, he might be able to provide us with some greater knowledge of the German plans for Russia. Would you do that for us?"

This time Robert smiled. "For us? Not in a million years! For you? Probably."

"I like that, Robert. Most of this human intelligence game, 'humint,' as we call it, is based upon human-to-human contact and trust. Please talk to Juan again, and get back to me. One more thing we would like to know from you. FDR signed the Land-Lease Act. Does this mean that the Yanks are coming?"

"I would bet my life on it. The German and Japanese constant heavy bombing campaigns against civilians and cities are accelerating the process of turning U.S. support towards Britain and China. Back in the Great War, when you were just a little girl, America finally decided to go to war against Germany, not for love of Britain and France, but because the Krauts were killing Belgian civilians and sinking civilian ships. But it will take a little more time to ignite the Yanks. And maybe some precipitating event."

"That is very good news," she said. She put out her hand, and Robert shook it warmly. And she held on for another minute or two.

They both stood up. Robert paid the bill.

"I am here almost every Friday night," she pressed a small piece of paper into his hand, "but here is my personal phone line. Whichever line of communication is best for you. If you want to set up something more private, just let me know." She held her hand in his for a moment, looked at him, smiled a little, and returned to her friends. As Robert watched Sarah walk away, he felt again a little tinge of that nagging loneliness. He did like to watch Sarah walk, but not away. And he was already plotting their next meeting. Juan was now his secret weapon.

10

Robert Seeks Some Feedback

22 March 1941, London

Robert and Juan sat facing each other again in the small Savoy room at a table with coffee and biscuits. Both wore dark suits. Robert appeared relaxed and earnest. Juan was very clearly nervous and twitchy. He held a biscuit, but didn't eat it. He did sip some coffee.

"Thank you for taking this meeting on such short notice. I'm sure it was inconvenient for you."

"I was happy to hear from you, Robert. I thought that our last meeting did not end so well. I appreciate these clandestine meetings put you in an uncomfortable situation. I am hoping you were able to make headway with the right people to address my earlier 'message.' Time is now even more critical."

Robert paused for effect. Why was Juan so nervous? This was not Juan's mission. He said he was just a facilitator. But there was something more.

"Juan, this is such a sensitive subject, I want to be very candid with you."

Another long pause.

"I have not approached the king. I do not know him. Nor have I approached his inner circle. It would put you and me in jeopardy to do so. But I can tell you this. For me to consider seriously the prospect of passing your message to higher circles, I would need to be able to provide my contacts with some justification for advancing this mission. Some quid pro quo."

Juan stared Robert down for a few minutes. "Such as?"

"Information to support your mission here. The German Government is giving every indication they plan to destroy the military forces of the U.K., and then invade the Island. Under this scenario, an appeal to the king for a separate detente would be regarded here as a cruel hoax, a deceptive diversion, or worse. I do need further intelligence from you to give credence to this effort. I do not know the scope of your mandate, or what you can share. But as you can see, I do need something more."

Another very long pause. Juan's lankiness made his nervous mannerisms more obvious. He put down the uneaten biscuit and glanced around. He took more coffee, then looked hard at Robert.

"There are a number of guideposts that should be evident to your sources—whomever they might be. From what I do know about you, Robert, I believe your 'sources' in the U.K. are largely British Government functionaries, not members of nobility or royalty. If I am right, they must be aware of political and military facts and assumptions that lead to certain conclusions. *First*, the Nazi-Soviet Pact signed on 23 August 1939 was designed to facilitate the division of Poland. That has been accomplished. *Second*, any pact signed by the likes of Hitler and Stalin is worthless. The Soviets are moving heaven and earth to arm the USSR. It seems highly unlikely that the Soviets are doing so in order to invade Britain. They have only one possible target-Germany. *Third*, the core strengths of the German military forces, as we have all seen, are its tank and infantry forces, each of which requires literally thousands of horses. The logistics of transporting and supporting such forces for an invasion of the UK are highly problematic, but such forces are ideal in pursuing a land war into Poland and beyond. My friends and 'contacts' in Germany are the officers who do and will command these infantry and tank forces. And they are very well aware of the fact that they will soon have to deploy and command these German forces in a major military campaign against the USSR. Your British friends must be aware that Germany has moved substantial forces into eastern Poland and elsewhere to fend off, or perhaps launch a pre-emptive strike on, the Soviet forces. I am not in a position to give you more background to underpin the credibility of my message, with perhaps one possible addition."

"You present a credible scenario, Juan. I see why elements of the German military would have concerns about the prospects of a two-front war. It was a losing venture twenty-six years ago, although the Eastern Front did collapse with the creation of the Soviet Government. What is the 'one possible addition' you mentioned?"

Juan sat quietly, deep in thought, sipping his new cup of coffee. He hoped to convey to Robert that by revealing his "one possible addition," he was really sticking his neck out. If his "addition" turned out to be true, he would establish considerable credibility. But, if not, he would look very foolish. In the end, he decided to reveal it. His orders from Berlin were to establish credibility and so far he was failing to do so.

"I have good reason to believe that a very senior member of the Fuhrer's inner circle may very soon make a personal effort to contact the inner circle of King George with the same message that I have given to you. I am dealing with some very murky reports and suspicions here. I cannot be certain about this information. But it is well known among the inner circle that the Fuhrer is very interested in finding a resolution with England, and it is very well known that his inner circle is hyperactive in finding ways to curry favor with the Fuhrer, no matter how bizarre a result that might produce."

"I gather that if there were to be such an overture, even from a high-placed person, Hitler would not openly endorse or embrace it?"

"Most assuredly not. He would want it to appear that the concept of a separate détente with England was *presented* to him by England. Not *offered* by him to England."

"And how soon might this clandestine overture be received here?"

"Very soon, based on the points I made to you at the outset of our discussion today."

"Thank you, Juan. Our conversation does provide me with some color of credibility. Further evidence of credibility would be provided if this 'senior member of the Fuhrer's inner circle' were actually to appear. I need to determine whether or not I can do anything with this information to advance your message. I am still very dubious that King George would be inclined to give the universally detested German Fuhrer any assistance in expanding Greater Germany. But you also have a point that these seemingly endless confrontations with Germany will be costly beyond belief to the United Kingdom. Leave it with me. I will be back in touch with you."

"Robert, there is one element here that I feel I should underscore. And I want to be crystal clear. All of the information which I have received and all of the information that I have conveyed to you, comes exclusively from highly-placed German military sources. Neither I nor Dr. von Buckholtz have any 'close friends' in the German Government. There are reasons for that, of course, but that is another very long story."

"You have told me that. Thank you." Robert thought for a moment, and then asked, "If Germany were to attack Russia, when do you suppose that might happen?"

Juan looked at Robert, and said, "That I do not know, but the messenger might know. Someone should ask him."

This time they parted with a warm handshake.

After Juan left the room, Robert sat back down to finish his coffee and munch on another biscuit. He thought about Juan's message and mannerisms. He could plainly see that Juan was a puppet. So, von Buckholtz might be the puppeteer. Fair enough, he thought. Von Buckholtz set up the meeting. But Juan was too nervous to be delivering someone else's mail. Juan has some skin in this game. There is a deeper plot here, and therefore some risk, Robert thought to himself.

11

Juan Reports to Base

23-24 March 1941, Lisbon

When Juan returned to his room at The Savoy, it was foremost on his mind that he needed to check in with Berlin. The meeting had not gone as planned. Robert was clearly skeptical of his message, and even of Juan himself. As a result, he felt that he had to take a risky step, predicting a highly secretive, private approach to King George VI by a very senior member of the Fuhrer's inner circle, although no such approach might be made and no such envoy might arrive to deliver it.

The result of such a failure would sink Juan's entire effort to build a bridge to US intelligence operations in London.

Juan felt that he had to cross that bridge. But Berlin might disagree.

He could not make a call to Berlin from London, even if he wanted to, so the next day he flew to Lisbon, where he checked into the Hotel Atlantico. He would have preferred his favorite hotel, the Palacio Estoril, but he knew it would be crawling with British agents. At least most of the agents hanging around the lobby and lounge at the Atlantico would be Germans. A call to Berlin for instructions from the Atlantico would be the rule, not the exception.

Once settled in his room, Juan called Sonja, Dr. von Buckholtz' personal secretary, and asked her to set up a private call with the boss. Two hours later, Sonja, a statuesque blonde from Eastern Germany, called back to say that the call was set for 2:00 p.m., Berlin time the following day.

Precisely at 2:00 p.m. the next day, Sonja rang with Dr. von Buckholtz on the line.

"Hello Juan. I am very anxious to hear the outcome of your meeting with my friend, Robert Johnston. And how is he, by the way?"

"He is well. And very well connected into the London scene. Everyone in London wants to connect to the White House, and Johnston is the man of the hour."

Juan carefully recounted their discussion at the meeting and explained his dilemma on predicting a messenger who, and a message which, might never materialize.

In the silence that followed, Juan could hear that von Buckholtz had muffled his phone, and was speaking to someone in the room with him. Then von Buckholtz spoke again.

"Juan, I do agree. You took a big risk. But I suppose you had no choice. If we hope to establish a close link to Mr. Johnston, we must show some credible information to him. It is a high stakes game for us. If all else fails, Juan, and the messenger and the message fail to materialize, I am sure that we can generate both a messenger and a message from our own resources. So, do not let it concern you. In the meantime, keep your oar in the water in London, and find out as much as you can for us."

"I have broken the ice with Johnston, as you directed. But he is no fool. He told me that he has no direct access to the king, nor to the king's circle of friends. I cannot be sure if, or when, he will get back to me. But if he does, can you give me some instructions as to the information you seek from him?"

Silence again on the Berlin end of the line. Muffled talking. Maybe arguing. Then silence again. Then Dr. von Buckholtz spoke again, sounding as if he were interrupting or perhaps overruling the "other voice in the room."

"On 11th of March, just two weeks ago, President Roosevelt signed the U.S. Land-Lease Act. It was a shocking move against The Third Reich, and broke all of the promises he made to the millions of German-Americans when he was running for office. The Fuhrer, in his "wisdom," is dismissing any U.S. contribution to the U.K. war effort, but our group is very concerned. If the U.S. launches a major campaign to provide substantive military supplies to the Allies, it could make a huge change in the tide of the war over the next several years. We need a window into the White House as to their long-term plans regarding Land-Lease. Will it be just some old U.S. destroyers, or will it be thousands of planes, tanks, guns, and ships? Robert Johnston could be that window for us. He lived and worked in Germany. I know for a fact that he admires the German people. Not the current Nazi government, but the people of Germany.

He might be a receptive target for us. In addition, Johnston is well placed to pick up very useful information on British Bomber Command plans, equipment, technology, and capabilities. I personally feel the Bomber Command will become an ever-growing threat to Germany, especially if the Luftwaffe has to turn most of its attention to dealing with other military objectives. Juan…hold on one minute…"

More muffled conversation on the Berlin end.

"Juan. It would be helpful here to know how much support the British can and will provide to the Greek Army. Picking up the pieces from the disgraceful defeat of the Italian Army is proving to be a major diversion for German troops, which are needed elsewhere."

"Thank you, doctor. I'll do my best."

"From what you have told me, it sounds as though the time may not be propitious to rely heavily on Robert Johnston. He seems to be highly preoccupied. Back off of him for the moment. He will soon see that your message and messenger were accurate. You now have plenty of other sources in your London network. Focus on them. The approach to Johnston can await further developments in Germany and the US. That will take time. And, Juan?"

"Yes, doctor?"

"What you are doing is very dangerous. Be very careful. We cannot protect you in London."

"That you for the warning. Frankly, I'm more worried about the Gestapo on my trips to Berlin."

"You should be. But our group here in Berlin does have some control of the Gestapo side of the equation. We can deal with them."

12

Bomber Command – The Search for the Truth

10 April 1941, London

Professor Lindemann was in his office with Aaron discussing the success, or lack thereof, of the British bombing campaign over Germany.

Lindemann sat at his desk looking very displeased. He was reviewing reports from Bomber Command.

"As usual, Portal was right," he said to Aaron without looking up at him. "When Churchill ordered Bomber Command to concentrate on defending our seaborne supply lines, Portal said Churchill was doing Bomber Command a huge favor. The bombing raids on German oil facilities were ineffective. But the PM didn't issue the new directive to save face for Bomber Command. Since the fall of France, our shipping has been hammered. Nearly nine hundred British Allied and neutral ships have been sunk. We cannot protect the convoys by sea, nor by air. And not just U-Boats. Two German battle cruisers, *Scharnhorst* and *Gneisenau,* have been single-handedly sinking our merchant ships at will. Our old warships cannot even catch them! And *Bismarck*—the formidable new German battleship—is almost ready to set sail. German long-range bombers— *Focke Wulf Kondors*—are now also an active threat. Spencer Haythornwaite and Robert Johnston were correct in their advice in the meeting back on February 23rd. We do need to focus Bomber Command on the German threat to our vital supply lines. I am finding these daily Bombing Command diary reports on bombing raids on Germany to be completely frustrating. No one knows the true facts. Bomber Command reports from pilots tell us that their raids are highly successful, but do they even know?"

Aaron waited a moment to ascertain whether Lindemann was seeking his opinion or asking a rhetorical question. Then he spoke, "I am very concerned about the accuracy of any of these Bomber Command reports on the success of their raids. Most of the raids are at night, of course. Visibility is either scant, or non-existent. Navigation aids are primitive, at best. The aircrews have limited training in both navigating and conducting bombing missions. They have little or no training at all in assessing bomb damage. They are very concerned about their own lives, and so eager to return to base. They may see some lights on the ground as they are flying. They may see some bomb flashes near these lights as they are heading home. But that is all they know. The German reports from the bombing scenes are intentionally unreliable and mostly fabricated."

"I agree," Lindemann snorted. "What we need is reliable photo reconnaissance and independent analysis. It is counterproductive to have Bomber Command grading its own papers. I do have a plan, but it is risky business. I strongly suspect that the closer we look at the success of our bombers, the more disillusioned we shall become."

There was knock on the door, and Lindemann's secretary announced Capt. Haythornwaite had arrived, along with David Miles Bensusan-Butt who was assigned to Lindemann as a personal assistant, on loan from the Admiralty.

"Gentleman. Thank you for coming today. It is a pleasure to see my two favorite Navy men."

Haythornwaite had a big laugh. Butt wasn't sure if he was allowed to laugh at or even with Lindemann, but he did so anyway.

Lindemann continued. "Dr. Solomon and I have been discussing the present state and the future progression of our illustrious Bomber Command. We need an independent assessment. Who better to provide this than David Miles Bensusan-Butt, a Navy man who is also an economist!"

Butt's face flushed in shock. Haythornwaite couldn't help but laugh again. He was happy to see Lindemann stick it to Bomber Command, which had been hogging all the glory.

Lindemann explained that what was clearly needed was a thorough and important assessment of the effectiveness of the RAF Bomber Command bombing runs over Germany, and why he wanted David Butt to do it. Butt was impartial. He did not have a horse in this race.

Aaron felt a pit in his stomach. He knew that David Butt was extremely talented, knowledgeable, and insightful. But he also knew that this study would be highly critical and negative, and therefore very unpopular at Bomber Command. No one wanted to tell the Emperor that he had no clothes. He was also sensitive to two factors that Lindemann, in his wisdom, probably overlooked.

First, David Bensusan-Butt came from a half-Jewish family. His mother Ruth Bensusan-Butt was known to Aaron because she too was a Jewish doctor. Aaron also knew that Ruth Bensusan-Butt was a Socialist.

Aaron considered raising the issue of Butt's family in private with Lindemann after the meeting. Everyone was virtually certain that Butt's report would be poorly received. And having the author of the report be a half-Jewish person from a half-Socialist family would not improve its reception by Bomber Command. But he decided that it would be better not to raise these sensitive issues. Lindemann was known to be anti-Semitic. Jews were already "suspect" in England for allegedly ducking military service. So, having one Jewish officer raise an issue about another Jewish officer being given a sensitive and critical assignment because of that other officer's Jewish faith was a non-starter. And he also suspected that David Butt would be highly incensed at being disqualified for this critical and desperately needed assignment on account of his mother.

Butt was a brilliant Cambridge man, and well suited for the assignment, so Aaron held his tongue, offering instead to give Butt any assistance he might require. But everyone in the room was virtually certain that the report was going to be a blockbuster, and that only Frederic Lindemann, Lord Cherwell himself, had the courage and wisdom to commission it. Aaron Solomon also surmised that the search for the best and most defensible use of their growing fleet of RAF bombers would continue for years. There were no easy answers.

13

A Visit from Sarah

13 April 1941, London

At 5:00 p.m. on Sunday afternoon, there was a triple light tap on the door of Robert's house. When he answered, he found Lt. Sarah Leach standing there. She was wearing an unbuttoned coat over a brown sweater and a brown loose skirt, which ended just below her knees, and low heel brown shoes. Almost like a public school uniform. The outfit looked good on her. Robert wondered if there was some significance to the fact she was not in her military uniform, as this visit was more or less an "official meeting," but also, "unofficial channeling."

She wasn't wearing a big smile, but she did look happy to see him. He was certainly happy to see her.

"Lt. Leach. Or perhaps I should call you Mrs. Leach, as you have "donned your mufti.""

At this, she did laugh.

"You are so very Shakespearean. Please don't call me Mrs. Leach, whatever I am wearing. Or not wearing. I am not married. Never have been. Might never be. Leach is my father's last name. And no man in his right senses would put up with the demands of my current assignment. Thank you for inviting me to meet with you on a dreary Sunday afternoon."

By this time, she was in the living room, and Robert was taking off her coat.

"Some wine, and cheese and crackers?" he asked.

Sarah looked around his room and took notice of the music playing from his gramophone. Great taste in music, she thought, and started to hum along to Peggy Lee singing Duke Ellington's "I Got It Bad (and That Ain't Good)."

Sarah turned back to Robert.

"Oh yes, please. Wine would be very nice. It has been a dismal few weeks. The Germans invaded Greece, after the Greeks defeated the Italians, just as I predicted at the tea trolley, and Yugoslavia, and Rommel is preparing to attack Tobruk, and it looks like Iraq will join the Axis."

"I expected that you might be coming here straight from your never-ending spy work, so I ordered a little supper for us. If you are headed off to a dinner meeting after our meeting, I certainly understand."

"That was thoughtful of you, Robert. I have no plans, at all. When you called, and told me that we should meet at a private place where we could talk freely, I hoped that meant that we would have some time to talk, reflect and digest your issues."

"You were right. As usual. Let's start by digesting a little supper."

As they ate and sipped wine, Robert proceeded to tell Sarah all of the details of his second meeting with Juan. Sarah listened intently, looking into his eyes.

"Juan seemed a little surprised, even maybe a little annoyed or disappointed, that Britain's MI5 and MI6 hadn't picked up on all the chatter by themselves," Robert concluded as he finished the story.

Sarah sat quietly and considered all Robert's input.

"The information Juan relayed to you is known by both MI5 and MI6, but there is no way Juan could possibly know that. The core nature—the core value—of an effective intelligence function is to pick up bits of spotty information and then "connect the dots" to produce a valuable revelation. This input from Juan is invaluable. Absolutely invaluable. It helps us confirm that *we* have correctly connected the dots. The Wehrmacht already know a thousand more dots about German military moves than we know. The more dots we can glean, the easier for us to connect them. And now we can see that we have made the correct connections of the dots we have. Nice work Robert. We owe you! There will be a German invasion of Russia. And very soon. And that, my dear American friend, is a huge reprieve for the U.K. Thank you!"

Robert smiled. He started to stand up from the table, and in doing so, knocked his fork off the table. It fell to the floor. Instinctively, both he and Sarah reached for it. As they grasped the fork simultaneously, Robert got the fork, and Sarah ended up with Robert's hand in hers. They both raised their hands but they both held on, and by the time that their hands were back on the table, Robert's hand was still holding the fork, and Sarah was still holding Robert's hand.

They took a long look at each other.

Robert stood up, walked over to his sofa, and sat down on the end. Sarah stood up. Their glasses of wine were having some effect. She kicked off her shoes, and sat down on the sofa, pretty close to Robert. Too close for a business meeting.

"You keep your home very warm, Robert. Don't you like our London weather?"

"I do find the weather here cold and wet. I am guilty of keeping my thermostat a bit high. Should I turn it down for you?"

"No, no. I'll adjust."

Sitting on the sofa, Sarah brought her knees up close to her chest, pulling her now bare feet up on the sofa. As she did that, her loose woolen skirt tumbled into her lap, exposing most of her legs up to her mid-thighs, which were bare. No stockings.

"This will cool me off. All these woolen clothes can get a bit itchy."

She retrieved Robert's hand and held it. Then she looked at him with her large cat-like eyes. Enchanting him with those eyes.

If Sarah was cooling off, Robert was heating up. He found himself looking at Sarah's legs.

"It's nice to see bare legs. In the States, women wear stockings most of the time."

"It's almost impossible to get stockings here. But they do provide warmth and support. I seem to have banged up my right knee, on one of my recent assignments. I'm not sure if it shows but it does hurt."

Robert put his free hand on her right knee, gently squeezing here and there.

"I had several knee injuries during my college sports days. Where exactly does it hurt?"

"Right there, where you are squeezing. Just above the knee cap."

"Quadricep tendon. My specialty." He gently massaged it.

"How did you injure your knee, Sarah?"

"On a top-secret Mission. Very hush-hush." Sarah closed her eyes. "That feels good. Message therapy is definitely the right sideline for you, Robert."

As they sat there together, the massage area on Sarah's thigh expanded. Soon enough, Robert was massaging both of her thighs, well above and below her knees. As he did this, Sarah held him gently, but tighter, and moved closer to him. Her skin was smooth and soft, and her thighs were shapely and muscular. Her calf muscles tapered down to the ankles. He wondered whatever her assignments might be, they seem to require some muscularity, and risk of joint injury. Neither of them spoke until Sarah broke the silence.

"I will head over to our office and report all of this to the duty officer. There are a few open points which I guess we should consider before I leave. Who is this soon-to-arrive messenger from The Third Reich, and when is he coming? And do we need to verify that Juan is not acting as a double agent to put us on the wrong path?"

"No idea of the messenger. Juan seemed not very sure about that piece of the puzzle. Could Juan be a double agent? Sure. I have known the Gleiss people very well for many years. It makes no sense that they approached me to bring this elliptical message to King George, and even less sense that they would bring their story to me, of all people, to convey false intelligence to the U.K. Regarding the messenger, it will certainly add a level of confirmation of if a messenger from Germany shows up here seeking a meeting with King George. Sounds farfetched, but we shall see.

"I also think that Juan's stated facts speak for themselves. If large numbers of German troops are massing near the Russian border, it's a little crazy to think that the Germans are doing that in preparation for an attack on England."

"I agree. Without going into detail, I have reason to believe that MI5 has picked up reliable information that confirms possible German intentions to enter into conflict with the Soviets, either defensive or offensive, and Wehrmacht grave concerns about a two-front war. Nevertheless, this approach from the mysterious Juan Frederico does appear implausible. It smacks of a hidden agenda. I'm going to head for the office. Will I see you soon? I hope so. Another dinner somewhere?"

"You bet. I'll call you."

Sarah headed toward the door. Then she stopped, turned around, and returned to Robert. She took his hand again and held it tightly, looking at him very intently. Those deep blue eyes. Looking at him.

"This was a wonderful meeting, Robert. Very wonderful. Thank you."

Robert found himself unable to respond. The new and intimate connection with "The Ice Princess" had made its mark on him.

14

Hannah Bores into the Refugee Problem

20 April 1941, London

In the morning, Hannah and Amanda met for lunch at a small pub. This was their third or fourth lunch together since first meeting last November. They were becoming close friends. They hugged and sat down. The contrast in their respective appearances was striking. Amanda glowed with bouncy exuberance. Her long hair was light brown to blondish, and she had big blue eyes. She was well-dressed in a matching outfit that showed her trim figure. The engaging look of a young woman who was carefully groomed and well cared for. She was happy and youthful.

Hannah was equally striking, but in dark brown and black clothes. Amanda thought perhaps Hannah's clothes had come from one of the Jewish refugee agencies that gathered clothing and other day-to-day items for the many refugees who had escaped the growing Nazi peril on the continent. But Hannah wore them well. Very well. Her short well-trimmed brown hair showed off her large brown eyes and her tall and slender stature. Her figure was becoming more womanly as she was maturing rapidly. Her long, straight chiseled nose and high cheek bones framed her almond-shaped eyes and gave her a noticeably serious and almost exotic air. But most striking about Hannah was her deep intensity and intellect. When she looked at you, and spoke, you knew that you would be well advised to hang on her every word. And so, you always did.

Amanda smiled broadly. "I haven't seen you in almost a month, but it appears that you have grown taller, and thinner!"

"Well, taller and thinner are probably the last two things I need. At least you didn't say "older!"

They laughed.

"Looking 'older' when you are twenty, maybe twenty-one, isn't so terrible. Anyway, the War is aging all of us."

"Amanda, I am sensing that you are off on another adventure. Am I wrong? You appear even cheerier than you did at our last visit in March."

"Hannah, you are amazing! You read me like a book. Yes, my wonderful mother was able to get me into an assignment with Princess Mary's Royal Air Force Nursing Service, the nursing branch of the British Royal Air Force. I feel so proud of the organization that I'm ready to pop out of my shell."

"Oh Amanda, that does sound wonderful. Do you have some nurse training in your background?"

"None at all. But I am in training now. And a big part of their critical mission is to bring wounded flight crews back to England for treatment here. I am also involved with the air and ground transportation activities. Who knows, I might even get some flight training one of these days. Our ground forces are no longer involved or engaging the Germans on the continent, after Dunkirk, but our very brave and very young RAF pilots and crews are taking the fight to these damned Nazis every night, and many of our boys are paying a terrible price for it. Often crash landing in France, and then picked up by friendly French farmers, who sneak them back into England."

"Good for you, Amanda. The British people are such a formidable force. How well you all stand together, and pull together, and fight together."

"And too often die together. The nighttime bombing of London by the Luftwaffe has become almost unreal. Are any bombs hitting your neighborhood?"

"We have not been hit yet. But the prognosis is not good. How about you?"

"Not yet. I cannot believe how many people in so many places are suffering and dying because of just one German madman!"

Hannah sat silent for a moment, head down. Then, without lifting her head, she spoke quietly.

"It is not just one German madman. In 1932, the Nazis held the largest number of seats in the Reichstag. Hindenburg appointed him Chancellor in 1933. He is now supported by a great many German men and women who believe deeply in his vision for Greater Germany. People need to remember that the Germans have been seeking to dominate all of Europe since Otto von Bismarck in the 1870s. It is their dream scenario. Until the Third Reich, my family always loved Germany and the Germans. We felt at home there. We even felt "German." I took my private English language study course mostly with German gentiles. But in 1934, things began to change. Rapidly, I saw many of our former friends in Dresden turn on us like savages, I could not believe my eyes. There was raw hatred and disgust on their faces when they stared at us. And you could sense that they had been hiding it for years. Waiting for a chance to spill it out on us. I will never forget the look on their faces. It burns in my memory. Never. It is not just one German madman. And the Luftwaffe aircrews who are dropping all those murderous bombs on us, they are not just following orders. They have all become dedicated killers, and they will never back down. Not until the German war machine is pulverized."

Hannah's face froze and her body stiffened. You could see and feel her anger.

"Oh Hannah. Too horrible. We're so focused on our own problems that I have ignored all that you and your family and your people have been through. Being attacked, confronted, and insulted by your countrymen, being torn from your families at an early age. And are still going through. And not knowing when you will reunite with your family. Who are these awful people? What did they do? Were they once really your friends?"

Hannah looked down at the table, almost as if to hide her face.

"We thought they were all our friends. Maybe we were wrong to think so. Certainly, there were some friends, some families, who stood by us—with us. They were some very fine people. But many turned against us. Harshly. The German language is more guttural than French and English. When those awful people get madder and madder at us, their voices sound deeper and even more intense. *Geh raus! Geh raus! Schweine-juden! Geh zuruck in dein Land. Du bist hier nicht willkommen!!*"

Hannah spoke these words in perfect German affecting a slight Bavarian-Austrian accent in order to mimick the accent used by Hitler in his many speeches. Each word was like a stab wound.

Amanda and Hannah realized they had an audience. Two attractive young women in a restaurant will always draw a certain amount of attention. But as Hannah lowered her voice, to discuss events in Germany, and focused upon the abhorrent conduct of some of these Germans who were now the blood enemies of the U.K., the two young ladies drew even more interest. Some of the diners fell silent, hanging on their every word. Straining to hear. When Hannah started speaking German, it hit the nearby diners like a lightning bolt.

In the ensuing silence, all eyes were on Hannah.

A well-dressed middle-aged woman hesitantly spoke first.

"Did you recently flee from Germany? It must be unbearable for people there who dare to disagree with those Nazi monsters. We hear all those terrible stories. But the stories are too incredible for decent people to believe."

Eight or ten diners at nearby tables were all now listening to the exchange.

Hannah explained that she had left Dresden in late 1938 and had no first-hand knowledge of conditions in Germany now.

Other diners asked her about her family and her friends still in Germany.

Hannah explained that she had not received any news from or about her family for a year. She feared for their fate. With the small but growing audience of restaurant diners, Hannah then described the current predicament of the Jews now living in France.

"Jews in occupied France have now become subject to the law on the status of Jews passed by the Vichy Government under Petain in October 1940. Jews there were deprived of their civil rights, and now are being rounded up for internment. Just last month the Vichy Government set up the General Commissariat for Jewish Affairs to seize Jewish assets. In occupied France, of course, the fate of Jews is far worse. Many have been deported to concentration camps in Poland."

It was a very disturbing lunch.

As Amanda sat with Hannah, listening to her every word, it slowly dawned on her that Hannah was a truly galvanizing and captivating speaker who could inspire a great deal of support for the Jewish refugees.

She would one day have a large following. And her cause needed all the help it could get. As she soaked in Hannah's charisma, Amanda spoke quietly, almost to herself,

"Tyger tyger, burning bright,
In the forests of the night,
What immortal hand or eye,
Could frame thy fearful symmetry?"
[William Blake, 1794]

15

A Bad Day All Around

10 May 1941, London

Sargeant Woodcock's phone at Fighter Command Control Center rang shortly after 10:00 p.m. Not surprising, as the Duty Officer, his phone rang on many evenings to alert the center of incoming German bombers. Woodcock was a beefy fellow, who also could be short tempered. He was all business. Reports were piled up on his aged wooden table.

"Woodcock," he answered.

"This is Network 47, Durham. We've picked up an incoming on radar. We assigned it Number 42. It appears to be a solo. Coming in near Alnwick, on Scotland's east coast. Moving very fast. Our observers had a visual. One of their new ME110s."

"That can't be right. Too far north. That plane could never make it back to Germany from there. And it could not be one of ours. Maybe a lost bomber?"

Network 47 responded, "I'll check back with you. We have some more spotters standing by farther west. Stand by. Just now two more spotters confirm a ME110. Speed over 300 miles per hour. Small and fast. That is no bomber."

Fighter Command No. 13 Group dispatched a Boulton Paul *Defiant* Mark I two-man interceptor night fighter from No. 264 Squadron. With a max speed of 250 mph at low level, it couldn't catch up to the raider, let alone intercept it. In addition, two *Spitfires* from No. 72 squadron, already in the air, were then dispatched. With a max speed over 300 mph, they might catch up.

Woodcock was getting annoyed. "Look, I don't know what you are seeing up there, but everyone here now thinks I'm a total idiot for wasting my time on it!"

The mysterious aircraft flew over Scotland's west coast, turned back east, and flew back to Scotland, dropping fast. Another observer spotted it. He also identified it as a German ME110.

Woodcock had by now lost interest in raider No. 42. His phone was ringing off the hook.

Radar stations further south were reporting hundreds of German aircraft flying west from the coast of France. This was alarming. There was a bright moon, and the sky was very clear. A perfect combination for a heavy bombing raid. But where?

Back at RAF headquarters in London, Captain Sherwood stood at the huge aircraft plotting board surrounded by a small army of privates and corporals holding sighting reports. Sherwood, who resembled a bespectacled high school math teacher, was plotting courses, speeds and numbers. He had boundless energy and scribbled down numbers with impressive agility, all the while standing in front of a sixteen-by-twenty-foot plotting chart fastened to the north wall of the plotting room.

"All right. All right. Slow down. I only have two hands. This is one of the biggest German raids ever. We are already tracking over three hundred bombers."

"Cargil, how many RAF fighter intercept messages have you sent? I'm not getting many reports of RAF fighter intercept aircraft."

"Colonel Stoke told us to give the RAF fighter intercept information to Percy, Brown, and Parker. They are all coming up to join you on the plotter platform, to add in the interceptor spotter points. There's too much plotting information for one man to handle."

A look of frustration and annoyance swept across Sherwood's face. He knew he had been scolded for being too slow, and he didn't like it. Sherwood also knew that "four on a plotting board" was two too many. And, sure enough, very soon the plotting board was a jumbled mess.

Several hours later, at Bomber Command, Air Marshal Portal, sitting together with No. 5 Group Commander Norman Bottomley, Harris, and Peirse at 3:00 a.m. reviewing the bombing reports. Portal was steaming mad.

"This is brutal. The Germans are not making any effort whatsoever to target military or industrial facilities. Look at these damn reports: Westminster Abby! The Tower of London! And Whitehall! Is this an assassination attempt?"

Harris chimed in. "Hamburg."

Portal looked at him. "What?" The look on Portal's face conveyed surprise and irritation. He knew that Harris could often be "Peck's Bad Boy," and his frequent brash behavior could annoy or embarrass others.

"Hamburg. We can get there. We can put a couple hundred bombers over Hamburg. It is their second largest city, and the largest port on the continent."

Peirse weighed in. "We are trying to maintain the bombing campaign with one hand tied behind our back. Bomber Command is currently under very strict orders to concentrate our fire power on maritime targets. Their U-boat campaign is strangling us."

Portal looked at Harris. "Your passion for bombing Hamburg first and Berlin next is well known. Harris, of course, we agree with you. Maybe a year from now we'll be able to put one thousand bombers over Hamburg first, and then Berlin a bit later, but not this month."

Peirse interjected, "I'm pretty sure we can put together a couple hundred bombers and pay a few noteworthy visits to the Hamburgers."

"Then do it," Portal said. "Go get those Hamburgers. But don't stop our maritime campaign to do it. I'd better have a word with the Professor first. He can clear it with the PM, if he thinks that is necessary."

A young corporal came in, and handed a white paper message to Portal, who opened it.

Portal frowned, "What the hell is this? Fighter Command is reporting that a German ME 110, one of their newer modifications, crash landed in Scotland last night. The pilot bailed out and was picked up. He claims to be Hauptmann Alfred Horn, with an urgent message for "the Duke of Hamilton," who is actually in the RAF. The local police think this pilot might be German Deputy Fuhrer Rudolph Hess!"

"Maybe a double. Possibly a diversionary tactic," speculated Harris. "But who knows? I assume they took this pilot to MI5. They usually have a good nose for these things. In any event, let's be sure to get our hands on that newer modified German ME110. An impressive airplane. We need to study it."

Harris and Peirse returned to their offices to catch up on a little sleep, and then went to work on a Hamburg bombing plan.

Bottomley, who Portal knew was about to be appointed Deputy Chief of the Air Staff, replacing Harris who was being sent to head an RAF Delegation to the U.S., sat looking at Portal, awaiting some reaction.

Portal said, "Bottomley, my friend, whatever may be your or my private thoughts as to the military prowess of Marshal Harris, he is most assuredly a master politician. He knows all too well that, especially after this day of massive bombing of London by German bombers, the British people and their feisty prime minister will be frothing to bomb and burn German cities."

Bottomley responded, "Amen to that."

16

MI5 Gets Strange News

12 May 1941, London

On the Monday following the worst bombing that London had ever experienced, the city was a mess. The situation at MI5 was only slightly better. Many members of staff were out, tending to their damaged homes, wounded friends, and suffering family members. MI5 Director General Sir David Petrie, who had just replaced Acting DG Oswald Harker in April, sat in his office rereading a short message on a piece of white paper. Lt. Leach sat on the other side of his desk. He had called her in to see him after he had read the message the first time.

Sarah was growing impatient and annoyed, waiting to hear the reason for their early morning meeting. But she was well trained. Her body language, eyes, and attitude did not betray her inner thoughts. Her sixth sense told her that whatever was written on the little piece of paper was significant. Petrie did not play games.

He looked up at her. She hoped he might read the message.

"Sarah, according to his notes, you spoke with Acting Director Harker back on March 21st about a meeting you had with Robert Johnston. Do you recall that discussion?"

"Like it was yesterday. Robert disclosed to me—which I, in turn, disclosed to Acting Director Harker—a meeting that Robert had with a Spanish citizen, Juan Frederico, seeking Robert's help in making a connection with King George, in order to explore a possible détente between Germany and the U.K."

"Robert? You are on a first name basis with Johnston?"

"Yes, I am. And after several very instructive meetings with him, I think I have succeeded in getting him to call me Sarah."

"Good. This message I received this morning tends to confirm that Robert may be an excellent source for information from the east, as well as from the west. A rare combination these days."

Sarah sat motionless and expressionless, giving Petrie time to play his hand as he felt appropriate.

"According to what I believe you told Harker, this curious fellow Juan Frederico had two items of significance to convey. *First*, that some group of well-placed Germans, presumably military and industrial, believe that Adolf Hitler wants a separate detente with Britain to pursue his hunger for Russian territory, and *second* that Britain should be expecting soon a high ranking 'messenger' from Germany to deliver this message to King George. Right?"

"Yes. Right."

"Amazing. Well, it does now appear that, just as predicted by this Frederico fellow, such a messenger has appeared on Scottish soil, and he does have such a message for the king."

"The message and the messenger are not the critical elements in the equation," Sarah noted quietly, but firmly. "The appearance of the messenger does tend to corroborate the essence of Juan Frederico's story. Important elements in the German hierarchy, including presumably the messenger, are extremely concerned that Adolf Hitler's strategy is to invade Russia very soon, and that monumental effort spells out the long-term demise of the military forces of the Third Reich, unless the Third Reich can cut some semblance of a separate peace deal with the U.K. Do you agree that we need to send the message up the chain of command, Director?"

"Yes. We did send that story up the pipeline very shortly after you gave us your report in late March. Without getting into detail, I think you might know that we have some collateral corroboration of German plans to invade Russia."

"I have picked up a few hints along the way. I also have picked up on the mandate that any discussion of this possible German invasion is strictly taboo. So, I guess my lips are sealed."

"Excellent. But I will share one very Top Secret piece of information with you, personally. Because you personally were a big part of it. I have been 'reliably informed' that a message was, in fact, sent from the top inner circle at Whitehall to the top inner circle at the Kremlin, to alert them to a possible German surprise attack. Who knows if anybody at the Kremlin ever read it. There was absolutely no response from the Kremlin."

"Thank you, Director. It does mean a great deal to me that you would share this with me."

"You earned it. Can you try to reach Robert Johnston today? And ask him to come over here to meet with us? MI5 and MI6 are trying to figure out how we can get more information out of this flier, whoever he might be. Precise Russia invasion plan dates. Troop deployments. Location of Panzer units. Establishment of German army headquarters locations would be extremely valuable to us. And maybe most important of all, relocation of Luftwaffe units from their recent deployments in France back into eastern Germany or Poland. Any German invasion of Russia will consume the Luftwaffe for weeks, maybe months, maybe longer. It now seems clear that your "Robert" is a very valuable ally, indeed."

"Yes, Director. I will try to reach Robert Johnston today."

Several hours later, Sarah ushered Robert into Petrie's office.

"Mr. Johnston, so good to meet you. Fortunate for us that you survived the heavy bombing over the weekend. Did your area suffer any extensive damage?"

"Thankfully all seems well in our neighborhood. And please call me Robert."

"Certainly. Robert, the information you shared from Juan Frederico regarding a message and a messenger from Germany appears to be accurate."

He handed the white piece of paper to Robert.

"The messenger is Rudolf Hess? I'll just bet that Hitler and his inner circle are having a fit about this. I cannot even imagine Adolf Hitler selecting Rudolf Hess for an assignment of this importance. Then have him fly himself to Scotland to pursue a meeting with someone he barely knows? According to our reliable sources, Rudolf Hess is no longer a part of the Hitler Inner Circle. He is now very much a fringe player."

"We are picking up on the consternation in Berlin. They are busily 'disowning' Hess. But this chain of events does give further credence to the suspicion of an imminent German invasion of Russia. When and where, we don't know. Can you get to Frederico and ask him when and where this invasion is scheduled to commence?"

"He tells me that he does not know, and if he did, he wouldn't be able to tell me. That data would be Top Secret, and probably has not been decided yet. Why is it urgent for His Majesty's Government to know the exact date and place?"

"If we have some reliable information on the exact date and place, we might want to pass that intel on to the Russians to enable them to mount a better defense."

Sarah sat still. Robert looked at the floor for a few minutes. Without lifting his head, he said, "I have to tell you, I think this is a terrible idea. FDR already sent a warning to Stalin. Because he did, I suspect that the PM did so, also. These messages to the Kremlin concern me."

Sarah and Petrie were surprised at Robert's candor.

"Robert—please continue," Petrie said.

"Unless I am gravely mistaken, Britain stands right now on the precipice of a monumental defeat at the hands of a Germany insistent at dominating all of Europe. The one event that could snatch victory for Britain would be a major invasion of Russia by Germany. Almost without doubt, a move toward Russia would tie up a major portion of the German Army and Air Forces for years, throwing a lifeline to Britain. Presumably why the Wehrmacht sent Juan to see me.

"For this to play out even more to our benefit, it seems to me *critical* that Hitler's fundamental rationale be proved correct. The invading Germans must find the Russian Army totally surprised, and totally unprepared. The German Panzer divisions must be able to penetrate rapidly far into Russia. Only then would their lines of communication and supply be extended beyond the point of no return, and only then would the Russians be capable and motivated, with their bottomless pit of land mass, horrendous weather and road conditions and limitless manpower from the Far East, be able to grind the German Army into bite size pieces.

"Don't kid yourselves. Stalin is every bit as monstrous a leader as Hitler. Maybe even worse. At least Germany comes from a background of western democracy. Russia is an Eastern Empire. As bad as they come.

"Let these two monsters chew each other up, as they surely will. We can and should assist the Russians in destroying the German ground and air forces, but not until we let them both get so deeply engaged in a mutual conflict from which they are totally unable to disengage. If this invasion actually is a surprise to the Russians, then the Russians will pay a terrible price up front, but the Germans will pay a much higher price later. In both cases, it couldn't happen to nicer fellows than Adolf Hitler and Josef Stalin. And that is how we save Britain from a fate far worse than death."

Petrie was stunned, and silent. He looked at Sarah for help.

She picked up the director's signal and sat up in her seat. She had slumped down as she heard the "course correction" delivered by this handsome Yank. She forced a smile.

"Decisions as to who tells what and when to the Kremlin are made in much bigger offices than these humble spaces, but clearly MI5 and MI6 need to reconsider our advice to Whitehall. I think Robert is right as rain on this. Thank you, Robert, for being such a good guest to your British hosts."

"You are very welcome," Robert added with a wry smile. "If you really need to know the date and location of the German invasion of the Soviet Union, I have reason to believe that your Swedish, Swiss, and Spanish friends can probably give that to you. I am sure they know."

Petrie and Sarah said nothing in response, but looked hard at each other. Sarah knew very well of Petrie's reputation for being a rugged and kind-hearted Scot, with ample reserves of physical and moral strength. Sarah liked and admired Petrie, and she could see that Petrie was going to take Robert's advice. They both knew that Robert was "setting them straight." His point was—"You should know this without me telling you!" Never an easy message to give or receive. But, after all, they did ask for it. Petrie and Sarah smiled broadly, as if on cue, and thanked Robert warmly for his candid and well taken advice.

17

Operation Barbarossa – An Update from MI5

1 July 1941, London

On 27 June, six days after the German surprise attack on the USSR, Sir David Petrie sent a message to Robert requesting a meeting at MI5 on Tuesday, 1 July. Robert was not surprised. He was sure that Petrie wanted to know how this monumental event was affecting U.S. reaction to the war—a view from the "inside" that Robert could hopefully provide.

When he walked into Petrie's office, Petrie stood up and cheerfully shook Robert's hand. Sarah was there, in uniform, looking very crisp. She, too, stood up, and gave Robert a warm handshake.

"Robert. Thank you for coming in. How are you? Busy, I'm sure!"

"Busy. Yes. Very busy. It seems that the world, or at least the war, had suddenly been turned upside down. And the general mood in Britain has certainly brightened."

"It surely has. Can you give us some insight on how this massive invasion has changed the view for Washington?"

"I can tell you what I know. The US relationship with the USSR soured badly following the Soviet occupation of Eastern Poland and the Winter War against Finland. Roosevelt openly condemned the Soviet Union as 'an absolute dictatorship as bad as any in the world.' What you probably do not know is he told his insiders that he was far more concerned about Nazi Germany. He carefully kept his powder dry regarding the USSR. There were secret negotiations between US Under Secretary of State Sumner Welles and Soviet Ambassador Constantine Oumansky to lift the US embargo on USSR this past January before the invasion. Welles warned the Soviets at that time that the Germans would attack them. And, Roosevelt provided for the possibility of US aid to the USSR in the Lend-Lease Act.

"The US War Department has advised Roosevelt that the Soviets won't last more than six weeks. Roosevelt disagrees, and is sending Harry

Hopkins, his trusted advisor, to talk to Stalin in Moscow. My people predict that Roosevelt will push the US to support the Soviets because then Soviet troops, rather than US or UK troops, will bear the brunt of defeating the German Army. The invasion does push the US more into the war because now Germany has set a clear course for its own destruction. I'm sure you both know the German invasion of Russia was the 'worst kept secret' of the war, and the person in this equation who dislikes Stalin the most is your beloved Prime Minister."

Big laugh all around.

When Robert finished, both Petrie and Sarah were beaming. This was excellent news for the future of the UK. After some further back and forth on this subject, Robert said, "Forgive me for asking, Director, but I do have a personal request."

"Of course, Robert. We owe you."

"Maybe two requests, then. What is the real story behind the loss of HMS *Hood?* The "Mighty Hood", the largest battleship in the world. Called "The Pride of the Royal Navy." She was sunk in three minutes flat by the German Battleship *Bismarck* on 24 May in the Battle of Denmark Strait, with a loss of over one thousand four hundred sailors. How did this happen? As a navy man, I am really shocked. And how did you manage to take down *Bismarck?*"

"We were all shocked at the sudden loss of *Hood*. Both *Hood* and *Bismarck* mounted eight 15-inch guns. It should have been a fair fight. It appears that a lucky shot from *Bismarck* hit either *Hood's* aft magazine, *Hood's* torpedo locker, or the inside of one of *Hood's* gun turrets. As a result, *Hood* blasted apart and immediately sank. It is possible that we will never know the answer. The smaller HMS *Prince of Wales,* with only ten 14-inch guns, most of them out of commission, took up the fight with the much larger *Bismarck* all alone. Although *Wales* was unable to fight for long, being heavily outgunned, she did damage a *Bismarck* oil tank, which cut *Bismarck's* speed and range. As a result, *Bismarck* was ultimately unable to escape the pursuing combined forces of the Royal Navy cruisers, battleships, carriers, and destroyers, all of which were chasing it back to Germany. They overtook *Bismarck,* and on 27 May, the *Great and Mighty Bismarck* sank into sea, taking about two-thousand sailors down with her. We did our best to rescue survivors, but German U-Boats chased us off. The bottom line: We could afford to lose *Hood*. Painful, but expendable. The German Navy could not afford to lose *Bismarck*. On the great maritime chessboard, *Hood* was a Castle piece for us, but *Bismarck* was the Queen piece for them."

"Most enlightening." Robert looked at Sarah. She returned his look, with a glowing catlike probe. It made Robert buzz.

Petrie took it all in. He understood that there was chemistry between the two. A man of enormous integrity, Petrie looked at Sarah, and felt just a stab of jealousy. She was a prize "catch," and Robert was clearly a lucky fellow.

Sarah and Robert left Petrie's office together, chatting with each other like old friends.

18

The Atlantic Charter

15 August 1941, London

Six weeks later, at 2pm on Friday, 15 August, Robert took a preplanned call from Donovan. Before putting the call through, Kathleen Scott placed some hot tea and a plate of biscuits on Robert's desk.

"Will you be needing anything else?"

"No. Thank you, Kathleen. Let's see what Big Bill has to say."

They smiled at each other knowing Donovan's love of drama and intrigue. Kathleen walked out, and gently pulled the door mostly closed, but left it slightly ajar. Robert noticed and smiled.

"Hello Bill. Good to hear from you. Any good news?"

"Yes. I think so. The president is elated that the US and the UK have agreed to the Joint Declaration by the President and the Prime Minister, setting goals for the world after the end of the war. It is a huge commitment, Robert. No territorial aggrandizement. No territorial changes against the will of the people. Restoration of self-government. Reduction of trade restrictions. Global cooperation on economic and social conditions. Freedom from fear and want. Freedom of the seas. Abandonment of the use of force. And disarmament of aggressor nations. Amazing commitments."

"I read that statement in the press here. I don't think anyone here really grasps the scope and reach. Or if they do, no one really believes it."

"That's why I called," said Donovan. "Most administration people here have real doubts that any of these measures will survive the war. Most significantly, do the British inner circles understand that this joint declaration means the end of the British Empire, the establishment of a world order organization similar to the League of Nations, and a permanent military alliance among the Allies? This is bigger than the war itself. What are you hearing in London?"

Kathleen poked her head in the door, and looked at Robert. They both knew this was a political discussion, not military intelligence. Fair game for her, too. Robert waved her in, and pushed the biscuits in her direction. She took one and listened.

"Bill, I do agree with you that this is a bold and exciting commitment. Public opinion here supports it. And Churchill himself seems to be a strong advocate. But insiders see it differently. It is a mechanism to drag the US formally into the war. Much like Lincoln agreeing to free the slaves to get more northern and international support for the Union in the American Civil War. Churchill would change his name to Eva Braun to get FDR to declare war on Germany.

"The cynics here see a myriad of downsides to this joint declaration. They predict that Germany and Japan will see it as a clear attack on them. Plans are already underway to drop leaflets over Germany assuring Germans that they will not suffer 'economical discrimination' when defeated. The Soviet Union will certainly ignore it entirely. The Poles, if the Allies win the war, hope to take over vast pieces of Eastern Germany."

Kathleen, a very bright and inquisitive young woman, and always an avid reader of world politics, was listening intently. Using his handy steno pad, she jotted down a few quick notes which she quietly handed to Robert:

"Even Churchill will eventually back away from some of the implications—most notably as it might apply to independence for India. And Mahatma Gandhi will jump on it to attack British rule. Gandhi has never supported the Allied war effort."

Robert paused in his call to read her note, and nodded in agreement. He then said to Donovan, "Earlier this morning, my very able and well informed secretary Kathleen said to me, "…" He then read her note over the phone.

Robert said, "I fully agree."

Kathleen sat back, beaming, and helped herself to another biscuit.

Donovan thought for a few minutes, and then responded. "Well enough, Robert. I cannot disagree with any of these reservations, but from the US viewpoint, the joint declaration will help push the US into the Allied camp, and that is very good news for me, and for you, and for your ever-loyal and very lovely Kathleen. Give her my best, please."

After Robert hung up, he and Kathleen happily finished up the remaining tea and biscuits.

19

Operation Barbarossa –
Mid-Term Assessment

30 September 1941, London

Lindemann reconvened his Brain Trust with one addition. German Army operations were the main topic of the discussion, so Major General Hastings Ismay, British Military Chief of Staff, was invited to join the meeting. Born in India, educated at Royal Military College, Sandhurst, "Pug" Ismay, as he was called, was Churchill's chief military assistant. He was always at Churchill's side during the early war years. With almost forty years of active service in the British Army, he had extensive experience in army operations. For this reason, Lindemann had asked "Pug" Ismay to join the meeting and bring a couple of very seasoned British Army officers to chart the progress of the German army in Operation Barbarossa. Colonel Stone was a tank commander, and Major Dutton was an infantry officer. Colonel Stone and Major Dutton had brought a large chart to plot German and Russian army positions, at least as well as were known by British army intelligence. The chart presented a vivid and shocking view of the seemingly dismal situation faced by the Soviet Army. The Germans were everywhere.

Major Dutton opened up the briefing. Dutton looked younger than his age. Tall and lanky. Well-built and deadly serious.

"Early on the morning of 22 June 1941, one-hundred German divisions, including ten to fifteen Panzer Divisions, invaded the Soviet Union, in three prongs spread from the Baltic in the far North to the Black Sea, which touches the northern border of Turkey. The Germans typically have about 15,000 men in an infantry division, and about 12,000 men and 300-to-500 tanks in a Panzer Division, for a total of 1,500,000 men. There appears to be another fifty divisions, with 1,000,000 to 1,500,000 men in reserve forces. We can surmise that the Germans have over 3,000 tanks and some 2,500 planes now in Russia. These German troops were supported by additional divisions from Finland and Romania.

"This three-prong attack encompasses a frontal distance of some 1,800 miles. The size and scope of this invasion by an army, seen by many as the best army in the world, is simply unbelievable. Even more unbelievable is the fact that the Soviet army and air forces appear to have been totally surprised and totally overwhelmed. How could they not see this coming? They were warned!

"The Luftwaffe almost immediately destroyed all of the Soviet aircraft and airfields. With virtual total control of the air and no organized and prepared Soviet army to stop them, the German Panzer units traveled rapidly across broad stretches of Russian territory. German Army Group North, the northern prong, headed straight for Leningrad. German Army Group Center, the middle prong, headed towards Minsk and Smolensk, on the way to Moscow. German Army Group South, the southern prong, headed for Ukraine and Odessa.

In just three or four weeks, these German army units penetrated more than 400 miles into Soviet territory. By then they were deeply committed to the Russian offensive. They seemed for the moment to be unstoppable."

Colonel Stone picked up the commentary. Stone was more compact, typical of a tank commander who had to spend long hours in a small tank. He exuded a sense of humor. Often smiling.

"But by late July, and into August of 1941, Russian resistance began to stiffen, and unfortunately, our information about the overall situation became murky.

"As Soviet resistance grew stronger, the advance of German Army Group North and German Army Group South slowed considerably. On orders from the Wehrmacht—or maybe Hitler, himself, we have no way of knowing precisely—the 3rd Panzer Unit from the Center Group was sent north, and the 2nd Panzer Unit from the Center Group was sent south. The German Army Center Group was left with only infantry divisions. The advance on Moscow lost momentum.

"At that point, the Germans were heavily overextended. German Army Group North and the German Army Group Center stalled. But

German Army Group South continued to advance and captured an astounding 4-to-500,000 Russian soldiers.

"And the Russians have been burning and stripping everything as they retreat. A highly effective Scorched Earth Policy. This leaves these vast German Armies overexposed and soon facing a forecasted unusually harsh Russian winter.

"That, gentleman, is pretty much where things stand at the moment on the German Eastern Front."

Those who had attended the first brain trust meeting back on 23 February, who had heard Bronowski's prediction on the fate of the German Army if they invaded the USSR, now looked at him to gauge his reaction. The others followed and all eyes were on Bronowski. Bronowski's eyes twinkled. He looked a bit like a jolly old Saint Nick. "Yes," he said. "It will go poorly for the Germans, now forced to spend this winter in Russia. The Wehrmacht knew better. Their Fuhrer put them into this trap."

Lindemann smiled, just a bit, and then nodded in agreement, annoyed again. His usual "default" look. He turned to Ismay, who sat quietly waiting to hear what he had to say.

"It is welcome news that the Russian Army is holding its ground," said Lindemann. "But news from other theatres of this war are not so cheery. Our British Army is holding on in North Africa, but we can see that Rommel is gearing up to move on Egypt and the Suez Canal. So, there we are playing defense. The Royal Navy is holding its own in the Battle of the Atlantic, but just barely. Our shipping losses are mounting. There, too, we are playing defense. This brings me to RAF Bomber Command, our only current offensive weapon. The timing of this meeting is an excellent opportunity to update all of you on the report that I delivered in August.

"The effectiveness of our Bomber Command against German targets continues to falter. Not good at all. This report, the Butt Report, named after the primary author, my very able assistant David Butt. Some of you have already seen it. His report, dated 18 August 1941, reveals that over Germany only one-in-four crews dropped bombs at night within five miles of their targets. In heavily defended areas, it was only one-in-ten.

Overall, only five-percent of dispatched bombs even came close to hitting their targets."

For most of the assembled group, this was not surprising news. Many had read the report. All eyes were now on Pug Ismay.

"Good that you communicated the report, Professor Lindemann. It does confirm what many of us have suspected. But Bomber Command is the only offensive weapon we can deploy right now. We need to stand strong in the ring, and hope to land a few lucky punches."

Not all present agreed with Ismay's assessment, but they did know that Ismay spoke for the prime minister and the War Cabinet. At least for today, he had the final say. The meeting then adjourned.

20

Hannah Comes to Tea

15 October 1941, London

The black cab dropped Hannah at 2424 Kensington High Street. The house was impressive, even intimidating. A white three-story townhouse, with plants on the first story terrace. Corinthian columns framing the shiny, black front door. Well-trimmed hedges and potted plants in the front yard. A black, shiny metal picket fence with a heavy metal gate bordered the sidewalk. It was 4:00 p.m., and London was getting dark, its usual fall punishment for being so far north. Undaunted by all the elegant exterior trappings, Hannah pushed open the metal gate, walked up the short path to the door, and knocked several times using the heavy metal knocker.

Amanda answered the door, with a big smile and a very warm embrace.

"So nice to have you here! I feel as dumb as a dodo for not having you over long ago. But with my new nursing activities, I seem to have no time for fun anymore."

She grabbed Hannah's arm, and the two of them entered into the large elegant living room. The furniture was posh and plush, the windows were wide and high, with heavy black-out drapes pulled aside to let in the now rapidly disappearing fall sunshine. A large tea cart stood at the ready with a silver tea service and water vessels, china cups, and several dishes with biscuits and cakes. Count Basie's "Jumpin' at the Woodside" was playing from the shiny, brass gramophone that was situated on a wooden console in the far corner of the room.

Hannah realized there were too many cups and cakes for just the two of them, so others must be joining. As the young women chatted away about how much more pleasant life in London had become with the Luftwaffe bombers diverted to the Russian campaign, members of Amanda's family began to wander into the living room, approaching the heavily burdened cart, but cognizant of the protocol to wait until their young guest had been offered some tea and cake.

Amanda introduced her father and mother, British Navy Captain Spencer Haythornwaite and Pamela Haythornwaite, and Amanda's younger sister, Alice, as well as two other afternoon visitors, Sir Reginald Bullock and his wife, Lady Sandra Bullock. The Bullocks appeared to be contemporaries of Captain and Mrs. Haythornwaite. Both of the Bullocks had very plummy accents. Hannah wondered if they might be semi-royals.

As it was Sunday, the guests were dressed in elegant casual, after-church attire. The men in blue and grey slacks and blue sport coats with gold buttons. The ladies in red and green dresses.

Hannah was dressed in dark brown colors, a full, pleated linen skirt and a light weight wool sweater. She might have felt underdressed, or out of place, or awkward, particularly as the others had recently come from church, but she really didn't have an extensive wardrobe.

But she didn't have time to feel awkward because the Haythornwaite family and friends filled Hannah's hands and her plate with hot tea and too many cakes, and gushed over her like she had just arrived from Jupiter.

If the truth be known, except for Amanda, none of them had had an opportunity to interact with a real-life German-Jewish refugee. And it became quickly evident that this particular refugee was a gem. Young, articulate, bright and well able to manage two or three topics, and two or three cakes and cups of tea all at once, as each of the other guests peppered her with rapid and direct questions.

Captain Haythornwaite was anxious to hear Hannah's views on whether the German people really supported the Fuhrer, and all of the bold and aggressive moves he was making to turn the Third Reich into a boiling cauldron, pouring hot molten metal onto the rest of the Western world.

"Can they not see that this man is truly mad? If it was not bad enough that he tore the German people apart, pouncing on so many minority groups who had been living in peace in what they thought was their own country. Now he is inflicting his lunacy on millions of people living in other countries as well. Under our Mutual Assistance Agreement with the Soviets, we hear endless stories of the mass murders of Soviet citizens by German soldiers. I wonder if the German people know, or even care?"

"I left three years ago," said Hannah. "And my family and I lived only in Dresden. But it was very clear that many of the German people we knew were strongly in support of the current internal and external policies of the government. More recent emigrants who I have met have confirmed this."

Hannah was impressed by the military bearing of the captain and his knowledge of the situation created by German government policies. It pained her to think how this British Royal Navy captain would have so enjoyed spending a few hours talking to her father. And she wondered if she would ever see her father again.

Amanda, her mother, her sister, Alice, and Mrs. Bullock, questioned Hannah about her life growing up in Dresden, and now living in London with no family. This personal attention and all of these well-meaning questions were starting to make Hannah uncomfortable. Her family situation, and her time spent in the UK, were fairly straightforward, but like most immigrants there were some background facts and issues that were not so straightforward. To take the attention off of herself, Hannah directed the conversation to the current fate of so many European refugees, many Jewish, but many from other backgrounds.

The tea and the cakes were disappearing rapidly, but a nicely dressed and very efficient service lady came in frequently to replenish the cart. As the conversation began to wind down, Sir Reginald, who had been listening intently, but talking very little, opened a new chapter.

"Hannah, this has all been interesting and enlightening. Thank you for sharing your fascinating but sad story with us. I was intrigued to learn that your family is from Dresden. My wife and I spent a great deal of time in Saxony. We especially fell in love with Dresden. An incredibly charming medieval city. I wonder if any of us will ever see it again."

With that painful question, everyone was looking at Hannah. She blushed, because the words made her wince. She knew an answer was expected.

"No," she said. "I believe that none of us will ever again see Dresden. Certainly, not the Dresden we once knew and loved. Dresden is changed forever. This war will end, but the pain and the stain, and the bane of the Nazi atrocities will last for a century."

Everyone nodded in agreement. With the Haythornwaite family paying close attention, the Bullocks and Hannah shared a number of their happy memories of Dresden and Saxony.

Around 6:00 p.m., Hannah turned to Amanda. "Thank you, thank you, thank you, for such a very special afternoon. Wonderful company, and such very nice hot tea and cakes. I've eaten enough for a week! I do now need to head home. The Hawkins, my host family, will be expecting me. I'm usually home much earlier."

"Hannah, the least we can do is offer you a ride home," said Sir Reginald. "We have a car and driver here. He can take you wherever you wish. Lady Sandra and I will be visiting a little longer here. So, it is no imposition."

After politely declining twice, Lady Sandra insisted, so Hannah finally agreed. She said farewell to all, walked out into the now dark and chilly London night. The driver in a grey chauffeur uniform opened the door for her and she climbed into the backseat of the Bullock's Daimler. He closed the door behind her. He introduced himself as Bruno Kreisler and asked for her address.

As they drove away, Hannah said, "Mr. Kreisler, I think I detect a German accent, along with a German name?"

"Yes. A Berlin accent. My English is still not so good. Have you ever visited Germany?"

"Actually, I was born there. In Dresden."

Hannah then continued their discussion in German.

When Kreisler learned from Hannah that she came from Dresden, Kreisler lit up, as he had often visited Dresden while working for the Bullocks.

Hannah explained that she had come to London in 1938.

"Well, Miss, are you familiar with the Innere Neustadt District of Dresden? The Bullocks took a house there in 1930. During those several years, they hired me as their driver. I drove them all over Saxony."

"Please call me Hannah. 'Miss' sounds too formal," she laughed. "We did not live in the Innere Neustadt District, but I do know it. It is very beautiful. We lived in the Sudvorstadt District, near the University Quarter. My father was a physician and a professor. He made medical calls to people's homes all over Dresden, often in the Loschivitz District and the Innere Neustadt District, and the Weisser Hirsch District.

"On weekends, when we were not attending school, my father would sometimes take my brother and me with him on his house calls. He was a well-regarded physician. I hope this doesn't sound like bragging!"

"So many years ago. Interesting though. Maybe he even made a visit to the Bullock family. If so, I'm sure that I would have picked him up, and then taken him back home. What is his name? Is he still practicing medicine there?"

"His name is Doctor Jacob Hanauer. He is not practicing medicine in Dresden. Not legally. The Third Reich passed several laws in 1934 barring Jews from several professions, including medicine. These restrictive laws were not widely publicized here in Britain."

Hannah's disturbing comments changed the tone of the polite conversation. Kreisler grew silent, focusing on his driving and navigating the darkening evening—looking for the address Hannah had given him.

The car pulled up in front of Hannah's home. The driver confirmed the address, and then came around to open the door for Hannah.

"Thank you, sir. This is a very nice way to travel. Do you recall ever hearing of my father? He had a fairly well-established practice in Dresden when you were there."

"Doctor Jacob Hanauer? I do not recall that name, but I will ask Sir Reginald if he recalls the name."

"I have not heard from my family in over a year. I am very worried about them."

Kreisler stood by while Hannah entered her home. Then he drove off into the dark night.

As Hannah entered the house, and took off her coat, she could hear the Hawkins back in the kitchen. She felt a twinge of anxiety. It had been a fine visit and a fine day, but she wondered if it were wise to share so much personal information with so many people who hardly knew her. Her memories gave her only physical discomfort and mental anguish. Not an experience she wanted to repeat. She put on her best smile and walked into the kitchen with a warm greeting.

21

MI5 Update on Operation Typhoon

1 December 1941, London

Robert joined Sir David Petrie and Sarah in Petrie's office at MI5. Sarah had provided Robert an updated "inside story" of Operation Typhoon, the revitalized German assault on Moscow which had mysteriously halted in July.

"Robert, we are anxious to hear any news from the White House on current views of the war situation," Petrie said. "Anything you can share?"

"All eyes are on the Soviet defense of Moscow, but the sinking of HMS *Ark Royal* came as a huge shock to our government."

"Yes. A shock to us as well. One torpedo from a U-boat. It struck *Ark Royal* amidships, creating a huge hole to the water line. Captain Maund ordered All Stop to the engine room, but the communication lines were cut by the torpedo's blast. By the time the engine room stopped the engines, the ship had taken on too much water. Fortunately, the entire crew was rescued by HMS *Legion*. More nasty news for the Royal Navy. But better news may be on the horizon. The Germans appear to be faltering outside Moscow."

"I have been trying to keep abreast of things at Moscow, but the reports in the press and even from my friends in the U.S. are spotty."

"The southern prong of the multi-prong German invasion seems most important to the Germans," said Petrie. "It's where they continue to advance. They took Rostov, on their way to the Caucasus. Not clear they can hold Rostov, as they are overextended. The Russians are counterattacking there. In the northern prong, they have settled down for a long winter siege of Leningrad. Their troops are north of the Arctic Circle. It is the middle prong, the German Army Group Center, which holds the greatest interest for us.

"To support Operation Typhoon, the Germans sent the two Panzer units back to Army Group Center—one from Group North outside Leningrad and one from Group South outside Sevastopol—to strengthen Army Group Center. 4th Panzer Army did get within twenty miles of the Kremlin, but 2nd Panzer Army failed to take the town of Tula.

"The German Armies are huge, under the direct command of Field Marshall Fedor von Boch, one of their best. Even more surprising, 2nd Panzer Army, commanded by the Panzer 'Super Star' Generaloberst Heinz Wilhelm Guderian, 'Hammering Heinz' as they call him, failed to take Tula, though it is one of their best Panzer Units with an amazing battle record.

"We have reliable intelligence that the Russians either became aware or else maybe made a deal to secure the continued neutrality of Japan in its relationship with Russia. At peace with Japan, the Russians were free to begin a massive effort to transfer a large number of their far-eastern divisions to the Russian western front to attack the Germans. With the Germans worn down, worn out and greatly outnumbered, they are on the defense. We can now state, with a high degree of confidence, that Operation Typhoon will fail. Moscow will not be taken. At least, not in 1941. Probably never."

Robert was listening intently. Thoroughly engrossed. Sarah was looking at Robert. She was almost smiling.

Petrie continued, "So, things on the Eastern Front are progressing largely as you and Bronowski and others predicted. Please pass on much of this as you deem appropriate to your colleagues in Washington. It is very good news for us."

"There is a strong likelihood of good news at Moscow, but the Fuhrer has staked the future of the Third Reich on defeating the USSR. He cannot and will not give up quickly or easily. We are far from the final chapter of this intriguing saga."

Sarah had been listening intensely. "That makes sense, Robert, but like a patient in intensive care, even a brief taste of potentially good news for Great Britain is itself good news."

That broke the ice, and everyone laughed.

"Let's reconvene in a week on 8 December. By then we will have more definite and conclusive evidence of the outcome of Operation Typhoon.

We here at MI5 regard this operation as one of the most critical battles of the war."

Robert nodded in agreement. "Absolutely," he said.

Sarah escorted Robert out of the office complex. Once outside, she offered her hand. "Thank you. We need you."

Robert took her hand, and shook it gently, but then held onto her hand for another minute or two. This time she did smile.

"Lieutenant, you have a nice smile. You should use it more often!"

"Thank you. I don't get many opportunities to smile in this job. Nor do I get many compliments on my appearance!"

22

A Day That Will Live in Infamy

8 December 1941, London

By the time that Robert arrived at MI5 on Monday, all of London was buzzing over shocking news of the Japanese surprise attack on the US Fleet at Pearl Harbor. But, for the wrong reason. Yes, it would certainly push the US further into a military alliance with the UK, but at a terrible cost in US lives.

Sir David Petrie and Lt. Sarah Leach stood up when Robert walked into Petrie's office. In fact, they almost saluted him.

"Incredibly terrible news, Robert. Truly unbelievable. Is it as bad as we hear? Have you heard anything from your home sources?"

Robert was visibly upset, but before he could respond, Sarah spoke.

"Robert, I am well aware of your deep affection for the United States Navy. The pain and injury that has been inflicted upon your countrymen and your country is incalculable. Our deepest sympathies to your lost seamen, airmen, and Marines. We have heard that there were several thousand lives lost on sunken ships."

As was often the case, Sarah's words struck Robert very deeply. It seemed as though she alone in all of London understood that the Japanese attack on Pearl Harbor was, to any American, first and foremost an attack on all of the things that the Americans hold dear. The first thoughts on the mind of every American on Sunday morning, 7th December were deep sorrow and remorse and anger, and revenge, revenge and revenge.

Robert was spitting mad. "Dammit! We tried our very darndest to stay out of the war, which is now boiling both the Pacific and the Atlantic Oceans, and these Japanese warmongers stabbed us in the back. They never even bothered to declare war on us, they just flew into Pearl Harbor on the Christian Sabbath, a day that we Americans hold dear, and dropped bombs and torpedoes on the fine ships and sailors of US

Pacific Fleet, lying peacefully at anchor in the harbor. They will pay for this. They will pay a terrible price for this."

Robert Johnston cared deeply for his British friends and sided closely with them in their fight against the Nazis, but that was not his first thought after the Japanese Sneak Attack on Pearl Harbor. Not even close.

And only Sarah. Sarah. On this large island, seemed to understand that.

"Thank you, Sarah. America and Americans will never be the same. That attack yesterday flipped a switch and the resulting electric current surged throughout the United States. We went from cool white to fire-engine red. The entire world will soon gape in awe at the vengeance that will come."

He was deeply depressed.

Without so much as looking at Petrie, Sarah reached over to Robert and put her hand on his forearm. She held it there for several minutes until Robert was able to calm down.

Petrie knew enough, and had just seen enough, to realize that he should say nothing to allow Sarah to calm Robert.

In a few minutes, Robert spoke again.

"I do know this much. It was a devastating attack. I am sorry to say this, but it seemed to have been modeled on the British attack on the Italian Fleet at Taranto. They sunk at least five of our eight battleships and ten other ships. Almost all of our two hundred military aircraft were destroyed. Total casualties are not known, but it appears that over two thousand were killed, and another thousand wounded.

"The Fleet was crippled, just as the Japanese intended. I have been told definitively that President Roosevelt will appear before a joint session of Congress this morning to request a Congressional Declaration of War against Japan. We expect that congressional approval will be immediate and unanimous."

"So sorry about this, Robert." Unlike many of the MI5 operatives in 1941, Petrie was not a combat veteran. His thirty-six-year career was in the Indian Imperial Police. His typical reaction to events, such as Pearl Harbor, was not how the event would affect the British Military situation, but rather how it would impact the people affected. He understood instinctively that a man like Robert would take this sneak attack very personally. And he also felt an instinctive affinity to Robert. "We are all so worried here about our own ghastly problems that we often overlook the suffering and loss of our friends. We all hope the payback will be swift and painful. I am able to tell you that today Britain will also declare war on the Empire of Japan. Good riddance to them. They are attacking British bases as we speak."

"Does this leave the U.S. with many warships in the Pacific? MI5 is hoping that you can give us a strategic overview of the situation." Sarah asked.

Petrie interrupted, "Would you mind if we invite some others of our MI5 analysts to hear your assessment of the Pearl Harbor implications? We think that you might also want to hear some of our new intelligence on Operation Barbarossa."

"Yes, of course. Invite whomever you wish to join us."

A number of other senior military and intelligence people, who had been asked earlier that morning to "stand by for a Pearl Harbor and Barbarossa briefing," then joined the meeting. Some in military uniform, some in civilian attire. Introductions were made all around. Robert was impressed with Petrie's tight organizational skills.

Robert then spoke. "Director Petrie and Lieutenant Leach asked for an assessment of the status of US Navy assets remaining in the Pacific after the Pearl Harbor attack. Let me give you some preliminary thoughts on Pearl Harbor.

"The Japanese Battle fleet is impressive, large and modern. The enormous success of this attack was no fluke, or stroke of luck. They used their first-line aircraft carriers, *Akagi, Kaga, Hiryu,* and maybe also *Soryu, Shokaku,* and *Zuikaka,* probably commanded by Vice Admiral Chuichi Nagumo, under overall command of Admiral Isoroku Yamamoto, Commander of the Imperial Japanese Navy.

"Yamamoto may well be the best naval force commander in the world. He got a good part of his education in the US. For many years, we all thought he was a friend of the US. Rest assured. We will pay him back for this.

"That huge assembled Japanese fleet sailed across the eastern Pacific under cover of warm storm fronts, because trade winds always traverse the Pacific Ocean from Asia to North America. The fleet must have traveled at least 3,000 miles. Undetected. Amazing! These carriers launched over 400 planes, mostly *Mitsubishi A6M Zero* fighters, in two waves. The planes carried Type 91 aerial torpedoes armed for air drops in shallow water."

"Quite right," Sarah piped in. "It does sound like the British attack at Taranto last November."

Robert nodded, and then continued. "You were right, Lieutenant, when you predicted that the British Royal Navy taught the world a lesson at Taranto. Unfortunately, only the Japanese were watching. And they are fast learners. Most of the damage to the US Pacific Fleet resulted from the damage and loss of our eight battleships. The Japanese regard our battleships as their primary targets, because the Japanese make battleship warfare a priority. Time will tell if they are correct in that assessment. The Japanese have been on the offense in the Pacific for some years. A future war with Japan seemed very possible. For this reason, the US placed embargos on Japan, and froze its US assets. Our Pacific Fleet was moved from San Diego to Pearl in April 1940 for the same reason. The Japs interpreted the move as being designed to cut off the supply of oil from Southern Asia to Japan. But I can tell you that, under current US Naval strategy, the US did not intend to sail our battleships out further into the eastern Pacific to attack the Japanese under any circumstance. Much too risky. Ironically, the seven US Carriers, three of which had recently been anchored at Pearl Harbor, were fortuitously not at the scene. The Japs knew this when they attacked us. To them, battleships are far more important than carriers. Dumb. Very dumb. Four of our carriers—*Ranger, Yorktown, Hornet,* and *Wasp*—had been sent to our East Coast to help deal with U-Boats. Our other three, *Enterprise, Lexington,* and *Saratoga* were out on a mission. So, our entire Carrier Fleet was intact. We suspect that the absence of our three Pacific carriers and the threat they posed to the Japanese carrier fleet, caused the Japanese to terminate their attack after only two attack waves. As a result, the base fuel and torpedo storage facilities, and the maintenance and dry dock operations, were largely untouched. Another saving grace, most of the seamen were not onboard the battleships because they had weekend liberty on shore. Otherwise, our casualties would have been much greater. These were three critical errors because these unscathed assets will be vital elements for future US Naval Operations against Japan.

"On the negative side, the Japanese are now attacking US bases in the Philippines and many British bases. That is the extent of the information I have received so far. Our primary assets there now are our carriers and our submarines. A double threat to the Japs. The net result of Pearl Harbor is that the Japanese pushed a very reluctant United States headlong into a life-or-death war with Japan. A war that the Japanese cannot possibly win. And I suspect all maritime powers can kiss all their old battleships 'goodbye.' Submarines and carriers will now rule the Seven Seas."

The assembled British intelligence officers and civilians made extensive notes. After an hour of further discussions on the ramifications of Pearl Harbor, the Brits took the floor.

Petrie was about to begin, when one young Brit asked, "Just wondering. Didn't US radar operators pick up all those Japanese incoming aircraft?"

Robert responded, "Good question. Yes, they did. Unfortunately, the Duty Officer thought that the first wave of incoming Jap fighters was a squadron of our own B-17s flying in from the US, so no alarm was sent."

Petrie cleared his throat and the young officer, who looked very earnest and very nervous to be butting in, squirmed in his seat. Petrie gave the young officer a hard look, as if to say, "This is not the time or place to cast aspersions on the US military." Others present looked at each other, shaking their heads in disapproval of the question.

"We want to give you a further update on the German eastern front," Petrie began. "We have good reason to believe that, over the long run, the German eastern front might have an even greater impact on this now global war than the terrible events at Pearl Harbor. Major Ralph Hugo, can you please give us the latest developments from the German assault on Moscow?"

Hugo, in full army uniform, appeared to be a professional senior officer; his accent betrayed an aristocratic background. Tall and thin, his uniform was meticulous, and his delivery was studied.

"Happy to, sir. About one week ago, Soviet troops retook the city of Rostov. This suggests the German Army Group South is struggling, but we don't have clear intelligence on that. Regarding German Army Group Center. They abandoned their attack on Moscow last Friday. The next day, the Soviets launched a major counter-offensive in the area. This will be a very unpleasant winter for those German troops. These are the facts on the ground. Our MI6 colleague, Ted Burgess, will provide a strategic analysis."

Burgess was dressed in a black suit with a white dress shirt. He was a small man, clearly not a combat army veteran. He appeared to be an academic, but he had a sly twinkle. He had been taking copious notes on Pearl Harbor.

"Thank you, Mr. Johnston, for that background on Pearl Harbor. An enormously informative summary. Let me fill you in on some Eastern Front analysis. We should first run through the chronology. Our sources tell us the German invasion of Russia was actually scheduled to begin in early May, which would have reduced the risks involved in poor weather in fall and early winter. It appears that Operation Barbarossa was delayed when Germany had to send troops to Greece in April to counter the British troops.

"This delay was extremely costly to the Germans. The Panzer Units initially advanced rapidly, but heavy rain and extremely muddy ground conditions in July slowed them down considerably. August weather conditions were better, and the Germans had an opportunity to move on towards Moscow, but for reasons we do not understand, they stripped Army Group Center of two Panzer Divisions, so the advance on Moscow was slowed to the pace of German infantry divisions.

"By the time Group Center was restored to its original troop and tank levels, the Germans had lost two critical months of decent weather. Winter came early, and this particular Russian winter is looking to be *especially* severe," he said with that usual twinkle in his eye. "Though Christmas is fast approaching, the German troops are still in their summer uniforms. Little or no winter clothing. Most of their military equipment is also summer gear. By contrast, the Russians are very good at fighting in winter conditions."

"Another critical element—the Russian reserves. The Germans appear to have grossly underestimated their size. They knew of the 100,000 to 150,000 Soviet reserve troops in western Russia, but they were unaware of an additional 100,000 to 200,000 troops held in eastern Russia. The unexplained delay of the advance on Moscow gave the Russians time to mobilize their Eastern divisions and transport them to the city.

"The reserves were needed. We believe that the Soviets suffered between 500,000 and 1,000,000 killed, missing, wounded or captured. German troops were permitted— or encouraged—to be brutal to the Soviet citizens in the areas they conquered, and to the hundreds of thousands of Soviet troops they captured. We are getting reports of tens of thousands of deaths of captured Soviet troops."

"This widespread brutality has proven to be an error of monumental consequence for the Germans because Soviet civilians and troops now believe that surrender to the Nazis is not an option. The invading German troops are now seen as alien creatures. They give no quarter. So, it's a fight to the death. And that seems to be exactly what the Soviets are doing."

As Burgess spoke, no one in the room moved in the packed quarters of Petrie's office. One officer asked, "How do we know these details? Are we sure of our facts?"

Burgess responded, "Our sources are deemed reliable."

There was that twinkle again. Sarah and Robert looked at each other.

Burgess sat back into his seat and took a few sips of water from his glass. He wanted to be sure that he had everyone's attention. He had saved the best for last.

He stood up again, trying hard not to smile.

"This final piece is soft intelligence, but we have reason to believe, from Russian reports, that the Germans have suffered well over 500,000 killed, missing, wounded and captured. The German divisions are now one-third full strength. The Luftwaffe has also suffered enormous losses of aircraft and crews, and harsh weather conditions are making it extremely difficult for the Luftwaffe to operate out of their forward bases in Russia. From what we can see, a major German withdrawal is very unlikely. Hitler hates withdrawals and, clearly, he is in charge. Any attempted German withdrawal at this point runs the risk of a major catastrophe for German

Army Group Center. Trying to backtrack over such great distances, passing through extremely hostile Soviet territories, hampered by terrible weather and poorly uniformed and equipped troops, hotly pursued by now superior numbers of Soviet divisions, could quickly become the rout of the century. Exactly what happened to Napoleon in 1812."

With this bombshell, there was another hour and a half of discussion about war strategy. Finally, the meeting ended. Everyone filed out of Petrie's office, leaving just Petrie, Robert, and Sarah still sitting there. Petrie turned to Sarah,

"Lieutenant, please escort our honored guest out of this MI5 labyrinth. Robert, thanks so much for joining us. There is a great deal to digest on all sides."

As Robert and Sarah walked down the corridor, she pulled him into her office, but left the door open to avoid any suspicions.

"Robert, I am dying to hear your reaction to the meeting today. Can you share?"

They both sat down.

Robert looked at Sarah for a few minutes. He did enjoy looking at her, and she didn't seem to mind at all.

"Petrie is nobody's fool. I think you now have the right person to head MI5. He orchestrated that meeting well. I walked in focusing entirely on the three thousand US servicemen and women killed and wounded at Pearl Harbor. I left with the grim realization that our losses are miniscule compared to the millions killed and wounded on the Eastern Front. Churchill is right in his assessment that The Empire of Japan is a sideshow. We must focus primarily on dealing with the Third Reich. I am absolutely certain that the US will quickly endorse this priority."

Sarah sat silently looking at Robert, then nodded in agreement. They agreed to meet soon for dinner.

23

A Cozy Dinner Date – Christmas Eve

24 December 1941, London

Ten days after the meeting at MI5, Sarah and Robert met again at the Old Bell Tavern. At their quiet dinner, after taking Robert's hand several times, Sarah listened as he told her of the developing scene in the US mobilizing for war. As they finished dinner and prepared to head off to their respective homes after a long day, Robert asked Sarah if she had any big plans for the Christmas holiday.

"I do not, except that I always spend the afternoon of Christmas Day visiting with my parents. My father has been incredibly busy this year with his Royal Navy assignments, and my mother always seems to have a very full schedule. It is a fun and calm Christmas Day with them. Too bad my brother cannot join us this year."

"You're right, Christmas is a time for family, but my family seems a bit 'remote' these days. I have always enjoyed Christmas music, especially on Christmas Eve. We used to go as a family to the Christmas Eve service at our church," said Robert. "Would you join me for the Christmas Eve service at St. Paul's? We could have a late dinner at one of the pubs in the area afterward."

"It would be an honor to be your "substitute family" this Christmas Eve," she said. "Am I to be your sweetheart, as you Yanks like to say, or maybe just an adoring London debutante?" She laughed.

Robert faked a scowl. "Actually," he said, "you remind me most of my elderly aunt from Scarsdale."

On Christmas Eve, they arranged to meet on the steps of St. Paul's. Not an easy reunion, as there was a crowd that evening. They eventually found each other, walked in, found two seats, and sat down.

Sarah took Robert's hand.

In keeping with tradition, the service featured English Christmas carols. Sarah knew most of them and sang along. Robert enjoyed watching

Sarah sing. It was a side of Sarah he had not seen before. She had a nice voice and sang well. But then everyone sings Christmas carols pretty well. It was clear that Sarah enjoyed the service.

At the end, Sarah and Robert sat quietly, and then walked around inside the church while the crowd headed out the main exit and dissipated. Then they walked out.

On the steps of St. Paul's, Sarah looked up at Robert. The solemn Christmas service had moved her deeply, but she was also enthused and intent on spending more time with Robert.

"You mentioned dinner at a pub, Robert. Is that still on offer? I have a few suggestions. Places you might like."

"London pubs are always good fun, but it was so nice—for me, anyway—to have dinner with you at my place that I have laid in some food for us there. Maybe I'm just being selfish. You are an experienced pub crawler, so you would probably prefer a night on the town."

"Not a chance. Dinner *avec tu chez vous* will make this a very special Christmas Eve. I've borrowed an MI5 car from the car pool. It's a cold night. I don't want to pass up an offer for a visit to your warm home. Your warm meal. Your warm hands. And some cold wine!"

Robert smiled. "I can guarantee one, two, and four on your priority list. Not sure about number three. My hands are pretty cold right now!"

"That's not good. Maybe, after dinner, we can find a nice warm place to put those hands of yours, to restore healthy circulation."

"I'm beginning to comprehend that you are a very intelligent Intelligence Officer." Robert paused. "Let's hurry through dinner!"

Entering his home, Robert helped Sarah remove her winter coat. When he looked at her, standing in his living room, he could not take his eyes off of her. And she did not want him to. She glowed.

Sarah wore an elegant well-fitted emerald-green long dress with a belted waist to show off her fine figure, and a red scarf. She did look Christmassy. She held out her arms, and turned slowly around, like a fashion model, but with a warm smile.

"Are you really a British Navy lieutenant? You look a lot more like a photographer's model from a Life Magazine advertisement."

Sarah smiled and looked very pleased.

"I am excited to do it up a bit. I have noticed that you do usually look me over once or twice when I am in uniform. But I was hoping, am hoping, that you will take even more notice of me in my "Sunday Best." I'm not sure who designed that British WREN Uniform, but she or he should be required to wear it non-stop for one year. It would be a fitting punishment. No pun intended."

Sarah and Robert worked as a team to pull the various portions of their Christmas Eve dinner out of the fridge, reheat things, and lay the table. Their teamwork seemed automatic and instinctive. Odd in that they had never worked together in the field.

"Let's sit down and enjoy the meal. I, for one, need a drink. May I offer you a glass of expensive wine that I bought just for you?"

"Just for me? No one ever bought a bottle of expensive wine for me! A bottle or two of beer, but never an expensive wine. Thank you."

Robert poured two ample glasses.

"Here's a toast to your prime minister, and to our president, who are tonight bonding with each other in the White House. Good health! Long life. And good luck to them both."

"And Happy Hunting!" Sarah added. "There are a great many German and Japanese soldiers, and sailors and airmen standing between us and our return to the lives we once knew."

"Agreed. Happy Hunting to us all!"

Robert watched Sarah as she sipped her first taste. Just a sip.

"Oh, so good Robert. What is this?"

"It is a 1941 Giacomo Conterno Monfortino, a dry red wine from Italy. I really should let it sit for three years, but what the hell? In the words of Virgil, *Tempus fugit!*"

They clinked their glasses. Sarah said, "And here's to Virgil's 'Georgics.'"

They both emptied their first glass. And Robert poured two more glasses for them.

"Please allow me to propose my own toast to the US president and Congress for declaring war on Germany. What Amazing Grace for the UK and its allies!"

"Hitler didn't give us much choice. He declared war on *us* first. What a blithering idiot. The decision was almost as dumb as invading Russia."

As they sat and enjoyed the meal, the red wine and the Christmas spirit drew them into a discussion of their prewar lives.

"My parents both grew up in London and were introduced to each other by their parents. All very proper. My father graduated from Britannia Royal Naval College. Sometimes called Dartmouth. But of course, they would enjoy meeting a Princeton Man."

Robert laughed. Sarah continued, "My brother Tom never liked the thought of sea duty. So, he broke my father's heart and went to Royal Military Academy Sandhurst. Father did eventually forgive him. Tom is now serving in North Africa. I attended Oxford, but then was able to take some courses at the Naval College in 1939 and 1940. That did please my father. And, so now I secretly suspect that I am his *favorite* child," she laughed.

Robert smiled.

"It's your turn. Spending Christmas thousands of miles from your home must be difficult. Have you spoken to your family today?"

"It is difficult to get a line on 23, 24, 25 and 26 of December. So, we spoke on the 22nd. They are all fine. Ellen's parents live close by, so they have Christmas dinner there, with Mark and Nancy, and our pet dog, Tinker Toy!"

"Please tell me about Ellen and your children."

"You and I never really discussed them, did we? Ellen and I married right after college, over twenty years ago. Our daughter Nancy is in college now. Mark is finishing high school and then wants to enter the Navy. They are facing a very uncertain world and an uncertain future. But if we can all pull together, maybe we will end up with a better world, and a better future. Time will tell. Ellen strongly objected to my remaining in London and getting involved in the war effort. So, she flew home to New York and filed for separation. That is where things stand today."

Sarah became quiet. She looked down at the remaining food on her plate, and pecked at it thoughtfully with her fork, while sipping the remainder of her second glass of wine. Sensing the awkwardness of his recent comments, and hoping to break the silence, Robert went on.

"Marriage can be difficult in the best of times, and sometimes impossible in the worst of times. Like these times, as an example. Have you ever thought about it?"

"Thought about it? Yes. A few years ago. A good man proposed marriage. A very good man. James. It is a complicated story. James was then a major in the British army. Still is in the army, in fact. He is now a Lt. Colonel. Tank Corps. And I was in the military. Intelligence division. Still am, of course. This war was coming at us like a juggernaut. For two very rational people it seemed like a crazy, crazy time to get married. And we were both so very rational. Still are. Maybe too rational. He and I are both a little less rational now. And we are both currently pursuing our 'careers' in high risk zones. James checked all the boxes for a perfect British husband. Right family. Right schools. Right army unit. And a right fine guy. Maybe that was the problem. No mystery. No magic. No intrigue. Every good love affair needs some intrigue. Some 'hint' of impropriety. He was and is also a good friend. Almost like a brother. And, of course, we were introduced to each other by my brother, Tom, who worships James."

"Is James still in the picture?"

"Sort of. I did have dinner with him earlier this year. April, I think. He was home on leave. But he did not speak again of marriage. Nor did I. We were lovers once, or at least we made love several times, several years ago. But now we are friends. Good friends. But just friends. He is in the British 8th Army in North Africa. With my brother, in fact."

They cleaned off the table and put the dishes into the kitchen sink.

Robert took off his jacket and sat in his usual and favorite spot at the end of the sofa, looking at Sarah as he did. Then he jumped up and put a record on his old gramophone. It was Paul Whiteman *Rhapsody in Blue* by George Gershwin from 1924.

The Gershwin melody made Sarah melt. She sat down next to Robert, but maybe six inches or so away. Her serious mood from St. Paul's had now returned.

"Robert, you and I are growing closer, thrown together in dark, cold London, during Dark Cold War Days and Dark Cold Times in general. Is it uncomfortable for you, in view of Ellen and Mark and Nancy?"

"Yes, and no. Ellen is over there. In NYC. I am over here, in London. Last year it was just a simple matter of geography. A mere four thousand miles of very treacherous ocean filled with U-Boats. But now it is so much more. We were then an ocean apart. But today we are quite literally worlds apart as though she were on Neptune, and I on Jupiter. We are now separated on so many planes. On so many spheres. On so many levels. It was once there and then. And it was fine. But today I am here and now. And so are you. And so are we. Here and now. With maybe just a 'hint' of impropriety! I suppose I might travel to Neptune one day. Maybe I will. But at the moment I am on Jupiter. 'Therefore, what God has put asunder, probably only God can join back together. Mark 10.9.' Or words to that effect."

Sarah moved in close. And kissed Robert on the lips. For the first time.

After sitting for a few minutes, she said, "If you would like for us to sit together for a spell like this, would you mind terribly if I take off this dress and hang it up? I plan to wear it tomorrow for Christmas dinner with my parents, and I don't want to look like I slept in it all night. I have only one or two fancy dinner dresses."

"Good idea. Makes perfect sense. Let me get you a sweater. I don't want you to get as cold as these darn hands of mine."

Robert stood up to go into his bedroom for the sweater, but quickly realized that was a big mistake because Sarah had also stood up to take off her dress, and focused her eyes on Robert as she began that slow process. She unbuckled her belt and put it aside, then she reached behind her and unbuttoned each button. Then she slowly stepped out of the dress, and laid it carefully over a chair. She smiled, and help out her arms. "Since you seem to be into planets, here before you is Venus on a half-shell. Sandro Botticelli. The Birth of Venus!" She smiled.

"Absolutely," responded Robert. And only then did he go for the sweater.

Sarah put on Robert's big cardigan sweater, and they both sat back down together again.

"Let's try to warm up these cold hands that have been annoying you all evening!"

Sitting to his left at the sofa, she took his left hand in her left hand, and she placed his right hand just above the middle of her right thigh.

"How does that feel, my American friend?"

"Both hands feel warm, but the right hand feels warmer."

"You are a 'hard man' to please."

"Please keep trying."

After a short period, Robert noticed that Sarah was dozing off, periodically.

"I think you are getting tired. It has been a very long day, and it is now pretty late. Would you like to spend the night here?"

"Sure. That would be very nice."

Sarah pulled a toothbrush out of her large handbag, walked into the bathroom where she brushed her teeth, using Robert's toothpaste, and climbed on top of Robert's bed, still wearing her under garments and his cardigan sweater. In five minutes, she was sound asleep.

Robert, seeing that their brief romantic interlude had now ended, brushed his teeth, using his own toothpaste, changed into his pajamas, stretched out on the sofa, and promptly fell asleep.

Robert awoke gradually on Christmas morning, to the sounds of Sarah in the kitchen. She was making eggs, toast, and coffee. She stopped and gave him a nice hug, and they both sat down to a warm breakfast. It was Christmas Day, 1941

After breakfast, Robert went back into the WC to begin to clean up. Sarah was right behind him.

"This is quite an elegant tub. May I try it on for size?"

Robert was a little startled. He was not accustomed to sharing his tub. But he was a gentleman.

"Of course. Try it out!"

Sarah looked delighted to do so. Brits love their tubs.

She turned on both the hot and cold spigots to start filling the tub. Then she spied his huge bar of soap. "Oh good!" she said. It was hard to find large bars of soap in England these days. She dropped the bar of soap into the tub as it filled. Smart girl, thought Robert, now she can have a sudsy bath.

When the tub was full, she turned her back to Robert, pulled off his sweater and her undergarments, and silently slipped into the tub.

"Oh my God. This feels so good. You are a very lucky man. What a wonderful large tub!"

Sarah washed herself from stem to stern, including her hair. Then she stood up in the tub, her back to Robert again, and took Robert's large bath towel to dry off.

Robert wasn't sure if he was expected to look at her, or not look at her. She was only six or eight feet away. He decided to look. She was in great shape. Slender and firm, but curvaceous.

She started to pull the drain plug.

"Ah, just leave it. I might as well just use the same bath water. You look pretty clean."

He stood around, expecting her to vacate the bathroom, so that he could get into the tub. He had forgotten from his days of living with Ellen that women never actually vacate the bathroom. Never.

Finally, fearful that the tub water was losing its heat, he peeled off his pajamas and modestly stepped into the tub. It was a little embarrassing, as he had gotten a little excited watching Sarah towel off.

If Sarah did notice, she didn't say anything.

Robert got out of the tub, grabbing his now somewhat damp towel from the hook when Sarah had replaced it.

She was getting dressed. In the bathroom, of course. It was now the warmest room in the house.

As he tried to shave in the bathroom mirror, he had to stand behind Sarah, who was putting on her lipstick and combing her hair. It was very clear that Sarah had taken over his bathroom, so Robert quickly exited. He finished dressing for Christmas Day and then stuck his head back into the bathroom. Sarah was back in her green dress. Looking very fresh from hanging up all night.

"That old bathtub looked a lot better with you in it," Robert noted. "The scene reminded me of these wonderful Italian paintings of bath scenes in early Rome. It is heartwarming to see that you are so 'at home' with sharing a bathroom with a man."

"Well, you are a gracious host. There are very few WCs at MI5 and MI6, and very few women, so we usually have to share the bathroom facilities with our male colleagues. It probably does make them a bit nervous, or uncomfortable, but honestly women have a different attitude towards coed use of bathrooms."

She thought a moment and then added, "I just thought of a short poem that pretty much sums up the attitude of women who share bathroom facilities with men –

No thoughts of sex in the bathroom, my dear;
We have more important business in here!"
They both had a good laugh over that. Then they hugged goodbye.

"Robert, what a wonderful Christmas Eve. I will never forget it. I am glad that you are here on Jupiter—at least for a while. And you, my bathroom tub-mate, are my favorite alien. I especially love that little Jovian antennae that pokes up every now and then!"

24

Queen Victoria Hospital – Christmas Day

25 December 1941, London

There were no German bombings on Christmas Eve or Christmas Day, 1941. That alone was cause for joy at Queen Victoria Hospital in East Grinstead, Sussex. But there was an additional treat.

Princess Mary's Royal Air Force Nursing Service (PMRAFNS) had organized a small Christmas celebration for the sick and wounded RAF pilots stuck in the hospital over the holidays. Many of the nurses dressed up and came bearing cider and home-baked cookies and small gifts.

A number of London families were also invited, including Royal Navy Captain Spencer Haythornwaite, his wife, Pamela, and his two daughters, Amanda and Alice. Amanda was wearing her new nurse uniform. Pamela Haythornwaite, realizing that nothing would cheer up the cooped-up pilots as much as a bevy of young women, suggested to Amanda that she bring along her impressive young friend, Hannah.

Hannah was thrilled and delighted to come along. Christmas Eve and Christmas Day was always a depressing time to be separated from family, or even worse to have no family. And for Jews living in a Christian country, it was worse still.

The lonely young pilots could not have cared less whether Amanda and Alice and Hannah were Christian, Jewish, Muslim or Hindu. They were very pleased. Charming, bubbly, attentive, talkative and interesting women.

For Hannah, it was uplifting. A number of the mostly young pilots were intrigued to learn that she was German and yet was not a Nazi, hated the Nazis, and seemed so very human. And she spoke English like a British noblewoman. Hannah made the pilots feel that maybe the German people they were bombing weren't all evil after all. Perhaps, there were "a few good Germans" over there.

Two of the young pilots were anxious to talk to Captain Haythornwaite, himself a decorated Royal Navy pilot.

"Captain Haythornwaite, so nice to meet you. I am Todd. My friend here is Ben. We got a little banged up in a bombing raid two weeks ago, but they tell us that we'll be back in action in a month or two. We don't get to meet many Navy fliers. How you can fly a bomber off a carrier with such a short runway? It just doesn't seem possible."

"Good to hear that your stay will be short even if the ward is currently filled with these pretty young nurses."

The pilots both laughed.

"Sometimes we fly off the carriers. Sometimes we get shot off with a big catapult. But that's when the excitement begins. If we don't have enough of our own engine speed to stay aloft after we take off the carrier, then we drop into the drink, and hopefully some small ship will pick us up out of the sea. But even if they do get us, our plane is lost. Flying anything off a carrier is lunacy, for sure, but that's why we are paid so much!"

Another big laugh.

"But I would rather take off from a carrier one hundred times than have to fly one bombing mission over Germany. Anti-aircraft fire, Luftwaffe fighters, long-range flying, poor navigation systems and aging bombers. You are a tough bunch. I take my hat off to you!"

Both pilots smiled at the captain's kind words.

"Thanks, sir. It means a lot coming from you!"

Two of the pretty young nurses came over bearing cider, cookies, and big smiles.

Alice, Amanda's seventeen-year-old sister, was standing very close to Hannah. While Hannah answered questions about recent life in Germany from several eager young pilots, Alice noticed four doctors of various ages, standing somewhat stiffly in their long white coats, taking in all the action.

Alice pulled on Hannah's arm. "Hannah, have you noticed those four men? Do you think they are flight surgeons?"

"I have never seen a flight surgeon, but that is surely a skill in demand around here. They look fairly unapproachable!"

With people starting to notice them, the four white coats started to feel a bit awkward. Two of the older ones walked over to the group, dragging the two younger white coats along with them.

"Hello, young ladies. We didn't mean to cause a stir. We are the staff doctors on duty, here to make our afternoon rounds. But our patients don't seem to be very anxious to talk about their medical problems today, so we have been hiding in the corner.

"I am Dr. Archibald McIndoe, these are my colleagues Dr. Thad Conegy, Dr. William Smith and Dr. Aaron Solomon. Welcome to you all. You have definitely brought a good measure of Christmas cheer to this often-gloomy ward. Thank you!"

Dr. McIndoe, a physician in his early forties, smiled warmly. He was very comfortable chatting with the young pilots and young women. The other three doctors were much younger, and so somewhat reserved. Accustomed to treating mostly airmen, the women made these three doctors nervous. But Dr. McIndoe's good charm and kind open fellowship broke the ice for all them. Very soon all four doctors stood around chatting, laughing, smiling, imbibing cider, and munching on cookies.

While they were hobnobbing, one of the senior nurses pulled Dr. McIndoe aside.

"Doctor, one of your patients has been asking repeatedly to see you. I am certain you won't be surprised to hear that it is Flight Lt. Hillary. And I am also certain that you will want to see him, as I do believe he is one of your favorites."

Dr. McIndoe smiled, and responded, "Of course I want to see him." He then turned to address the group. "Flight Lieutenant Richard Hope Hillary is indeed one of my favorite patients. Australian by birth, Hillary was a very dashing and handsome Oxford man before he joined No. 603 Squadron RAF Fighter Command. His impressive record as a Spitfire pilot was cut short when his plane was shot down in September 1940 by a Messerschmitt Bf 109 flown by Hauptmann Helmuth Bode, one of Germany's ace pilots. Hillary was pulled out of the North Sea by a lifeboat from Margate Station. He suffered terrible face and hand burn injuries. I have been treating his burn injuries extensively. Hillary has become a legendary RAF pilot model. After he was injured, on his good will tour of the U.S. this spring, Hillary attracted the romantic attention of the very beautiful, and famously exotic, Bombay born Hollywood movie star, Merle Oberon. This only enhanced his legendary stature. It is also generally known that Hillary is now writing a book about his experience. So, I must say hello to him."

Dr. McIndoe excused himself and headed over to Ward 3 to check up on Hillary. The remaining group chatted on about Hillary, and then moved to other subjects.

During the introductions, Hannah had picked up on the name of the "Doctor Aaron Solomon." She slowly moved in his direction. Although Dr. Solomon seemed to be the least chatty of the four doctors, she was attracted to his shy good looks and quiet, thoughtful demeanor. Alice tagged along, enjoying her time in Hannah's orbit.

"Hello, Dr. Solomon and Dr. Smith. I feel like maybe we have invaded your peaceful domain. I hope you don't regard us as a disruption!" she and Alice laughed.

Dr. Solomon smiled. "I would say that these quiet corridors need all the invading and disrupting they can get. I am absolutely sure that your visit today has significantly speeded up the recovery time of these flyboys with clipped wings."

They all laughed.

Aaron turned to Hannah and Alice. "It is hard to fully relate the heart-warming impact your visit has on these young pilots, and on us doctors as well, particularly having Captain Haythornwaite come to spend Christmas with us. He is a revered figure. I actually attended a couple of meetings with him to discuss urgent issues at RAF Bomber Command.

"We have also heard that the captain has his two daughters here today, of whom he is very proud. Alice, you might be one of them, but Hannah, I suspect you are not, because I overheard you telling the pilots about your experiences growing up in Dresden. You are a friend? A refugee?"

Pleased by Aaron's warm words, Hannah responded. "Yes—both! And I feel so fortunate to have been invited here today. It does give Christmas a special meaning to be brought into its afterglow."

They listened attentively while Hannah explained her background.

Across the Ward, Amanda found herself "captured" by four wounded RAF pilots. Two were Brits. One was Canadian. One from New Zealand. As they spoke, the young pilot from New Zealand pointed out to her that Dr. McIndoe was a New Zealander and founded the highly regarded

Guinea Pig Club for burned pilots. Members of the club had tried many of Dr. McIndoe's innovative and often very successful burn treatments. Hence the term, Guinea Pigs. It began to dawn on Amanda that maybe being a young nurse to these dashing young, wounded RAF pilots did have some benefits beyond public service.

As they chatted on and on, she noticed out of the corner of her eye that Hannah and Alice were getting a whole lot of attention from the two young doctors. RAF Pilots are heroes during wartime, but doctors are heroes almost all of the time. She wanted a piece of that action.

"Excuse me for a few minutes, gentlemen. I better rescue my sister and my guest before these young doctors sign them up for Late Night and Weekend Nurse Assistant Duty!"

When Amanda approached the foursome, she found that Alice was focused on a Dr. Smith, inquiring into his background and experience. Smart girl. But Hannah and Dr. Solomon seemed to be wading into a more serious discussion.

"Dr. Solomon, given my background, I was wondering whether you might share my Hebrew Heritage?"

The doctor smiled broadly. "Yes. Indeed, I do," he said. "My father has always claimed that our family are direct descendants of King Solomon, often called Jedidiah, and therefore of Jedidiah's father, King David, and Jedidiah's mother, the glamorous Bathsheba; the Queen consort of Israel in 1,000 BCE. How my father might have traced that origin back 1,000 years before the birth of Christ has always been a mystery to the rest of the family. But King Solomon-Jedidiah had a great many wives and concubines. He must also have had a great many offspring. So, I guess it is also possible that I am actually a descendant of Naamah, the daughter of the King of the Ammonites. That may be a longer answer than you were looking for," he laughed, and then continued, "I'm so very sorry to hear your description of the treatment of Jews in Germany, and about the current state of affairs for tens of thousands of Jewish refugees."

"It is a desperate calamity," said Hannah. "I wish we could convince our friends here in Britain to admit a great many more of them."

Dr. Solomon thought for a few minutes. "This is such a complicated issue. But it is also a very controversial issue, with incredibly strong and sometimes intemperate feelings on all sides. And I'm sure you are now seeing that the refugee problem is being intricately intertwined with the whole Palestine conundrum which is particularly explosive. Clearly you and I should talk."

Hannah looked at the doctor. "There are now several hundred thousand German-Austrian Jewish refugees. They have to go somewhere. Maybe some to Britain, and some to Palestine. But just ignoring the problem is not an option."

Aaron nodded in agreement. "There are strong currents of anti-Semitism here in Britain, and some of those adherents can become violent in their opposition to Jewish emigration. And there are others, not necessarily British, but persons having Middle Eastern connections, who can be equally volatile at any suggestion of increased Jewish incursions into Palestine. These are high stake games. People play for keeps. Be careful."

Hannah studied him for a moment, digesting his words. "Sound advice, Dr. Solomon. I will try to be more cautious. But it is clear to me looking around this hospital ward filled to capacity with badly injured young airmen, many of whom are my age, that people my age are never careful and seldom cautious. We are all in pain watching our world go down the drain!"

The doctor nodded again. "Believe me, I do feel your pain, and I too have given it a great deal of thought. I wonder if you and I could meet one day for a lunch to discuss the situation with all of its ramifications? We could learn a great deal from each other."

"It would be my honor. My friend and host here today, Amanda, will be working with you and knows how to reach me. And thank you for your considerate warning. I do sense the risk you describe. But I have nothing left to lose."

Aaron was stunned to hear Hannah say she had "nothing left to lose," but it was clear from her demeanor that she meant it. He said nothing in response.

As twilight approached, the visitors began the farewells and headed home, and the four doctors began their daily rounds, checking up on their cookie and cider filled patients.

25

A Year-end Pub Party – New Year's Eve

31 December 1941, London

A few days before New Year's Eve, Sarah called Robert to invite him to the MI5/MI6 end of year get together. It was all hush hush because spooks love secret stuff. But this particular party arrangement was probably not the best kept secret.

Robert met Sarah at the "secret little pub," where food could be had, and music could be played. They sat together, ate together, and talked on and on with the other members of the group. All those in the military wore their uniforms, including Sarah.

Robert took note of all the handsome uniforms. "This is quite a show. I feel like I am attending a Military Tattoo, and I've forgotten my bagpipe!"

"We are all so very proud to be serving our country right now," said Sarah. "It is a great honor."

Although it was a bit chilly in the pub, Robert quietly took off his navy-blue blazer, realizing that if he were wearing only his shirt and tie, it would not be so obvious that he was not wearing a uniform. Sarah realized immediately what Robert had in mind, and felt a little guilty herself for going out with him on a New Year's date in her uniform. What was she thinking? Reaching under the table, she took his hand. In this group, a public display of affection would have raised questions in the minds of those present. The perceived relationship between Sarah and Robert was strictly professional. If it came to be seen as personal, they would both suffer some loss of credibility, and Sarah might be "reassigned" to some other hapless Yank, now that London was crawling with Yanks. Neither Sarah nor Robert wanted that.

"You are doing your part, Robert. Being here in London at this time, in this role, has served both your country and mine very well. Bless you. And thank you!"

Robert choked up a little.

"One day the Brits should erect a statue of Japanese Admiral Yamamoto in Trafalgar Square. In four short hours on a sunny Sunday morning on the Island of Oahu, on 7 December 1941, he united your country and mine, and assured the eventual destruction of both The Empire of Japan and the Third Reich. No small achievement."

"Yes, he did. And he got a little help from his Comrade in Arms, Adolf Hitler, who declared war on America three days later. But I don't imagine that we will be erecting any statues to him!"

"One thing I can assure you, Sarah. Hitler has now sealed his doom. His war is lost. And so is he. And so is Yamamoto. The difference is that Hitler probably doesn't realize it yet. Yamamoto almost certainly does. On a happier note, my dear Sarah, I propose a toast to your 'good friend,' James and to your brother Tom. May they both have success and long life in North Africa, and beyond."

"Thank you, Robert. And good health to Ellen and your son and daughter in New York City. I am quite certain that your children miss you very much."

As the party petered out, Sarah and Robert slipped out quietly, one by one, and then headed over to Robert's home for a night cap. The weather that night was calm, and not too cold. They decided to walk a bit to enjoy the mild weather and take note of the other people walking about and celebrating the end of a dreadful year in Britain. They shared a few memories of past New Year's Eve experiences. Then they climbed into Sarah's borrowed MI5 staff car and drove to Robert's house. Once inside, Sarah drank some red wine, and became warm and affectionate. They both began removing clothing. Sarah gave him a long kiss.

"Happy New Year!"

Robert said, "Is that all I get?"

Sarah looked at him, both of them now seated close on the bed. Once again she drew him in with those big cat-like eyes. Once again he was locked in.

"Of course you can get more." She pulled him very close. "It is very late, but I can stay awake if you can. After all, I'm younger than you!"

They awoke many hours later, still knitted together in bed, and then shared a hearty New Year's Day breakfast of scrambled eggs, grilled ham, cheese and bread, and hot coffee. The sun was shining, to open a whole new year. There was change in the air. You could definitely feel it.

It was 1942.

1942

The US Enters the Fray

26

Bomber Harris takes Command RAF HQ

28 February 1942, High Wycombe

In February 1942 Sir Arthur "Bomber" Harris replaced Sir Richard Peirse as head of RAF Bomber Command. Peirse was a precision bombing advocate, and precision bombing was now out-of-favor. British Chief of Air Staff Charles Portal blamed Peirse for Bomber Command's lack of performance and he chose Harris to replace him. It also did not augur well for Peirse that U.S. General Hap Arnold, Chief of US Army Air Forces, was a strong advocate for replacing him.

Shortly after taking command, Harris had a visit from Professor Lindemann and a few others, including Dr. Aaron Solomon and David Butts. Suspecting that "The Prof" would come with a lot of difficult and annoying questions and criticisms, Harris "invited" a number of senior and junior Bomber Command flight officers to cushion the expected blow.

"Congratulations, Air Marshall. You are The Man of the Hour. If it weren't for RAF Bomber Command, the Germans might think that the Brits have already surrendered!"

"Thank you, Professor. Coming from you, this is a huge praise. We will do our best to get their attention."

Harris proceeded with brief introductions of the assembled officers. It was clear from Lindemann's facial expression and demeanor that he understood only too well why Harris had surrounded himself with his "Wolf Pack," but Lindemann was not going to pull any punches. He was very displeased and concerned about the past poor performance of Bomber Command under Peirse and apprehensive about its future prospects to show a dramatic improvement under Harris. He planned to air his concerns, Wolf Pack be damned.

Lindemann knew all too well that the problems of Bomber Command were endemic, and that simply replacing Peirse with Harris was unlikely to produce a dramatic improvement. He opened the discussion on a somber note.

"What are your plans for the next six months? Does Bomber Command now have the resources to make an impact?"

Harris more or less grunted his response. "The short answer is 'no.' The longer and more accurate answer is '*clearly*, no.'"

Harris was not a man to mince words.

"Let's recap where things at Bomber Command stand now," he continued. "Most of us here are aware of the bombing issues and many distractions over the past three years, but some of our young friends, being new to the force, are probably out of the loop."

Harris knew better than most people that the best defense is a good offense. So, he planned to tell his version of the story before Lindemann could tell his. Always a challenge with Lindemann.

"When German forces invaded Poland in September 1939, the RAF was prepared. Bomber Command had 280 bombers in five Air Groups, with *Bristol Blenheims, Vickers Wellingtons, Armstrong-Whitworth Whitleys*, and *Handly Page Hamptons*. But on that day, US President Roosevelt appealed to all warring countries to refrain from bombing targets where there could be civilian casualties. So, Bomber Command was effectively prohibited from bombing raids on German soil.

"Eight months later, on 10 May 1940, the Germans commenced their Western Offensive. Bomber Command was still restricted from bombing Germany. Insanity, of course. Then, on 15 May, the Germans bombed Rotterdam almost into smithereens, even though Holland had already surrendered! The British War Cabinet changed course 180 degrees and finally authorized bombing on German soil.

"By that time, Bomber Command was heavily involved in The Battle of France and suffering heavy losses. We lost almost 150 planes from 1 May through 30 June. And many more of our planes were lost from crash landings in England and aircraft fire over Germany. We were reduced by fifty percent.

"The Battle of Britain then waged from July through September 1940. We won, of course, thanks in large part to the now fabled derring-do of RAF Fighter Command.

"Luckily for us during the period from June through October, the Luftwaffe night bombing defense, mostly *Messerschmitt* 110s, was small and ineffective.

"Our bombing operations over Germany slowed considerably from October 1940 through February 1941. Sir Charles Portal left Bomber Command on 5 October 1940 to become Chief of Air Staff. Air Marshall Peirse took over as commander.

"During that period, Bomber Command was instructed to focus on German oil facilities. For these missions, we had about 150 effective aircraft, mostly *Wellingtons*. Our total strength on paper was about 500 aircraft. We had two hundred *Blenheims*, but they were of little use for long range heavy bombing missions. We had eighty-five *Battles*, but they were soon taken out-of-service. We had seventy *Haydens* and sixty *Whitleys*, all scheduled for replacement. And we had one-hundred *Wellingtons*. The weather through winter was terrible, virtually shutting down our bombing operations.

"In the spring and early summer of 1941, Bomber Command was diverted to attacks on German U-Boats. I think we performed pretty well, but the bombing of Germany itself was placed on hold again."

At this point, Harris stopped to drink a glass of water. He picked up his desk phone, and asked the corporal on duty to send in some tea, coffee, and biscuits.

Lindemann liked the idea of some refreshments, so he suppressed his desire to comment on the Harris monologue, and quietly enjoyed a cup of hot tea. Aaron and David Butt were a little surprised at this unusual silence.

Sensing a tactical, if perhaps temporary victory, Harris continued his story.

"In the summer and fall of 1941, Bomber Command returned to its pressing mission of bombing Germany. *Stirlings* and *Halifaxes* were very good, but we did not have many of them-about fifty in total. By that time, German air defenses were very much improved using airborne radar. Bomber Command casualties increased significantly.

"Then in August 1941, the earth shifted under our feet. Our losses were unacceptable unless we could show impressive results. But the report from young David Butt, who has joined us here today, showed us that our results were disappointing.

"According to the Butt Report, for June and July 1941, one-third of all crews did not reach their targets. Only our best crews were given cameras to record their success. Of our best crews, often only one in four or five dropped their bombs within *five miles* of their targets, even then only on moonlit nights. Shocking and astounding. I don't have to tell you, Bomber Command was shaken to its core.

"Even worse, flight crews were balking at the risk of dangerous flights while they knew that often the raids did little real damage to their targets. Between July and November 1941, Bomber Command lost over 500 bombers! Put another way, we lost three or four percent of our planes on every nighttime mission, and seven percent on every daytime mission. On one single night, 7 November 1941, we lost thirty-seven aircraft.

"As a result of these unsustainable losses and poor results, the War Cabinet instructed Bomber Command to curtail operations over the winter of 1941/42.

"Months later, on 14 February 1942, the Area Bombing Directive was sent to Bomber Command from Air Ministry. The primary objective of bombing operations would henceforth be the morale of the German civilian population. On 22 February, I was given command here. That ends the telling of this convoluted tale."

Harris did not ask for questions, he just looked around the room, finally focusing on Lindemann.

Silence. None of the military men present was going to take on Harris, particularly on a subject where he was the undisputable expert and Harris was their boss. His report was a litany of bad news. The men in the room looked markedly downcast, discouraged and frustrated. If the appointment of Harris to Commander of Bomber Command was intended to inspire optimism, his words today were dark and ominous. The mood was funereal.

Lindemann knew it was his turn to speak. He also knew that Harris could probably out talk him, but he certainly could not out think him. Harris himself had described the sad story of Bomber Command better than Lindemann ever could. Lindemann said, "I rest my case. The past has been a failure. Where do we go from here?"

Harris was well aware that he could not redeem the past, but it was his job to brighten the future. So, he pressed on.

"Coming at last to the present, and the future," continued Harris, "we now have over 500 bombers. Mostly *Wellingtons* and *Hampdens*, and a few more *Whitleys* and *Blenheims*. We tried using America's *B-17s*, but we have had technical problems that hopefully our American friends will address. And we have two huge new assets. Our *Lancaster Bombers* are starting to arrive. A much much better aircraft. No secret about that. Our other new asset is secret. It is a complicated navigation system using three transmitter stations in England to create a navigation grid. We call it GEE after the first letter of grid. It will enable our bombers to find their targets and to return home. I am not permitted to give out any further details on GEE, but we have great hopes for the system. All that said, let me finish by giving you my thoughts on our operations for the next five-to-six months. There will be a number of very important changes.

First, we will focus on only one target on any given night. *Second*, we will only bomb on suitable nights. Clear weather and moonlight. *Third*, there will be much shorter bombing runs. Just two hours. Hit them hard and fast and leave quickly. *Fourth*, we will increase our use of incendiary bombs. Burning does far more damage than exploding bombs. Blow off roofs with bombs, then set neighborhoods on fire, and then bomb surrounding roads to keep firetrucks far away. *Fifth*, reduce the number of raids. Pushing out bombing runs under unfavorable conditions is a certain prescription for failure.

Now I want to hear some questions. I do not want Professor Lindemann to think that you have all fallen asleep! That's an order!"

Suddenly, hands shot up all over the room.

"Now that we finally have War Cabinet clearance to bomb German cities, when can we begin?"

"Very soon. This new Directive from the War Cabinet does not give us any new or better bombers."

"Are these Lancaster Bombers a significant improvement?"

"Yes. A very significant improvement."

"Will GEE work over targets in Central and Eastern Germany?"

"No comment."

"Why is there so much public acclaim for Fighter Command and so much public criticism of Bomber Command?"

"Because everyone sees RAF Fighter Command Spitfire and Hurricane fighters flying overhead shooting down German bombers and none of them see RAF Bomber Command Manchesters and Lancasters flying over Germany."

"Why does everyone think that fighter pilots are better pilots than bomber pilots?"

"Because they fly the Spitfire, the most beautiful airplane ever designed, and we fly the Armstrong Whitworth AW 38 Whitley Bomber, the most aesthetically unattractive aircraft ever flown."

The attendees pressured Harris for more and better insights. His rough and gruff military sense of humor seemed to put everyone at ease. Even Lindemann, who seemed pleased with the results of the meeting, sounded more hopeful for the future. He was in a much better mood. After another hour of discussion, the meeting adjourned. Lindemann and Harris went off for a private meeting.

27

Hannah Starts to Attract Attention

15 March 1942, London

Hannah, Amanda, and Alice attended another meeting at the British Foreign Office on King Charles Street in London. These meetings were intended to address British immigration policies and the Jewish refugee problem. Given the topic, it was not likely to be a pleasant meeting.

Hannah came as Amanda's guest. Amanda's parents, the Haythornwaites, had long family connections to the British Foreign Office, and hoped that Amanda or Alice would one day go to work there. This meeting was very different from many of the 1941 and early 1942 meetings and sessions regarding the European refugee problem. It was held in a government office. A very plain, drab grey room. There were a small number of British government bureaucrats presiding. They shared the characteristics of the room.

Without Amanda, Hannah would never have been able to attend this meeting. She was probably the only actual recent Jewish refugee there, and as such, would *not* have been welcome because of the sensitivity of the issue. No one other than Amanda and Alice knew of Hannah's German-Jewish background, nor of her recent emigration into the UK. The purpose of the meeting today was to explain and largely defend the current policies of the British Government towards refugees in general, and Jewish refugees in particular. The audience consisted of members of the press, other government officials, representatives of refugee agencies, business interests, local politicians, and other diverse members of the British public.

The audience was divided in its sympathy to the plight of the European refugees. Probably a significant portion of the British people felt that the refugee situation was awful, but that the British had not caused it, and there was only so much that Britain itself could do. As such, their sympathies for Hannah would also be mixed. Hannah could sense the tension. It did cause her discomfort, but she knew she had to rise above it.

Also present were four representatives from the British Home Office, headed by George Davis. They were responsible for immigration, and did their best to limit immigration. George Davis, a somewhat heavy set and pompous fellow, was determined to "Defend the Castle," but he was also fair minded and very professional.

Davis laid out his version of the situation.

"There had been roughly one million Jews in Germany and Austria before the Nazis came to power in 1934, and perhaps a third of them are still there today. The numbers are not entirely clear. Many thousands are quite simply unaccounted for. The Germans told us that a quarter-million Jews left Germany before the war. We have reason to believe that there are still 100,000 Jews in Austria and other areas which have come under German control. Perhaps up to 25,000 of these refugees were able to go to the US, 50,000 to Britain, 40,000 to France, 25,000 went to Belgium, 10,000 of them emigrated to Switzerland, and about 53,000 went to Palestine. The balance has been stuck with no place to go. A large group of 20,000 went to Shanghai, which had no Visa requirements. All of these numbers are estimates, and include some non-Jews, but they are mostly Jews.

"To make matters worse—far worse—other European countries including Poland, Romania and Hungry did not admit German Jewish refugees, and actually started pressuring their resident Jewish population to emigrate. These refugee problems have only worsened, year by year."

Members of the press attending the meeting were generally aware that there was a big story here. Largely unspoken. The Western Allies, including Britain, appeared to be standing by and ignoring the current catastrophic European refugee problem. So, they began, one by one, as is their style, to press the speakers to learn more.

"Why is Britain, with a population of 45,000,000, not admitting more than 50,000 Jewish refugees, only one-tenth of one percent of the British population?" one reporter yelled above the others.

Davis responded, somewhat flushed, "Please realize that Britain is currently fighting a war for its very survival. We feel great sympathy for these German-Austrian Jews and for the many other refugees of this wretched war. But our first obligation is to save and preserve Britain and the British people. We are already bearing the enormous cost of this war, and a great deal of the cost of feeding and housing the tens of thousands of refugees we have already admitted. We are also asking that the other major countries of the western world increase their own quotas to admit more of these refugees. But it just isn't happening."

Members of the Press were grumbling and buzzing amongst themselves. Other parts of the audience sat quietly, digesting Davis' rebuttal. The few Jewish members there, most of whom had families that had lived in Britain for generations, were reluctant to weigh in more heavily, sensing that the war and the refugee problem entailed a delicate balance.

Amanda, seated among her small group of young women, spoke out.

"Do you know, Minister Davis, whether or not Britain continues to have diplomatic contact with the German government through the Swiss government, and whether those channels might be used now to facilitate the removal of more Germans and Austrian Jews?"

"At this time, there are no diplomatic channels available to our government to facilitate the escape of German or Austrian Jews. Not through the Swiss, nor anyone else. Emigration of Jews from those countries is now barred by German and Austrian laws."

Hannah listened, but her temperature was rising. She knew all too well that it was not her place to speak at the meeting, but she had burning concerns that festered. As a passionate young woman, she had difficulty keeping her thoughts and emotions under wraps. It was painful for Hannah to remain in her seat, so she shuffled from side to side. She and Alice looked at each other, and then she and Amanda locked eyes. Hannah shook her head to show disagreement. An unspoken question from Hannah. *Should she speak out?* An unspoken nod "Yes," from Amanda.

"Minister Davis," Hannah began. "Were you at your present post in the summer of 1939 when the German Economics Ministry sent messages to your government through the US Embassy asking for British assistance in getting as many German Jews as possible out of Germany? To a great extent, these Jews were not admitted into Britain because the

British Government set strict quotas on the number of these Jews that could enter either Britain or Palestine."

Hannah's comments were shocking and disturbing news to many in the small audience. Most attendees were looking at Hannah and not at Davis. They were commenting to each other, within their respective groups. They all looked troubled. The government people did not look at Hannah. They first looked at the floor. Then they looked at Davis, awaiting his answer. Davis was starting to perspire. Amanda put her arm around Hannah's waist to show her support.

Davis was now out of his comfort zone. "I am not aware of these facts, if they are facts. How and when did you become aware of these reports?"

"I was living with my family in Dresden until late 1938. We were very aware of the efforts of the German Government to ship as many Jews as possible out of Germany. A great many were very willing to leave, but very few were admitted into other countries. So many remained in Germany. Effective last October, the German Government prohibited Jews from leaving Germany. So now it is too late for them. For all of them.

"I heard these reports from my parents in Dresden back in 1938. I have not heard from my family at all now for over a year. The bits and pieces of news that we do hear about the tens of thousands of German Jews remaining in Germany are very bad."

The non-government people showed great sympathy to the information and Hannah herself. The Press were feverishly talking notes, often looking at Hannah and smiling to show encouragement. The small number of representatives of the Jewish Aid Organization were nodding in agreement. Some members of the public and local politicians were exhibiting surprise, and a little shame. You could hear the muttering words like, "awful," "shocking," and "our own government!" and "what a brave young woman!"

The reaction of the group from the government was entirely the opposite. They were grumbling and talking to each other in hushed tones, annoyed at Hannah's challenge.

One of the officials said just loud enough so Hannah might hear, "I told you. We admit these Jews into our country to protect them, and they turn on us. Now they want us to admit more of them so that even more of them can turn on us!"

The meeting ended in some turmoil.

As everyone began to file out of the room, a number of people, particularly members of the press, tried to catch a few words with Hannah, Amanda, and Alice. They wanted more background on these young speakers, especially Hannah. Eventually everyone drifted outside into the chilly and darkening afternoon. The three ladies then found a pub and sat down for some tea.

"I am so sorry for speaking out. I know I embarrassed you. It was very rude of me. These people will never invite you back!"

To Hannah's great surprise, Amanda and Alice looked at each other for one moment, and then burst out laughing.

"We should be so lucky," Amanda said. "This is England, not Germany. Everyone speaks his or her mind. It is our nature. You just added a little pepper sauce to a very dull beef pie. Now they will pursue us with, "Please, please come to our next meeting, and please, please bring that very attractive and articulate young German-Jewish woman with you!""

Amanda looked to Alice, and Alice agreed. "Hannah, Amanda is right. The government people were annoyed at the three of us because they always hope for worshipful adulation when they speak, but they know that rarely happens.

"There is a tension here in Britain. We all feel it. We feel very sorry for the refugees, but very few countries welcome large numbers of refugees. We feel very sorry for the Jews, but most of the Jewish refugees do seem foreign and different from us. There is anti-Semitism here. Plenty of it. Just below the surface. We have a world of problems of our own."

Amanda and Alice both took one of Hannah's hands. Hannah felt very lucky to have these two supportive friends. But she also sensed that she had made some enemies today.

28

U.S. Eighth Air Force Bomber Command

14 April 1942, London

By early April, Robert was extremely busy making connections, developing his growing intelligence and military network and acting as a switchboard for British and American communication. Almost too busy to practice law.

One main draw on his time was the rapidly growing U.S. Eighth Air Force presence in London. On 11 April, he received a call from a Lt. Bart from the office of General Ira Eaker, the commanding officer of the new U.S. Eighth Air Force Bomber Command, asking if Robert would please come in for a meeting with the general. This was an unexpected honor for Robert. General Eaker was the new and rising star in the US Air Force, and everyone wanted to meet him.

Robert arrived at the High Wycombe Headquarters at 1:45 and was ushered into Eaker's office promptly at 2:00 p.m. Eaker stood up and greeted Robert warmly. Robert had heard one or two "well-born" RAF Generals refer sniffily to Eaker as "short, stout and bald, too chummy, and still in his cowboy boots." Eaker was short and balding, but remained behind his desk, so Robert was unable to confirm the cowboy boots rumor. He did not appear to be "stout." As for "chummy?" Time will tell.

"Mr. Johnston, I have heard so much about you," he said with a Texas drawl. "You have become the face of the US of A over here. I hear you even met with Hap Arnold and Tooey Spaatz last year when they were in London?

"An impressive duo of West Point grads who somehow went from being infantry mud crunchers to glamorous flyboys! I enjoyed them immensely. Please give them my regards."

"I suspect that you will be seeing them yourself pretty soon. I called you in here because, although I am "in command" of our new Eighth Air Force Bomber Command, I am sure as hell flying blind. I am not a fancy pants West Point man. My folks were poor Texas sharecroppers. I went to Southeastern State Normal School in Durant, Oklahoma. I was also an infantry "grunt" who ended up in the Army Air Corp, but *only* because I fixed some dumb pilot's engine. That was a mistake! And unlike tall, dark, and handsome Hap Arnold and Tooey Spaatz, I am a short, fat, bald guy!"

Robert smiled. He was well aware that Hap Arnold, Tooey Spaatz and Ira Eaker were often referred to as "The Three Musketeers."

"Well, they must have seen something in you they like, they certainly gave you a big job. Call me Robert. I only call people 'Mr.' if I don't like 'em!"

Eaker laughed. "Oh, sure," he said. "It sounds like a big job, but no one else was dumb enough to take it! Here's the real story. I have been sent to London to head up this so-called U.S. Air Force Bomber Command, but I am a *fighter* pilot and have never flown a bomber. Maybe that's okay because we don't *have* any bombers in our US Bomber Command to fly. Not a one! And Major General Chaney, Commanding General of U.S. Army Forces in Britain, wants to put me and my air operations under the command of his bunch of infantry people. *And* your buddy Arthur Harris wants us to become the RAF-North American Squadron and only bomb German cities by night. *And* the Brits want all of our *B-17s*, even though they don't like them and can't fly them. *And* the stuffy British government people talk to me like I'm some ingrate 1776 rube colonial militiaman. They are so damn arrogant! And they *supposedly* speak English here, but not like any English I ever heard before. I could sure use some helpful advice from a guy like you who knows the ropes."

Robert laughed, long and hard. "Welcome to England. Now you know why the thirteen American colonies revolted 170 years ago. The English are by nature bull-headed and arrogant and tough and plenty smart. Just exactly who we Yanks need at our side in the current alley fight with those pigs in Berlin. The Brits are for sure the best allies in the world. Bar none."

They both had a good laugh. Robert thought it impossible not to like Ira Eaker, even if he is short and balding. He was so warm and friendly and unpretentious. No wonder he felt that the Brits were so foreign.

"You can trust Arthur Harris," Robert continued. "He is about as tough as they come, but he is in the war to win. His predecessor, Sir Richard Peirse, was a very fine fellow, but probably the wrong man in the wrong job at the wrong time. As I recall, Hap Arnold was very *unimpressed* by Peirse. Although you and Harris are as different as night and day, both with very different bombing strategies, you can work with him. I predict that you and he will become close friends. His problem at the moment is that he does not have many bombers either. Maybe four hundred. Not more. And many of them are simply *not* fit for purpose. Pretty bad, actually. And they can seldom find their targets at night. They need many more bombers, and some form of trustworthy navigation system. They have high hopes for this mysterious new GEE radar system. We shall see.

"I suppose I'm more of a Navy man than an Army Air Corp guy, but your tall and handsome Billy Mitchell showed us all the wave of the future. Battleships, tanks, trucks, troops and even submarines are all vulnerable targets for well-trained and well-equipped air forces."

"What do you think of Chaney?" asked Eaker.

"The general? He's okay but he's not the man of the hour. I predict that he won't last much longer in his job. The commander of the U.S. Forces in Europe will certainly become the Commander of European Theater of Operations – a huge and impossible job. That commander will have to deal with Churchill, de Gaulle, the British Army, the Admiralty, the RAF, and a grand host of other prima donnas. It is a job for a diplomat as well as a general. Someone bigger than life. You would know better than I, but my sense is that your Hap Arnold is a lot more powerful than General Chaney, and Arnold is *not* impressed with Chaney."

"I think your assessment is spot on. I've heard the same myself."

"Since we're on the subject," said Robert. "Maybe you could tell me where the hell is the U.S. Air Force and when will it show up in England? The Brits are expecting to see the skies over merry ole England darkened by squadrons of U.S. bombers heading across the English Channel to flatten Germany and bring a quick end to this war. But my sources tell me that the 'Mighty US Eighth' Air Force is, at present, a paper tiger."

Eaker grimaced. "Your sources are correct. The U.S. had no Air Force until May 1940 when Congress finally authorized funding to build bombers after the world saw the Nazis flatten Rotterdam. By mid '41, we were building 400 to 500 bombers each month. We are on the road to creating a force to be reckoned with, but a long, long way from darkening the skies over England. We have to train crews and then ship—or fly—everything and everybody over here. It all takes time."

"I understand, but I'm not sure the Brits will. They need support now."

"Our first air combat groups should arrive at RAF Polebrook and Grafton Underwood in June. They will be *B-17Es* for the 97th Bomber Group. A month or two after that, we'll probably be ready to make a few small runs over Germany—more for PR than impact. I plan to fly myself on that first mission."

"So you support the Harris' initiative to bomb German cities?"

"Robert, I have to tell you that I have a significant difference of opinion with your British friends. I am a strong advocate of daylight precision bombing of military and industrial targets, not the nighttime carpet bombing of German cities embraced by Air Marshall Harris. My view is the view universally held by President Roosevelt and the entire command structure for the U.S. Army Air Corp."

"Explains why we're sending B-17s…"

"Exactly, we love our *B-17E* bombers. They are flying gunboats for daytime precision bombing. Why they are not so well-regarded by the Brits— they carry a smaller payload of bombs. Robert, I am impressed by the gravity and scope of your insights. It is comforting to learn that our newly formed U.S. Intelligence Service is so intelligent!"

"Nothing could be further from the truth," said Robert. "Our newly forming U.S. Intelligence Group has barely emerged from its cocoon. We rely heavily on British intelligence. By far the best in the world."

"Then you obviously have formed some very close relationships with elements of British intelligence. Good for you, and for us!"

Robert smiled, thinking about Sarah.

"True. I have formed a warm and worthwhile relationship with some elements of British Intelligence. It hasn't always been so easy. They are by nature a bit distant and frosty. But I have been able to get close to one MI5 agent."

"Excellent, Robert. Keep that agent close if you can. We need all the help you can give us right now. I feel like we have landed on Jupiter!"

Robert laughed heartily. Eaker was not quite sure why, but laughed along.

"We all feel like we are on Jupiter," Robert said. "I'll take that as a Direct Order from Higher Authority. I'll pursue that frosty British Intelligence Agent later this week to try to make further headway."

He smiled just a little, eager to see Sarah over dinner as planned for next Saturday night. Eaker probably didn't catch the sarcasm as he was looking down at his calendar.

"This talk has been great. Let's meet again in four weeks. I'll be in London then."

Robert agreed. He thought Eaker was an impressive man. If he was to be the new face of the U.S. Army Air Corp in Britain, there was definitely a light at the end of the tunnel. He also thought to himself, you know, I had never met an Okie I didn't like.

29

The Master Spy

16 April 1942, London

Since their New Year's Eve date, Sarah had become involved in several assignments. The first was pleasant enough. American forces had begun to arrive in London in January and she was assigned to develop contacts with them. Robert was very helpful. Sarah and Robert connected for dinner dates every second or third weekend during the winter months. All good, she thought. But she also fell into two other assignments, which were definitely not so good, and she was very careful not to disclose them to Robert. She knew that he would not be pleased because neither he nor the U.S. Government condoned assassinations.

Operation Flipper, the British plan to assassinate or capture General Irwin Rommel had failed in November 1941, but there were ongoing efforts to try again. Operation Anthropoid involved a plan to assassinate Reinhard Heydrich in the spring of 1942. Heydrich was a high-ranking German SS and Gestapo official who was heavily involved in the Holocaust, Kristallnacht, and The Final Solution. He was also the Officer in Charge of the Einsatzgruppen, which was responsible for the murder of more than two million refugees and Jews. As the acting Reich Protector of Bohemia and Moravia, Reinhard Heydrich was quite possibly the *worst* of the *worst*. The Butcher of Prague. Large teams of Brits and other intelligence officers were involved in both operations, so Sarah did not have a significant role. She was just one of many. But these assignments did require that Sarah not share all of her intelligence with Robert. And Robert began to pick up on that.

On 16 April, Sarah had been instructed to show up at MI6. No one told her why. She was told to wear civilian clothing. No surprise. MI6 always tried to keep a very low profile.

She sat quietly in the small room where she had been placed to await "her meeting" with no more information. After about twenty minutes, she was escorted into the imposing office of Major General Sir Stewart Graham Menzies, Chief of the British Secret Intelligence Service (SIS), commonly known as MI6.

Sarah was a little intimidated. But Menzies smiled at her.

"Lt. Leach, please sit down. Good to see you again. How is your old sea dog Father?"

"Holding up pretty well. He was hoping to retire to his hobbies at age sixty, but my mother suspects the Royal Navy might have other plans for him."

Menzies laughed. "Captain Benjamin Leach will probably be permitted to putter around his garden right after Nazi Grand Admiral Karl Donitz is buried in *his* garden in Brandenburg."

Sarah smiled. "May 'Der Lowe,' The Lion, Kriegsmarine Admiral Karl Donitz, rest very soon, in little or no peace, hopefully with his beloved Fuhrer at his side."

They both laughed.

"Are you back in good working order?" he asked. "I am told that you injured your knee a few months ago in our training program. Have you been receiving treatment for it?"

"MI6 has big ears. My knee seems to be on the mend. I am getting some treatment for it by a knee specialist."

She suspected that Menzies might know all about Robert, too. If he did, he did not seem to make the connection.

"How is your French these days? We have an assignment for you, which may require that you pose as a French housewife in Normandy for some period."

"My dialect is more Parisian. I probably sound more like Athos, Porthos, and Aramis than d'Artagnan, but I can fake it for a few days. Certainly, if the local audience is German soldiers, they will be more focused on my French housewife bosom than on my French house-wife accent."

They both laughed again.

"Can you give me some background?" she asked.

"I think I can, but please keep it to yourself. I don't want to share this with your friends at MI5."

Sarah felt that Menzies was a bit off putting. He seemed to be mixing professional inquiries with some personal inquiries. Menzies was now single. His first wife, the very high born Lady Avice Ela Muriel Sackville, had left him for another man. According to office rumors, he now had his eye on his MI6 secretary. It bothered Sarah that Menzies always seemed to keep his eyes on her and spoke slowly to drag out their meetings. But he was a man of considerable power and influence, and could easily make or break her career in military intelligence.

"The Americans, having just formally joined our war effort, want to invade France this fall. They are calling it Operation Sledgehammer. Being American, of course, they want to end the war quickly and decisively."

"How can they possibly do that? They have very little military equipment here, and virtually no troops!"

"So true. They plan to use our troops and just a little of their equipment to open up a very small beachhead in France to show Stalin that we are going to help him. It is lunacy, of course. And it will never happen. But we have to show respect for their plans. The alliance is not a matter of life or death for us. It is more important than that!"

"I understand, but will they be ready for an invasion by the fall?"

"Extremely unlikely. Next year is only remotely possible. Probably more likely in 1944. Whenever it does come, we will need help from members of the French Resistance in or near the coastline area of north-western France. That is where Lt. Sarah Leach comes into play. We need you to develop these contacts, here and in France. Just between us, there is a newly formed group here in London, Special Operations Executive (SOE), intended to organize and equip the French Resistance. This "group" seems to have ten or twenty different names. It is more aptly called EOS which would stand for Enemy Occupied Sabotage. In any event, you will be working with us and them."

"Well enough, Chief. If I can be of service, bum knee and bum French notwithstanding, just point me in the right direction. I am ready to go."

"Thank you, Leach. Your reputation as a tough cookie is well-earned and well-deserved. Or perhaps I should now call you, *une dure petit gateau!*""

Sarah smiled faintly at this "tough cookie" allusion. It was inappropriate and somewhat derisive. And it did not escape her notice that

Menzies put the emphasis on "cookie" with a big smile. She knew he meant it a double entendre. But she bit her lip, as was the custom for women when dealing with powerful men, and deflected his words as best as she could.

"I am not so sure about the "petit," she said.

They both had a nervous laugh.

"But Chief, from what I hear, there isn't much of a French Resistance. Would it make more sense to use de Gaulle's people, the Free French, to pursue these contacts?"

"The Free French have neither love nor respect for the current elements of resistance in France. De Gaulle has openly stated that he wants those who claim to be loyal to Old France to sneak out of France, come to England, and join his army. Good luck on that. Nobody really knows if there is a significant French Resistance. There is very little evidence, and reports are conflicting. We are hoping that you and maybe SOE—the Baker Street Irregulars, as we call them—can give us some answers."

Sarah thought it was very odd that the great and mighty MI6 needed to rely on the spanking new Baker Street irregulars to provide insight into the French Resistance. But again, she bit her tongue, which was now beginning to get sore from all the biting.

Menzies continued. "My view is that these resistance efforts and forces reflect the mood of the general population. It seems clear that overall French opposition in Occupied France is subdued. The German occupiers are going out of their way to be pleasant to the French people. That will not last long, because it is not the German nature as an occupying military force, and it is certainly not the typical Nazi style. But in the meanwhile, the French people will not get too riled up. As the Nazis become nastier, and the real possibility of an Allied Invasion of France grows, so too will the Resistance grow. As it increases in size and intensity, it could become very useful to us. Your assignment is to get us plugged in, keep us plugged in, and help us to grow the effort."

"I am eager for the challenge, Chief."

"Good. There's one additional hurdle in France. You are British. The French have not forgotten nor forgiven the British naval attacks on French Navy ships at Mers El Kebir at Oran, nor the British evacuation of Dunkirk, where we abandoned the French Army without even telling them."

Then Menzies handed Sarah a sealed envelope.

"Here is the address of SOE and a list of contacts in the greater London area who are current 'connectors' to French Resistance. Meet with each of them, check in with SOE, and learn what you can. Do not take this list out of this office. Memorize the list today, then give it back to my secretary in the same envelope. Use your meetings to start to develop a list of resistance contacts in France. Memorize those names and addresses as well. Stop by to see my secretary periodically so that she can make a list of them here."

"Understood and agreed," said Sarah.

"As an aside, I believe the same conditions I listed regarding La Resistance in France apply to the German resistance movement. As you yourself have reported, there is some German resistance now. We expect that it too might increase over time as the German war effort starts to collapse. The vicious Nazi internal security forces will undoubtedly keep it suppressed. But that is a story for another day."

Sarah nodded, eager to get out of Menzies' office.

"Leach. One last thing." Menzies paused, and looked at Sarah.

"Yes?" she responded.

"Your friend, the American lawyer, Robert Johnston."

Sarah was not expecting this. She waited quietly and patiently for Menzies to get to the point, but could feel that she was blushing slightly. The chief of MI6 was probably orchestrating her "interview" in such a way to see if he could make her blush. Like an old-style lie detector test.

"Is your relationship with Johnston official, or personal?"

Sarah thought for a minute.

"He and I like to refer to our relationship as 'unofficial channeling.' In truth, it has sometimes been official, sometimes semi-official, sometimes personal. And sometimes very personal."

"I gather you have high regard for him? I ask because I have received a number of reports. Some from you. He seems to be a solid fellow. I have been thinking about trying to bring him into MI6. What do you think?"

"Yes, I regard him highly. Very highly. Very smart. Very knowledgeable. Very dedicated to our cause. An elegant man of high integrity and a great catch for MI6. But no. Please don't go after him. We clearly have the best Intelligence organization in the world. The Americans have no Intelligence organization whatsoever. They are now desperately trying to build one, using a collection of mostly New York lawyers, like Johnston, and they really need him. Also, I have been able to glean a great deal of useful information from him, much of which he obtains from his own networks."

"And I suppose he gets some useful information from you? "

"Of course."

"I connected with your father several months ago at the Royal Observatory Naval Conference in Greenwich. I asked after you. He sounded very proud to tell me that you've been seeing a fine tank commander, James somebody, a close friend of your brother, Tom? I believe that James is in North Africa defending the Land of the Pharaohs from The Nazi-Italian Philistines. I find that military fathers are always keen to pair their daughters with military spouses, so be warned!"

Sarah laughed. "You are quite right. Both my father and my brother are desperately in love with James. Unfortunately, I guess I am the intended object of James' affections, and at present, as you may have noticed since you seem to be keeping close tabs on me, I seem to be married to MI5 and MI6. Time will tell with James."

"Your friend James and your brother Tom are currently serving under Claude Auchinelech. He is able but probably not the measure of Irwin Rommel, who is a true genius at tank war tactics. Luckily for Claude, his friends in MI6 are giving him some help. The Germans and the Italians tend to talk too much."

"Glad to hear they're getting support," said Sarah.

"Back to Johnston, what would you think of your sharing with him, in a low-key fashion, the fact of your new assignment? Since some of this invasion of France activity is to appeal to our American allies, he then might be in a position to pass on to Washington the fact that we are not ignoring their keen desire to take some pressure off of Stalin by opening a new front in France."

"I like the idea," she said. "And, so will he."

"Good. While you're at it, maybe he can advise you about that gamey knee of yours. I am told that he played some American football during his years at Princeton. I'm sure he's had more than his share of knee injuries. But please Leach, no mention to him whatsoever of SOE."

Menzies didn't smile. He seemed very matter of fact about the knee therapy suggestion. And he didn't look at her either. Sarah was relieved. She was pretty sure that she was blushing again. She also wondered whether Menzies had already signed up Robert into MI6.

There was a light tap on the door, and Menzies' longtime secretary entered gingerly.

"Yes, Miss Jones? What is it?"

She was a petite and attractive young woman. "An important call, sir." She walked up to Menzies and said something in his ear. While she was whispering in his ear, Menzies put his arm around her waist, presumably to hold her close to his ear.

"I must take this call. Sorry," Menzies said.

Sarah figured that the caller was the prime minister. He and Menzies were known to speak often. So Sarah took this as her opportunity to escape from Menzies' office, fearing that he might next be asking her for the name of her knee specialist. With a wave of her hand and a quick salute, she followed Miss Jones out of the office.

Sarah prided herself on being "cool, calm, and collected" in most settings, but as she walked out into the hallway she felt very flustered.

30

A few Hard Questions

18 April 1942, London

It was a clear Saturday night. The Germans had been bombing a number of cities, not just London. Robert walked into The Old Bell Tavern looking forward to spending some time with Sarah, but also looking forward to some red beef and red wine. A fine British tradition.

A few young RAF pilots hovered around the yellow jukebox in the corner of the pub, while their dates swayed in time to the dance song emanating from the glowing music machine. The Andrew Sisters' smash hit, apropos of the moment, "Boogie Woogie Bugle Boy," brought other diners from their tables to the dance floor. The "*toot toot toot, toot diddelyada*" lyrics created some camaraderie among the night crowd as everyone sang along.

"Hello Robert. I hear your days and nights are now filled with visits from your newly arriving American military friends. I hope that you aren't going to start losing the nice British accent that you have begun to develop—and your nice British friends."

"Hello to you, Sarah. I've been looking forward to our dinner. I hope that I have retained just enough of my British accent to make my dinner order comprehensible to Owen. I managed to miss lunch today, so I'll probably be grumpy until I am fed."

"You Yanks are so accustomed to eating three square meals each day. We Brits are not so fortunate. But that does make our dinner meetings all the more welcome. I will try not to get in between you and your slice of beef. You might bite me!"

They both laughed.

"An excellent idea! But it does sting a little to hear you confess at last that my main attraction to you is my enormous talent for plying you with fine food and wine. I foolishly thought that you enjoyed my immense charm, wit, and good looks."

"As is the case with any man who is kind enough to take a woman to dinner, his charm, wit and good looks will increase measurably with each morsel of food and sip of fine wine she doth consume!"

They ordered dinner, ate and drank, and discussed recent news, but nothing sensitive. As always, for the sake of discretion, they never touched nor made comments that might be misconstrued, or more accurately, correctly construed. But, towards the end of their dinner, Sarah very quietly told Robert that she had been to a meeting at MI6, which she found a bit disturbing. She said this with a troubled frown on her face. After paying the bill, Robert stood up, shook Sarah's hand, said his farewell, and headed out into the night.

Sarah stuck around briefly to chat with a few friends, said her goodbyes, and also departed. All very discreet.

Thirty minutes later they met in front of a small cheese shop, two blocks away, climbed into Sarah's borrowed MI5 car, and drove off together to Robert's house. It was 9:15 p.m., and very dark when they arrived.

Once inside the flat, Sarah gave Robert a tight hug and lingered in his arms. He kissed her warmly.

"How about a little nightcap and a few biscuits?" he asked.

"Wonderful!"

Robert put on a record. It was the Willie Lewis Band playing "All of Me." They sat together on the usual sofa, in their usual positions. Sarah took off her sweater, and then her dress. She said that the flat was warm, and that she didn't want to scrunch up her clothes. Robert helped her and didn't complain.

As her legs were now bare, Robert took the opportunity to carefully examine her knee. He squeezed it a little and she yelped.

"It does look a little better, but it is still too early for you to return to active combat duty."

"I am happy for you to explore, touch and even squeeze areas and portions of my anatomy, but please do go easy on that particular knee."

"Oh, fine. Let me see if there are any other areas of interest."

His hands gently stroked her legs.

As he did, Sarah unbuttoned his shirt, and helped him take it off. Then she placed her hand on his belt buckle.

"Do you want to take these off? It would avoid wrinkling them."

Robert nodded 'yes.' He stood up and took off his shoes and socks. Sarah took off his trousers, and hung them neatly on the back of the chair. Wearing now his cutaway 1940's military style undershirt, the type without sleeves, and his trim 1940's military style boxer shorts, he walked over and changed the record. Sarah was still sitting on the sofa in her underwear and her slip.

With Robert now watching her, she took off her slip, and he started back, intending to sit down in his usual spot on the sofa.

"You mentioned a disturbing meeting at MI6 and you looked pretty troubled. Anything you want to vent, or was it all hush hush stuff? If you can't tell me, of course I understand."

He was still standing, not quite sure if he should sit back down. Sarah was frowning again. She looked up at him.

"Meeting at MI6 was fine. I meet with them frequently. But for this particular meeting last Thursday, I was summoned to a private meeting with Stewart Menzies."

"The Chief of MI6? I hear he can be difficult."

Sarah looked up at Robert. She thought for a moment.

"Robert, let me ask you a question. Have you met recently with Menzies, or with anyone at MI6, or maybe MI5?"

Robert was a bit surprised. "No. I've never met Menzies, but his reputation precedes him. I've never met with anyone from MI6 to my knowledge, unless it was some undercover agent. All my meetings at MI5 are with you and your boss."

"Have you discussed me, or our relationship, or our little Saturday night dinners and rendezvous, or anything about us, with any of your 'buddies' at Bomber Command, or the new U.S. Eighth Air Force Group? Or anybody, at all?" She looked intently at Robert, and he felt the sting of her stare.

"No, Sarah. No. Never. Not in a million years. Surely, you know that. I'm surprised that you would even ask me. I would never discuss our relationship for a myriad of reasons. And I would like to know why you are asking all these questions. It obviously has a lot to do with your meeting last Thursday with Menzies."

Sarah thought for a moment. "I almost wish that you had answered 'yes' to my questions. Menzies asked me about you. He seemed to know a lot about you. Too much, really. He said he wanted to recruit you into MI6. Menzies asked about me, and about us. He seemed to know a lot about me, and about us. Too much. He called me 'a cookie.' He asked about my knee, and if someone was 'treating it.' It was very spooky. They have clearly been watching you, and me, and us. He knew about James, and Tom. He claimed that my father told him about James and Tom at a naval conference last winter. Menzies even remembered their first names! I don't believe for one minute that my father told Menzies about them. My father knows better. But I'm afraid to ask my father."

Robert was now feeling put upon. She had been "interrogating" him in his underwear. It was both demeaning and unnecessary. But he knew he had to let it go. Sarah was very upset. He knew that he needed to comfort her, not scold her.

"Sarah, of course Menzies is watching you, and me, and us. Of course, MI6 is spooky. They're spooks! Professional spooks. And so are you, young lady. And I too hope to become one under your fine tutelage. And you have made no secret about us, or your friend James, or your bum knee, for that matter. You and I are seen together frequently at the tavern, which is overflowing with your spooky 'buddies,' and most of the time you are limping a bit on the knee. And I have noticed that two or three of them have enquired after James, and your brother, Tom, and your knee. None of this is Top Secret Stuff, and none of this is any cause for shame. Unless perhaps you're now ashamed of our relationship. If so, we should end it now. Your work is far more important than you and me, Sarah. You know this, too."

Sarah sat and thought. Long and hard. Looking down at the floor. Then, her mood brightened.

"You, of course you are right. Absolutely right. It was just an upsetting meeting. I don't much like Menzies. He seems very devious."

"I guess it is not so surprising that the chief of British espionage would be a devious fellow. The PM obviously thinks very highly of him."

"True. But that is also very odd. Before the war, nobody paid the slightest attention to Menzies. Now suddenly he and the PM are bosom buddies. And I have some suspicions about that, too."

"Before we consider your suspicions, Sarah, I would like to make a point about Menzies and his ilk. Be warned. Espionage is a nasty business. And the deeper one gets into it, the nastier it becomes. That is why the U.S. avoided it for years. It eventually leads to murders, assassinations, government overthrows, dirty tricks, and most particularly, some very awful people. It is akin to practicing criminal law!" he laughed. "This terrible war has dragged us in to this espionage business, but it is not a 'walk in the park.' But if you don't have the stomach for it, then bail out now, before it consumes you."

"Ugh. I hadn't thought of it in those terms, but I guess your observations are accurate. I'll be okay. I suspect that it is in my bones. The loss of my privacy. I don't usually get upset, but you are right, it's getting colder and darker on the inside of the dreadful business. I have had some other recent assignments which were quite distasteful. On the bright side, however, I now have two very juicy assignments. The first assignment is to build up our British contacts with our friends and supporters in France for the possibility of an allied invasion at some unspecified date. For that assignment, which might involve foolhardy and a physically challenging boat, plane or car trips into France at night, I need two good knees, so I do need the constant attention of my American knee specialist who, I as I just learned from our new friend Sir Stewart Menzies, was trained in knee therapy on the playing fields of Princeton.

"My second assignment from MI6 is to establish, maintain, and nourish my close relationship with a certain US lawyer who has close ties to Washington, DC named Robert Johnston. So now I couldn't dump you, even if I wanted to. And you can't drop me either, unless you want me to fail in my MI6 assignment!!"

Sarah was smiling again. Robert was much relieved.

"There was something else that Menzies said, and it did not relate to my assignments. He was nattering on about James, and Tom, and General Claude Auchinleck, Commander in Chief of British Middle East forces. And then Menzies said, 'Luckily for Claude, his friends at MI6 are giving him some help. The Germans and the Italians tend to talk too much.' Those words burned my ears, because clearly British intelligence is learning something of great value from 'chatter.' Do you agree?"

Robert thought for a minute. "It was a careless slip for sure. He clearly trusts you. But it brings to mind a comment that I picked up a couple of weeks ago from one of my new buddies in RAF Bomber Command. Some of their units are bombing Nazi shipping and submarine assets in the Mediterranean, and he expressed some surprise that Bomber Command seemed to know where these assets were on the open sea. He even asked me, 'How do we know that?'

"Two possibilities. A plant somewhere in the German army or Navy High Command, or we are picking up their tactical messages. But supposedly the Germans have unbreakable codes."

"And there are some other clues, as well," Sarah said. "James and Tom have told me that Auchinleck seems to know ahead of time about Rommel's tactical maneuvers. Not usually enough to defeat Rommel, but maybe just enough to tip the advantage to our side. Eventually. And then there are the now almost daily meetings between the PM and Sir Stewart Menzies. Why do they meet so often? It smells like some critical MI6 intelligence breakthrough. Either a super spy in the Wehrmacht or some code breaking success. His words 'tend to talk too much' support a code breakthrough. And what are all those nerdy Cambridge mathematicians and all those attractive, upper class, young women doing together every day up at Bletchley Park?"

"Ah, yes. The 'Boffins and the Debs.' Hopefully, they are breeding a new crop of super humans to supersede all the German Aryans!" Robert laughed. "Bears watching. For sure."

He smiled and looked at Sarah. "Now can we please get back to my now official duty as the Keeper of the Royal Knee and provide a proper massage for those two legs so highly prized by British intelligence?"

Sarah readily agreed. Her eyes locked with his, with that silent tug. Did she purr? He wasn't sure.

31

These Are Our People

2 May 1942, London

Thursday afternoon, Hannah ran to catch her bus. A few weeks earlier she had learned a special subcommittee of the Coordinating Committee of Refugees (CCR) was holding a meeting. It wasn't open to the public, but she suspected no one would notice if she were to sit in, unless she were late.

Alice had called two hours before to ask if Hannah might want to take a walk and a stop somewhere for tea. Amanda was on duty that afternoon, which gave Alice a license to hunt down Hannah, her second favorite target for company.

Hannah suggested that Alice join her as a party crasher at the CCR meeting, and Alice happily agreed.

Since the meeting on March 15 in the government affairs office, Hannah had attended five additional sessions with one or more of the various groups in London addressing the growing problem of European refugees and Jewish refugees in particular. She attended the meetings as she would classes at a university. She listened intently. She took careful notes. She respectfully asked questions. She offered observations. And she caught people's attention. For better or for worse.

Today's meeting was different. Many of the participants were Jewish men, discussing Jewish refugee problems, from the Jewish perspective, including some British Jews whose families had been living and thriving in Britain for generations.

Hannah felt more welcome as these were, more or less, her people. Alice felt less comfortable. Her Jewish countrymen seemed foreign to her. But sitting next to Hannah, she relaxed.

The gentleman chairing the session introduced himself.

"Hello friends. I am Selig Brodetsky. I am a professor of Applied Mathematics at Leads University, Advisor on aerodynamics to the

British Ministry of Defense, and current President of the Board of Deputies of British Jews. Joining me here today is my good friend, and former President of the Board, Neville Laski, KC, a distinguished barrister and judge. He and I have been asked to co-chair our discussion today. The topic is the current prognosis for the tens of thousands of Jews from Germany and Austria, and increasingly from Romania and Poland, and even now France, who are desperate to find at least a temporary residence. Looking around today, I note some new faces and even a couple of very young faces. Faces of young ladies. So nice to have you here!"

Both Brodetsky and Laski were well known figures in the Anglo-Jewish community. Ukrainian born, Brodetsky was stoutly built and looked uncomfortable in his suit. Which he probably was. Laski, in the top ten of well-born Anglo-Jews (his mother was a member of the very distinguished Frankenstein family), looked like he was born in an elegant bespoke suit. Which he probably was.

Everyone present was very impressed that Brodetsky and Laski were chairing the meeting. Laski had served with the 6th Lancaster Fusiliers in the Gallipoli Campaign in the Great War and was now a King's Counsel. Like the much younger Jacob Bronowski, Brodetsky had been a Senior Wrangler, the title awarded to the top math student at Cambridge, Class of 1908. They both spoke with knowledge and conviction.

Professor Brodetsky, Neville Laski, and several of the members of the committee, laid out the grim facts.

"Among the few bright spots, very few bright spots," Laski noted, "is the recent interest shown by the Dominican Republic to admit as many as 100,000 Jewish refugees. It appears that over 400 have already settled there. The effort seems to have stalled for reasons that are not clear, but there does appear to be strong U.S. support for their placement in the Dominican Republic.

"As many of you know, Shanghai had been a welcome refuge for thousands of Jews over recent years. More than 20,000 are known to have settled there, and the true number is probably much higher. But now the Japanese are occupying Shanghai, and Jews are no longer welcome. Unfortunate.

"The purpose of this meeting is to share available information and then brainstorm solutions."

The meeting extended for another hour and a half. At that point, the speakers opened up for questions and discussions.

Hannah raised her hand.

"I heard about a report issued earlier this year from the British Government that said the Germans were trying to bring large numbers of German and Austrian Jews into Britain in order to fan the flames of anti-Semitism here, and that Jewish members of your Coordinating Committee for Refugees, perhaps even some of you, were sympathetic to the view. Reportedly, you did not want Britain to admit any more Jews unless and until you personally approved them. Is this true?"

This generated considerable murmuring and buzzing in the room. Several people were shaking their heads in disbelief, disapproval of the government and the committee, and maybe also Hannah.

Alice was proud of Hannah for having courage to speak up.

Neville Laski, no stranger to controversy, spoke up. "There is some truth in what you say, young lady." Silence befell the room. Laski continued, "These events occurred several years ago, and there were many surrounding facts that contributed to these concerns. There are a number of complications affecting the admission of German and Austrian refugees into Britain, Jews and others, at a time when Britain is at war with those two countries. Nazis propaganda has fanned the flames of suspicions that some of these German and Austrian refugees, Jews and others, are German spies. And admitting large numbers of refugees, including Jewish refugees into Britain, does precipitate anti-refugee and anti-Semitism reactions.

"You should also be aware that one of the critical factors in convincing nations to take in refugees, including but not limited to Jewish refugees, is who will bear the cost of feeding and housing them? The Jewish people here in Great Britain, including a number of us sitting here today, agreed to bear that cost before the war. The extent of this war, and the resulting huge number of Jewish refugees, has made that undertaking simply impossible. And there is only so much of that burden we can ask Great Britain to bear. The cost of the war effort itself is overwhelming."

The room nodded in approval. Several clapped and stomped on the floor. Several cries of, "Hear, hear," were heard, like a debate in the House of Commons.

Reflecting the practice in the House of Commons, Hannah then stood up. To be seen. To be heard. To reinforce her points. And maybe to impress the listeners with the growing force of her presence.

And they did look and listen in complete silence.

"Professor Brodetsky and Judge Laski, and other committee members. Thank you. The actions you have taken are enormous and impressive indeed. We all salute you. But the European refugee problem we are all facing today has only begun and cannot be solved with half measures, and the problem must be solved. Must be solved!

"From what we have heard here today, there are 300,000 to 400,000 Jewish refugees stranded in Europe. And many more on the way. They are stranded. These are *our* people. They might even include my parents, from whom I have not heard from in more than a year. And so now most of us young Jewish refugees are alone in this country.

We must now ask ourselves: Who are these stranded Jewish refugees? They are not just number estimates on a page of a report. These are actual living people. Where are these Jewish refugees? How is it that we don't even really know where they are? They are not invisible. They actually exist. Somewhere!

"How are these refugees surviving? Are they in refugee camps, concentration camps, living in forests? What shelter, food and water are being provided to them? How many Jewish refugees are there? We keep hearing, over and over, that no one knows how many of these Jewish refugees now exist. Can we really not do a better job of keeping track of them?

"What is to become of them? Wherever they are now, can they really survive there until the end of the war? I think we all know the answer to this question.

"And whose responsibility is it to address these issues? I think we all know the answer to this question too.

"These are *our people*. If we don't stand together to help them, no one will. No one will. You may not want them here, because some of them are different from you. They will change over time and become very much like you. Many are young men and women. They will join the fight against the Nazis. The Poles say that the Jews will not fight. That is not true. Jews do not want to fight with the Poles because the Poles are every bit as anti-Semitic as the Nazis. Sometimes even worse.

"But our people will fight in the British Army and Navy and Air Force. As will I. And if Britain does all it can to help rescue these people, the free world will rush to her side. Now and forever. We are all in this together."

She did not sit down. The others in the room were murmuring. Some nodding their heads in agreement, but some others shaking their heads. Her comments were clearly controversial.

After a moment, Alice stood up next to Hannah, and took her hand. Alice looked at Hannah, and then said, loud enough to be clearly heard, "You are not alone in this country. Not ever. An army of us stand with you!"

The stark contrast of those two young vocal women sent a powerful message. Alice had moxie and presence. Self-confidence. Fashionable navy-blue attire. Crisp British accent. Erect and elegant. Brimming with personality. Blue on gold, like a British Royal Navy Uniform.

Hannah was equally poised, also elegant, but severe. A dark brown dress and jacket. Steely eyed. Brown on brown. Like an RAF flight jacket.

Hannah and Alice. Pepper and Salt. Night and Day. Black and White. A Chess Set.

As everyone filed out of the meeting, a number of people came up to Hannah and Alice to express their support and sympathy. But there were also a number of others whose expressions and mutterings indicated that they neither supported nor agreed with Hannah's views. Their animosity was not veiled. Hannah had once again made some friends. But also, some enemies.

32

Cologne and Midway

8 June 1942, London

During late April and all of May, Robert had been focusing his time on the U.S. and U.K. bombing missions and issues. The Luftwaffe was intensifying the bombing of British cathedral cities and RAF Bomber Command was seeking permission from the British War Council and the Roosevelt Administration to bomb German cities in return. They got it. With the blessing of both Downing Street and the White House, Bomber Command launched almost one thousand bombers over Cologne on 30 May. Over six hundred acres of Cologne were devastated, compared to one-hundred-and-twenty acres of Luftwaffe bomber devastation in London in all of '40 and '41.

Ironically, that was Memorial Day 1942, so Robert and Sarah had a dinner date that night. And Sarah was in a very good mood. At 11:00 p.m., with insider knowledge that the RAF bombers were in the air, headed straight for Cologne, they toasted Bomber Command.

Nine days later, Robert was asked to join a meeting at Bomber Command to brief senior U.S. Eighth Air Force officers on the 30 May British bombing of Cologne and hear some insights into the Battle of Midway.

Sir David Petrie, Chief of MI5, was also invited to the meeting, as highly secret information was to be shared with Americans. Keenly aware of her tight connection to Robert, Petrie invited Sarah to join. Petrie also invited Lindemann, who brought along two young men whose opinions he valued, David Butt and Dr. Aaron Solomon.

The principal speaker was Air Vice Marshall Sir Roderick Carr. With his movie star good looks, always impeccable uniform, jet-black hair, and steely serious demeanor, Carr commanded attention.

"We sent a thousand bombers over Cologne. I am informed that your generals Arnold, Eaker, and Eisenhower were personally informed of the bombing by the PM at Chequers that very night. Here is the full story:

"First, for the saturation bombing of Cologne, we shifted to what we call a 'bomber stream.' The bombers all follow the same route. We do this to 'flood the zone' of the German defense sector box over which we are flying. For this to succeed, we must pass through the zone quickly. And we did. We have learned that each German defense sector has a set number of interceptors. A very effective strategy for Bomber Command. We lost only about forty bombers. Far fewer than expected.

"Second, For the saturation bombing of Cologne, we relied heavily on GEE, our new navigation grid. I cannot give you details on GEE, except that the 'g' stands for 'grid.' Many of you here are aware that it is a radio signal triangulation system, which I believe will someday be widely used in global navigation.

"Third, we sharply curtailed the allotted time over target. Previously, our bombers would allow up to four hours over target. For Cologne, we cut the time to ninety minutes.

"Fourth, we quadrupled the number of bombers. That turned out to be our biggest hurdle, rounding up enough bomber aircraft and crews. In the end, ironically, we found that our older bombers, flown by our younger student pilots, suffered lower casualties than our veteran operational crews. Why? Who knows. Maybe the student pilots were more cautious than some of our veteran pilots!

"Fifth, great effort was made to have the incendiary dropping bombers lead the procession of heavy bombers to mark the targets with fire bombs. This has the added effect of exhausting the local firefighters even before we started blowing up ground structures.

"All in all, the Cologne bombing was a major success for Bomber Command. For the really exciting news today – let us hear from our American friends about their *enormous* victory over the Japanese in the Battle of Midway."

The American airmen in the room were now jostling among themselves, trying to agree on who should present the incredible Midway saga. The most senior American officers present were all U.S. Army Air Corps, but every one of the American officers was also keenly aware of the never-ending deep and destructive competition between the US Army and the US Navy. And Midway was largely a Navy affair. Finally, General

Bermin Jones, U.S. Army Air Corps, the Senior Officer present at the meeting, took his pipe out of his mouth for a few brief moments, and broke the deadlock.

"U.S. Navy Commander Steves is here today. An experienced Navy aviator. Let's have him present the Midway story for our British friends. But first, I would like to ask U.S. Army Air Corps Major Brad Ember to remind everybody of the critical events of April 18, 1942, one of the events that helped to set the stage for Midway. The precursor to Midway was the Doolittle Raid over Tokyo—a rare Army-Navy inter-service operation."

Maj. Ember brightened.

All eyes turned to Maj. Ember. He was fairly short with a boyish look, blond hair and pale blue eyes. Ember was a good name for him because he was lively and sparky.

"Back in January 1942, right after Pearl Harbor, the top brass in the Army and Navy cooked up a very bold scheme to bomb Tokyo. Right out of a fairy tale. The raid could have been done from Russia with our *B-17* bombers, but Stalin was not in a position to take on Japan at the time. I guess he was right. Russia needed a détente with Japan in order to move the Soviet far eastern troops back to the west to fight the Germans.

"So, the US Army rounded up sixteen *B-25s*, and the Navy served up two carriers, *Hornet* for the bombers, and *Enterprise* for the fighters. After long and hazardous training, the carriers and the eighty B-25B pilots and crew were ready. The carriers followed the same sea route used by the Jap carriers when they sailed for Pearl Harbor in December '41, only in reverse, of course. The carriers managed to get within about 700 miles of Japan, when they were spotted by a Jap sub. So, the bombers took off early, and succeeded in bombing Tokyo.

"The material damage to Tokyo was light. Some people killed or wounded. Some fires. But its psychological impact was huge.

"The US planes had to be launched 300 miles farther east from Tokyo than planned. Their plan had been to launch the bombers only 400 miles east from Tokyo. So, after dropping their bombs on Tokyo the bombers ran low on fuel and were barely able to make it to China and Russian for landings. They all ran out of fuel and had to ditch.

"As a direct result of the Doolittle Raid, the Japs went absolutely berserk and immediately made plans to attack Midway without adequate planning, thinking that the US bombers might have come from Midway. The Japanese Navy also went scurrying all over the Pacific searching for the U.S. carriers — which were of course long gone — filling the Japanese airways with non-stop urgent messages. The Japanese Navy was forced to expand its defense perimeter, quickly putting Midway Island in its crosshairs."

Ember flashed a smile at Stevens. "Commander, would you like to pick it up from here?"

Commander Stevens took the floor. Older than Ember with greying hair, a thin mustache, and rimmed eyeglasses, he was not sparky like Ember, but very matter of fact in his presentation. He spoke from notes, and never smiled, not even once. When asked later about his demeanor, Stevens remarked, "War is a deadly serious business. It was a great victory for the US, but thousands of lives were lost, on both sides."

He stood silent at the podium for several minutes, first organizing his notes, and then carefully looking around the room to assess his audience. Finally, he began speaking slowly and methodically.

"From very heavy radio traffic and Japanese Navy ship movements, we were fairly certain that the they were about to launch a major naval offensive somewhere in the Pacific. Pearl was a candidate, but too risky. The Japanese were hoping to lure the two active Pacific based U.S. carriers *Hornet* and *Enterprise* into a battle to overwhelm us with their vastly larger battle fleet.

"As a result of U.S. Naval Intelligence suppositions, suspicious and surveillance, it became more and more likely that Midway Island was the target. The typical Japanese strategy was to approach from the northwest, and so we sent spotter planes in that direction. Of course, the Imperial Navy was busily searching far and wide for *Hornet* and *Enterprise*. They were not aware that *Yorktown*, severely damaged at Coral Sea, was on its way back to join this battle.

"The Japanese fleet arrived at a point roughly 250 miles from Midway Island, with four of their seven major carriers, *Akagi*, *Kaga*, *Hiryu* and *Soryu*, almost exactly where we thought they would be. They launched their first attack before dawn on June 4. Over 100 planes from all four carriers. Midway Island picked up the incoming aircraft long before the Japanese planes arrived, and so Midway launched all their aircraft able to fly, in hopes of crippling the Japanese carriers.

"As it turned out, neither the US torpedo and dive bombers, nor the US *B-17* bombers, all launched from Midway Island were able to lay a glove on the Japanese carriers. The Japanese chewed up the American torpedo planes and dive bombers. The *B-17s* flew too high to hit their targets.

"However, by an amazing stroke of good luck for the U.S. forces, the Japanese decided to rearm their defensive aircraft with land bombs, on the very mistaken conclusion that the only major threat to the Japanese carriers would be another attack from Midway. They were totally unaware of the proximity of three American carriers. Not two American carriers, but actually three! Just then the US torpedo bombers appeared. A total surprise for the Japanese.

"The torpedo bombers from *Hornet* and *Enterprise* struck out. The heavy defense by the Japanese *Zeros* shot all of them down. But that defense pulled all of the *Zeros* down near water level, at the very time that the Japanese carrier decks were covered with Jap fighters ready to take off to attack the American carriers.

"Falling in close behind the US torpedo bombers, thirty-seven dive bombers from *Enterprise* arrived overhead, and an additional seventeen dive bombers then arrived from *Yorktown*. They struck fast and hard. Scoring many direct hits. Within hours, *Kaga*, *Soryu*, and *Akagi* were sunk. *Soryu* had also been hit by torpedoes from *USS Nautilus*.

The Japanese still had one remaining carrier, *Hiryu*, nearby. Unaccustomed to suffering naval defeats, the Japs were gunning for revenge. Eighteen dive bombers from *Hiryu* followed the US fighter planes back to *Yorktown*. Most of the Japanese fighters were shot down, but four made successful hits. Shortly later, several torpedo bombers also hit *Yorktown*. She was in bad shape. Barely afloat. On June 5th, a Japanese sub hit the crippled *Yorktown* with two torpedoes. *Yorktown* sunk the next day. The remaining Japanese carrier, *Hiryu*, was then struck by dive bombers from *Enterprise* and *Hornet*. It sunk.

"The loss of *Yorktown* was excruciating for the US, but the loss for the Japanese at Midway was catastrophic for the Japs. The best four of the Japanese seven major carriers, over 300 of their best planes, probably 5,000 of their best sailors, and hundreds of their best pilots.

"The U.S. can and will build many new carriers to replace *Yorktown*. I wouldn't be surprised if there is a new *Yorktown* within the year. But the Japanese have little or no industrial capacity to replace *Kaga, Soryu, Akagi,* and *Hiryu.* I bet that they never will. And they also lost many of their best senior naval officers and pilots."

The entire room of Allied officers and others were now standing, clapping, cheering, and stomping their feet. Many were even crying. It was clear to all present that the Japanese Navy could never recover from The Battle of Midway.

Sarah was very excited to hear all the good news from both theatres of the war. Unlike the dour Commander Stevens, she was smiling from ear to ear. But was also aware that there was, and would continue to be, plenty of bad news. Robert shared her joy, but he was wondering if he had lost any former navy buddies at Midway. And he focused on the grim fact that the Midway casualties on both sides were just the tip of a terrible iceberg. The future casualties of the two-front war would be unimaginable.

As the meeting adjourned, Robert was buttonholed by Brits and Yanks alike. Everyone was curious to get his take on things, probably in view of his Washington connections. Sarah waited patiently for him to free up. When he did, he came to her side in a quiet corner.

"Can we go somewhere for a coffee or a tea? Good news always stimulates my appetite!"

"Yours and mine, too. Let's escape this swarm of flyboys!"

33

Sarah Reads Between the Lines

9 June 1942, London

After breaking clear of the conference room and the crowd, Sarah and Robert headed for a close-by pub. They wanted very much to hold hands as they walked, but thought that might be indiscreet. Once seated inside, they rehashed the reports of the morning, from East and West, while maintaining careful respect for *confidential* and *secret* information. You never know who might be listening when you are out for lunch or dinner or tea.

The day was waning, so the late high tea became an early light supper. It was almost 7 pm as they walked out of the pub. Being June, it was still hours from sunset, but even so, body rhythms are largely guarded by mealtimes. And by cocktail hours.

First checking that there were no prying eyes or ears, Sarah gently touched Robert's arm, and spoke very quietly.

"I haven't really seen you for a bit. Might you have some time for me tonight?"

She looked more serene than playful. Robert didn't quite know what to make of her tempting invitation. He was certainly not going to turn it down.

"I have to take a call from Washington back at my office at 7:30 pm, but I will end it at 8:30. Can we meet at 9. Will that work for you?"

"That is perfect. I want to get out of this outfit beforehand." She paused and said, "Thank you, Robert."

"Thank you, Sarah. You are the bright spot of the week for me. As I'm sure you know."

Two hours later, when Sarah stepped into Robert's house, he removed her light raincoat and she gave him a long, hard hug. Robert noted to himself that her hug was maybe just a little longer, and just a little harder, than her usual "happy to see you" hug. Robert's gramophone was playing a recent Jimmy Dorsey favorite and Sarah wondered if the title of the song, "Green Eyes," was intentional or just a coincidence.

"Those cool and limpid green eyes—a pool wherein my love lies.

So deep that in my searching for happiness I fear that they will ever haunt me,

All through my life they'll taunt me."

Sarah cleared her throat. "Fitting."

"What's that?" Robert responded, clearly unaware of what she was referring.

"Oh, nothing," Sarah feigned disinterest.

"Since we weren't really able to drink some wine earlier today – against the rules, I guess. I took the liberty of cracking open a bottle. Will you join me?"

"Robert, you are always so thoughtful, and your wine collection must rival the wine cellar at Chequers!"

Robert poured, and they clinked their glasses.

"To Midway!" they said it in unison. Sarah drank half of her glass, and then poured more for herself and for Robert. He took the cue and drank half of his glass also.

Sarah munched on a few crackers with cheese, took off her dress, hung it up neatly and sat down at her usual spot on the sofa in her slip and undergarments, looking up at Robert as she did so. Robert took the hint and sat down beside her.

After nuzzling for a few minutes, she proceeded to unbutton and take off his shirt. She then undid his pant belt. He looked at her for a moment, wondering what was going on. But not being a fool, he stood up, and she removed his pants.

Sarah took off her slip. A little more nuzzling. Sarah could see that Robert, now in his trim boxer shorts, was getting in the mood.

Her eyes opened a little wider, and she gave him that look. "Robert, how much more do you *really* know about Midway?"

At that very moment, The Battle of Midway was not really the focus of Robert's attention. He looked at Sarah.

"How much more do I *really* know? You mean above and beyond all the details that we learned today from Stevens? Nothing really. Why?"

"There is a whole lot more to the story of Midway than we heard today from Stevens. I'm sure of it. Everything we heard could easily be, and probably will soon be, in all the newspapers. What do you really know about 'the rest of the story?'"

It was beginning to dawn on Robert that Sarah had set another trap for him, and that he had been all too ready, willing and able to fall into it. Once again. But he also realized that falling into Sarah's traps probably had more pluses than minuses. Still, he was learning a lesson. Sarah might be "our spy" but she was also "a spy" and Robert had a feeling that handling spies can be a tricky business, as well as a nasty business. Especially after a glass of wine when a very beguiling spy is sitting one foot away in her underwear.

While Robert's thoughts were on the spy game, Sarah's was focusing like a radar beam on Midway.

Sarah continued, "Stevens said, 'As a result of U.S. Naval Intelligence suppositions, suspicions and surveillance, it looked more and more like Midway Island was the most likely target.' And he said, "We discovered *Akagi, Kaga, Hiryu,* and *Soryu* just almost exactly where we thought they would be.' No way, Robert. There is simply no way that U.S. Naval Intelligence, which has never been the primary focus of the U.S. Navy, just 'surmised' by serendipity the precise location and the destination of the Japanese carrier fleet in the middle of thousands of miles of open, misty and choppy seas somewhere in the largest ocean surface on the planet. No way!

"Think this through with me, Robert. The U.S. Pacific Fleet has only three carriers. Two and a half, really. Would the U.S. Navy, your Navy, really risk sending their most precious carriers on Earth into the vast stretches of the Western Pacific, where they could easily be greatly outnumbered and outgunned by the Japanese Pacific Fleet, if they weren't virtually certain of the precise location and strength and destination of the Japanese Fleet? Not on your life. Somehow, the US Navy knew. They knew exactly, and they knew for sure. For absolute sure!

"Somebody or something must have narrowed the scope of their search. And we know it wasn't some random U.S. Navy Catalina flying boat, because they would have been spotted, shot down, reported back to the Imperial Navy. Nor was it a U.S. Navy submarine, because it would have been very risky for your submarine to send messages. The sub would have to surface to send ratio transmissions, both of which would make the US sub highly discoverable by enemy forces, and also alert the Jap fleet.

"An Allied spy in the Japanese Imperial Staff? That would really be unheard of. So, that leaves only one other possibility. U.S. Naval Intelligence, or someone, is deciphering the Japanese Naval codes."

Robert was stunned. Sarah must be right. Finding the location of the Japanese fleet in the middle of the Pacific Ocean, and ascertaining its destination, would be absolutely impossible without some very reliable intelligence.

"If you are correct about this, and I have to admit that the case that you have presented is pretty convincing, then that revelation is even more vital and promising to our ultimate victory over Japan than The Battle of Midway itself. And if you are correct, not one person in that room knew about it, including me!"

"Except *maybe* you, Robert. Top Secrets are *top secret*. And if you knew you would never tell. Not even me. But you and I do not need Top Secret Information to sort out this mystery. Just connect the dots!"

"Sarah, if your desire for our meeting tonight was to probe my knowledge of a possible U.S. cryptoanalysis breakthrough in the war in the Pacific, and it now seems crystal clear that was your objective tonight, was it really necessary to get me all stirred up, and then let me down, so that sleep tonight will be impossible?"

Sarah smiled. "Robert, my favorite spy! I just wanted to be sure that I had your full attention. But I can see that you have a point!" She looked at his him in shorts and laughed. "I will now turn my full attention to ensuring that you get a good night's sleep tonight. You men are such big puppy dogs!"

Sarah was smiling. She enjoyed outfoxing The Great Robert, and she knew she was on the right track regarding her suspicions about the role of Naval Intelligence in the Battle of Midway. Robert was not smiling. He did not mind at all being outfoxed by Sarah, it was not his first time, nor his last, but he wondered how she figured it all out, and he did not. And he was a little surprised, and maybe put off, by the fact that she had used her feminine wile and guile, plus their romantic relationship, to poke and probe him for information. He thought to himself, "This lady is a very clever, smooth, and charming operative. On the other hand, I have done more than my fair share of 'poking and probing' her mind and her body, and she and I are working together in pursuit of shared goals, and she is teaching me a lot about the Art of Spy Craft. So, I guess I will just relax and try to be a good "big puppy dog." That part sounds like fun!"

34

The Battle of Gazala

24 June 1942, Libya, North Africa

It was a warm, breezy late afternoon in the North African desert, about one hundred miles northwest of Cairo.

British Army Lt. Colonel James Carlton and Captain Thomas Leach, both assigned to the 7th Armored Division of the British Eighth Army, were riding in a half-track vehicle on a routine patrol about thirty miles west of El Alamein, searching for enemy incursions. With them in the M2 half-track were four enlisted riflemen attached to the 11th Indian Infantry Brigade.

Tom was driving. James sat next to him, peering intently through his binoculars looking for any signs of German or Italian forces. James spoke loudly to be heard above the sound of the noisy half-track and the desert wind.

"We have been given typical British Army Orders. They order us at 8:00 a.m. today to drive westward from our base camp to search for enemy units along this road. Then they call us in for meetings from 8:00 a.m. through 3:00 p.m., most of which are a complete waste of time, then they send us out at 3:00 p.m. to begin the 8:00 a.m. assignment. Now of course the sun is slowly setting in the west, and we can't see a darn thing, with the sun right in our eyes."

Tom laughed. "I don't know why you always complain to me. You are the one who sits on General Staff. Why don't you tell them we would be twice as efficient if they would reduce staff meetings by fifty percent?"

James smiled. "Surely you will learn, my young friend, that the British just *love* to meet and talk, and *meet* and *talk*. You need to become aware of to your ancestral proclivities."

"James, I am glad we have a few minutes. Stuffed down our rabbit-hole tanks during these massive tank battles, we don't have the big picture. We just engaged the Germans and Italians in a huge battle back in Gazala, the kind of battle we usually win, and we suffered a massive defeat. I don't have precise numbers. You probably do. But I do know that we sustained God awful casualties, lost hundreds of tanks, almost including mine. They took thousands of prisoners, and we lost Tobruk. I am holding only the tail of this animal, but my sense is that it is an elephant. A major defeat for us. What am I missing?"

"Nothing, Tom. Nothing at all. Gazala was probably one of the worst military defeats for the British Army ever. Rommel is an amazing tank battle tactician. No question about it. But we made a lot of mistakes. You may know that General Ritchie was relieved of command a few days ago. Auchinlech flew in and took Operational Command himself."

Suddenly, five or six rifle shots rang out. Several bullets pinged off the armored siding of the half-track. Several more shots whizzed by over-head. Tom instinctively whipped the steering wheel to the left, putting himself and the entire right side of the British M2 half-track to the side of the old road from which the gunfire was coming. This also protected James, who was the front left seat passenger.

The Indian infantrymen in the rear, using the armor-plated side as a shield, fired their old Enfield rifles in the direction of the enemy fire, which paused as the enemy shooters sought cover.

"Not a large number of troops," James said, staring intently through his binoculars. "Maybe eight or ten. They are Italian, judging by their uniforms. But there is a German officer standing behind them. He is looking at us with his binoculars. He doesn't appear concerned by our return fire, but they are at least eight hundred yards from us. Really out of our range. There are also several local men, probably Egyptians, standing behind him. It appears that they were having some sort of meeting."

"From the angle of their shots, some must be lying on the ground," said Tom, "which would give them cover and improve their aim. The Italians usually carry Carcano M38 carbines, with a maximum range of maybe one-thousand yards, so they will have a hard time hitting us at this distance. Our old Lee Enfield 303's have an even shorter range. Should we take them out with our mounted M2 machine gun?"

"No, Tom. Hold on. If we do that we will also take out a number of local Egyptians. It's not worth it. The Muslims on the western desert are already hostile to us because of the Palestine situation. And that is not our mission here. We only have six men, and they could have a lot more troops than we can see. We spotted them. That is our assignment. Let's just head back to base to report that they are here. Our job here is done."

Tom reached behind his seat and pulled out his own rifle.

James had seen it before, and never really noticed that it was *not* a standard issue British Lee Enfield 303. "What is that?" he asked.

"It's a U.S. Springfield M1903. I want to get just one shot at that Nazi officer before we leave. I can do it in about three minutes."

"Okay, but hurry up. Please."

James knew that Tom was a crack shot, and he figured the one shot could not cause much injury to the assembled Egyptian men. But the serious young Nazi officer was very far away even for a Springfield M1903. Even for Tom.

Tom took careful aim, and then fired. Through his binoculars, James could see that the Nazi officer was hit, but not fatally. He saw blood in the officer's left arm, but he was still standing.

"Good shot, Tom. You must be a direct descendent of Robin Hood!"

"No way! He was a Saxon. They were a nasty tribe of Germans. My people are Angles."

"Oh please. Your sister, Sarah, is clearly a great Saxon beauty! Anyway, let's get going!"

Tom told Corporal Guptan to fire a volley from the mounted machine gun aimed over the heads of the Italians. Then Tom wheeled the M2 around, and headed back east. The Italians all ducked, but James noted that the wounded German Officer never flinched. Tough guy, he thought to himself.

James and Tom and the four Indian Infantrymen were now traveling at least forty miles per hour back to base. It had been a risky sortie with a good tale to tell back at the Officer's Club that night.

"Where did you get an American Springfield? There must be a juicy story in there somewhere."

"There is, James, and especially juicy for you. But I promised Sister Sarah that I would not tell you that she gave it to me, because it would just annoy you."

"Another tricky bit from Sister Sarah. She does sometimes annoy me, but it is hard for me to stay mad at her for very long. I don't plan to make any negative comments about Sarah. You will always report them back to her."

As they sped further on down the dusty road, James finally asked, "Do you know where Sarah obtained your rifle?"

"I do. On orders from MI5, or maybe MI6, not sure, she has been working closely with an American lawyer in U.S. Intelligence. A well-connected man. The 'M's' regard him as having value to the British Empire, and so they ordered Sarah to 'keep him close,' so that we don't lose him. He sometimes gives her gifts. He gave her two American Springfield M1903's. She gave me one. To help me survive the war, I guess."

"Don't the bloody M's recognize *my* value to the bloody Empire? Why don't they instruct Sarah to keep close to me?"

Tom laughed. "I'm sure they do appreciate your value to the Empire. And that is why they do not fear losing you. And anyway, Sarah keeps close to you for her own personal and purely selfish reasons."

"I thought that the Yanks usually curry favor with our British girls by giving them chocolates, cigarettes, and stockings."

"That is often true. But as you may know, James, since you and Sarah do seem to be fairly intimate, Sarah doesn't smoke cigarettes, rarely eats bon-bons, and almost never wears stockings. But she does like guns. Take notice, friend, if your current plans regarding my Secret Service Sister Sarah include a marriage proposal. She does like guns!"

"You've now made me think twice about proposing on my next visit to London. What did she do with the other Springfield?"

"She kept it for herself, of course. Maybe to ward off suitors."

The half-track pulled into camp. The four Indian infantrymen said goodbye and headed back to their group area. James and Tom headed off to the open tent Officer's Club for some dinner.

They sat down at the far end of a long metal table and began to eat their dinner rations.

"James, can we pick up where we left off? The severe beating in Gazala?"

"Sure. But it's a grim."

Two other officers walked by and stopped.

"Mind if we join you? It looks like we four are having very late dinners tonight."

"Please sit with us. I'm James Carlton, and this is my young friend, Thomas Leach. We were on patrol to the west and came upon a small enemy detachment."

Tom said, "Hello!" and reached over the table to shake hands.

"I'm Lt. Duncan Phipps. 2nd New Zealand Division.

"And I'm Lt. Jay Pathok, 11th Indian Brigade. Four of our men accompanied you two on that patrol. Corporal Guptan said you made an incredible shot, and wounded a German officer. An excellent near miss from seven-hundred yards! Too bad you didn't kill him."

More handshakes and hellos.

Tom looked down at his plate as he picked away at his dinner.

"Thank you, Lt.," Tom replied without looking up. "But it was not a near miss. I aimed only for his left arm. Whoever he was, or is, he was not holding a weapon. He was attending a meeting of sorts. I am not an assassin. And he was a brave fellow. Never a flinch or a duck. Hardly blinked an eye. Clearly, he is one of Rommel's toughest young officers. I'm sure that he and I will meet again, in our respective tanks and sort it out on the battlefield, for all to see. If our tanks are equally matched, that will be his final battle. I'm sure of that."

Tom's admission left everyone speechless. But they knew they would place their bets on Tom in that future tank battle.

James broke the ice. "Tom is one of our finest tank commanders. No question about that. I was just revisiting with him our defeat at Gazala. Jay, you were there. And Duncan, you were at Mutreh. Should we talk about it? It is a sad story."

Phipps and Pathok nodded, and listened as they ate.

James continued. "I have heard many reports here that we lost Gazala because the Germans and Italians had more and better tanks. Not true. Rommel had about 500 tanks, but more than 200 of them were very poor quality Italian tanks. Mobile coffins. We had well over 800 tanks, although only a couple hundred were the better quality M3 Grant Tanks. We also had more troops there, about 100,000 to Rommel's 90,000. Since

Rommel was attacking our fixed defensive position, he should have had a 3-to-1 numerical superiority. He did not.

"What he did have was the tactical expertise to concentrate his total forces—armor plus artillery plus infantry plus air superiority—on our weak spots. That is exactly what he did. Ritchie had spread our defensive line too thin and was unprepared to cover the weak points in short order. Our reconnaissance was also very mediocre."

They all nodded in agreement. "What about their air cover?" asked Tom.

"Good point, Tom. Rommel's boss, Luftwaffe Field Marshall Albert Kesselring, was able to provide *both* supplies and air cover. Their aircraft outnumbered ours almost 2 to 1, and we had mostly very old *P-40 Kitty-hawks* and *Hawker Hurricanes*, no match at all for their *Messerschmitt Bf 109F* fighters."

"When we were out on patrol this evening, you mentioned something about the Auk—what was your point there?"

James smiled at his friend's keen understanding of the events.

"Right again, Tom. On 12 June, General Clark Achinlech—'Auk' as we call him—flew in to relieve Ritchie and take direct command. The right move, but way too late. We fell back, but our defensive position of Tobruk was a nightmare. We had totally ignored Tobruk for a year. It fell almost immediately with the surrender of over thirty thousand Allied troops. So, then we were forced back to El-Alamein, and here we sit. Waiting for the Desert Fox to reappear."

By now, five or six additional young, Allied tank officers had joined the little dinner party, listening intently to Lt. Col. James Carlton educate them on Ghastly Gazala.

"That is the sad story of Gazala. But the Western African Desert Campaign is a much bigger picture. And hopefully a much brighter story."

"Brighter how? I don't see how we'll get out of this mess," said Phipps.

"In the long-running pattern of history, dating back to the early days of the Roman Empire," said James, "control of North Africa depends on control of the Mediterranean Sea. The Axis Powers have had a leg up on us, because they control the Italian Peninsula and Sicily with sea and air bases.

"But we control Malta and Egypt, and we have a much stronger Navy and up until now, an equivalent Air Force. The entry of the U.S. will certainly tilt the balance considerably in our favor. The Yanks are sending us better and more tanks, and more fighters, and amazingly, a significant number of *Liberator B-24* bombers."

"Aye, but the Yanks promise the moon, will that be enough to defeat Rommel?" asked Tom.

"Rommel will be back. No question about it, Tom. But he will find us here with considerably more and better forces to defend Egypt. And there is one other consideration for the Axis forces arrayed against us here. This Russian Campaign. That campaign is a matter of life or death for the Axis. North Africa is a side show for them. They can afford to lose this North African campaign. And so, they will. They are stretched too thin now. We cannot afford to lose this North African battle. And so, we will not."

All the young officers returned to their units, now anxiously awaiting the return of the Desert Fox.

35

Chad and Harry

6 July 1942, London

The windows in the Burn Ward at Queen Victoria Hospital were open. There were a few electric fans, but it was still a warm and sticky day. Some of the young pilot patients had taken off their shirts. If they had chest or shoulder or back wounds, that was deemed to be acceptable. But some of the others were just trying to cool off.

The two attending doctors on duty paid no attention to these obvious breaches of military dress code. By and large military men serving together almost anywhere do not hassle each other about "proper attire."

As is always the case, throughout history, and possibly much earlier than that (but we don't know because there is no record of it) there was a military service nurse assigned to this ward. Assistant Matron-in-Chief Gladys Scripps, age fifty-three, made it her principal assignment to ensure that everyone in or near the ward was buttoned up. Including even On Duty doctors. She was off duty on this very warm day. And the young nurses who were on duty that day did not mind at all having the young men shirtless. Not at all.

Amanda was in her summer nurse uniform. She was in constant motion and perspiring. For the most part, she was following Dr. McIndoe, the great plastic surgeon, as he checked on each of his burn patients.

The doctor was finishing his rounds and about to head into surgery. His last stop was at the beds of Lt. Chad Clarke and Lt. Harry Noble.

"These two fellows look fine, Nurse Amanda. I think their burns and broken bones are progressing very well. Hopefully, they will not be requiring any further follow-up surgery."

After the doctor took his leave, Amanda finished her notes, and then turned to Harry.

"I saw that you had a visit last week from your parents, Lt. Noble. Were they comforted to see you doing so well?"

"Definitely. My father told me that I am now 'completely healed', and that I should 'get my butt back into the cockpit and stop all of this lolly-gagging!' He talks like that. He probably doesn't mean it. It is his usual way of saying, 'You look fine!'"

Amanda laughed and squeezed his arm.

"My mother looked more worried. She said, 'Please let your wounds heal fully. Please don't let them push you out the door and back into one of those dreadful *Hurricanes*. Just look at all these young burn victims!' She probably didn't exactly mean that either, because she knows all too well that our 'dreadful *Hurricanes*' are knocking down a lot of those dreadful Kraut bombers!"

Amanda smiled at Noble and then turned to Chad. "Lt. Clarke, I don't believe we have seen your parents here. Do they live far from London?

Chad looked over at Harry. There was a pregnant pause. Then Chad spoke quietly.

"You are kind to ask. And kinder still to notice who comes and goes to visit us fallen angels. Our home is in Coventry. Only about 85 miles from London. Same as Harry here. But both of my parents were killed in November 1940 in the horrible Nazi bombing of our quiet, little Coventry.

"Harry's parents ran into the bomb shelter that night. My mother had a touch of influenza, and was largely confined to her bed. She did not want to risk giving the bug to others in the small bomb shelter, so my parents both stayed at home. Harry and I are next door neighbors. Have been since we were born. Both homes were hit. A direct hit."

Amanda held back tears as she squeezed Chad's arm. How could she be laughing one minute and then crying the next?

"Go on, Lt. Clark. I'm listening."

"I am told that both of my parents died instantly together in her room, where Father had been tending to her. Now when Harry's parents come to visit, they treat us both as their sons. Our parents were the closest of friends since World War I. Our dads served together in France in 1917. It's a very long story."

Amanda broke down. She couldn't help it. "I am so sorry, Lieutenant. I had no idea. Please forgive my rude intrusion."

"Not at all, ma'am. It was the very kindest of inquiries. We very much appreciate all the attention here from the nurses and the concern, most especially from you. But I for one will be glad to check out of this hospital and climb back into the cockpit. I have a score to settle with Jerry and I intend to do so with a vengeance. Every one of their damn bombers I can shoot down in flames is payback for my parents and for all of our wounded and deceased friends and neighbors in Coventry. I'm sorry Nurse Amanda. This discussion touched a very sensitive nerve for me."

"I entirely understand. How fortunate that you have Lt. Noble and his family so close to you." Amanda was now crying. Not a usual sight in a hospital burn ward filled with badly burned young pilots.

Chad sensed that he should lighten the mood a bit. "Harry's parents are terrific. But Harry himself has always been a burden to me. As you can tell from our charts, I am six months older than Harry, and I have had to teach him so much, including how to fly airplanes and even how to talk to a girl! Now we just need to find a girl willing to talk to him!"

They all laughed.

"Lt. Clarke, we have all been wondering, these piles of official looking documents on your nightstand? They seem to consume the attention of both of you all day every day. What are they?"

"An excellent question. No one ever asked."

As he spoke, Chad started to pull out document after document.

"These are the official specifications for the *Hawker Hurricane*. A document for every change and modification. These documents are given to the manufacturer representatives, for their use when they talk to government and army officials, but most of us pilots don't get them. Not unless we chase them down relentlessly, which most pilots won't do. But if we are going to bet our lives on these planes, we need to know every detail. How to get their maximum speed, and for how long, and at what altitude, and at what climb rate, and from every dive angle, and from every turn. And fuel consumption. And flack vulnerability. And fuel burn rate. And fire hazards. And gun accuracy at what distance and speed. One mistake means one more lost RAF pilot. I know my days are numbered in the *Hurricane's* cockpit, but I intend to stretch that number to the max.

"The documents also describe in great detail all that we know about every German fighter plane we may or may not encounter. We need to know how fast they can fly, for how long, how much tighter can they turn, which areas of their planes are most vulnerable to our guns, and on and on.

"And, these documents over here," he said pointing to a different pile, "have substantial details on every German bomber. This time in the hospital is not just to heal these burn wounds. We need to learn as much as we can about how to be even better at our jobs. And we have learned a lot."

Amanda was dumbstruck. Most of the pilot patients were spending their healing time reading magazines and novels, chatting with nurses and patients and visitors, listening to the radio, or dozing off, while these two lieutenants were sharpening their teeth.

She said her farewells and started to leave. Then she stopped, and walked back, turning to Chad.

"Lt. Clarke. I'm so impressed by what you have told me here today. Just a thought. During your recovery time, might it make sense for you and Lt. Noble to spend some time each day teaching the other pilots here some of what you yourself are learning? Speaking as the Navy Junior that I am, you two might help to scuttle a few more German fighters, take down a few more German bombers, save a few more British lives, and extend the life expectancy of a few more British pilots!"

Chad and Harry readily agreed to Nurse Amanda's plan.

36

More News from Juan

18 July 1942, London

Juan and Robert met in their usual room at The Savoy. Juan was impeccably dressed, as always, and looked very serious and troubled.

"Juan, you must be keeping busy," said Robert. "I haven't heard from you in a long time. Is all well?"

"I have been busy with my usual job, and every couple of months I get tapped for one of Dr. von Buckholtz's special assignments. Often they are dangerous for me personally, but increasingly, I must say, I find them intriguing, and usually satisfying. The Axis military is having many successes, but it is increasingly difficult to like the Germans these days."

Robert saw an opening and seized it. Maybe he was learning good spy craft from Sarah.

"We should perhaps explore these mixed emotions. What exactly is conflicting you?"

"Since the last time we met, I have had a few run-ins with the Gestapo on my business trips to Germany. They are trained to be as unpleasant as possible. And I now have a much better understanding of the attitude of some high-level officers in the Wehrmacht towards these ever-present Gestapo pigs. I am quite sure that they have knowledge of my travels and have become suspicious of my motives and purpose. It will make my work more difficult, but I might have to avoid or curtail further travels into Germany."

"I have heard a number of similar reports of Gestapo harassment."

Juan nodded grimly.

"Robert, allow me to relate the reason for my requesting our meeting today, in great confidence. The message I brought to you from Germany last year was very accurate, and very sensitive, and very secret, yes? My message today also meets those criteria."

Robert sat silent for a moment, knowing that Juan was expecting a response from him.

"That meeting was more than a year ago. And there has been so much water under the bridge since then that I hardly remember. But the messenger did arrive as you foretold, in a very spiffy aircraft, and the message he carried was the message you foretold. But that was long ago, and a separate peace deal now is clearly out of the question."

Juan listened carefully. "That is understood. The reason for the Rudolf Hess trip to England—and it really *was* Rudolf Hess, not a double—was to advance a separate peace agreement with England, which was a real prospect a year ago. But, as you say, the prospect is even more remote, because Adolf Hitler is in full control of everything in Germany. I have a new approach. More dangerous. More dangerous for all concerned."

Robert nodded. "Go on…"

"There is a growing interest in the German army to remove Hitler from his current position as Commander in Chief, and then isolate him entirely from control of the German government and the German military. This group, which is composed largely of German army officers, is hoping to explore whether the English or the Americans or both might be interested in providing support or assistance in the effort. As was the case in the now-aborted Hess approach, the benefits to the Allies would be incalculable."

Robert thought for several minutes. He stood up, walked over to the window and looked out at the sunny, warm day.

"Juan, as I told you at our earlier meetings, I am not in a position to deal with this. I have no official role with the U.S. Government nor its military establishment, and I certainly have no position whatsoever with the British Government nor the British military establishment."

Juan opened his mouth to object, but Robert held up his hand.

"Nevertheless…I do have a few questions. Does the enquiry come from any duly recognized authority within the German army? Would it be a correct characterization to say that this comes from the German Resistance? Is the principal purpose of the effort to overthrow the currently constituted government of Germany? Is one of the objectives of this effort to assassinate Adolph Hitler, or any members of his inner ruling circle?"

"Robert, as you probably already know, under these circumstances these four questions are unanswerable. Certainly, unanswerable by me anyway. I do not represent these people. The purpose of my visit today is to see if you would be willing to meet with this person, who apparently does represent these people. If so, then this person might be able to answer your four questions."

"Are you able to tell me anything at all about this person? The last time we met that person turned out to be no less than the Deputy Fuhrer of the Third Reich!"

"I can tell you a little. I met him, albeit somewhat briefly. In view of the attention I sometimes receive from the Gestapo goons, it is risky for others to meet with me, even in Spain. But I thought it best to meet him in person before introducing him to you. Here is most of what I do know about him. He is young, maybe twenty-three or twenty-four. He is a junior officer in the German army, on active duty, although he was wearing civilian clothes when I met him in Madrid. He has seen combat, first in France and elsewhere recently. He did not say where, but presumably in the Mediterranean theatre. He was, intentionally, I think, a little vague on where for security reasons.

"He is one of the decreasing number of young German officers from an upper-class family. A family of wealth and stature. The ongoing effort of the Nazis to bring more and more 'common people' into the junior officer ranks has been diluting the ranks of the old Prussian and Saxon nobility in German military circles. He is highly educated. Speaks English fluently. He is nobody's stooge. He is a very impressive young man."

"That all sounds very interesting. You did not give me his name. Do you know if he is a member of the Nazi Party?"

"*He* did not give me his real name. If his name and his mission were ever linked, and then discovered, his life is forfeit. The name he is using for these discussions is Gunther. A code name, I guess. I did not ask him if he is a member of the Nazi Party, but I suspect that he is not, given his inclination, unless he joined as a cover, in which case it is irrelevant.

"Robert, I just want to say that, if you do decide to meet with him, I suspect that it will be a meeting you will never forget and a meeting you will never regret."

Silence.

"Where would I meet him? If I were to go to Spain for such a meeting, it would attract attention."

"He and I think you should meet him here. In London. Perhaps at the Savoy."

"He can get here?"

"He says he can. He has sources in Spain who can easily provide him with forged travel papers. I am told that it's not so unusual. He would claim to represent Gleiss. Just as I do. Or he could come ashore at night in a small boat. I am told that is also not so unusual. Tens of thousands of people enter and depart London every day. Most of them unknown, unknowable, and unnoticed. He wants the meeting. He will get here. Of that I am quite sure."

"Give me a few days to think about this, Juan. He knows that if he is caught here in civilian clothes, he will be considered a spy and probably shot?"

"I am sure he does," Juan said and then paused.

"Robert, there is one particularly noticeable characteristic about the young officer you will appreciate. He seems utterly fearless. He seems totally devoid of concern for his own safety. He is on a very critical mission for the Fatherland."

"Interesting. I suppose I, too, could be shot."

"I doubt that. You have a cover story."

"Juan, hear me out on this. What if I were to bring someone with me to the meeting? Someone who could give me some cover, and who might also increase the chances of getting this message into the right ears?"

"Who might that be? U.S. Military? British noblemen? British Intelligence Service??"

"Probably the latter."

"I would need to preclear that with Gunther. He is putting his life on the line here. Could I first meet this Intelligence fellow?"

"Maybe. I have to work this through. And it might be a woman."

"A woman? That is a shocker. I did not know that there were any women in the British Intelligence Service. Think it through, Robert. But if bringing this person will aid the mission, I would need to meet him, or her, first, so that I can talk it through with Gunther."

"Understood. I'll try to get back to you in a week or so."

Juan said his farewell, and left the room. Robert sat back down to think things over. On the one hand, he was not wild about the idea of getting involved in a half-baked, hallucinogenic Hail Mary to replace the all-powerful German Fuhrer, and he instinctively really didn't trust Juan. On the other hand, how could he say no? He decided to talk it over first with Sarah, and then with Bill.

37

Those Pesky Mosquitoes

27 July 1942, London

Robert was invited to British Bomber Command HQ along with a small group of U.S. Eighth Air Force Officers, to hear some reports on new bomber tactics and new bomber designs. It was all very "hush hush."

He was hoping he might see Sarah, but she was off on assignment. It set Robert thinking. These Bomber Command top secret briefings are always a thrill and an honor, now almost always with exciting news. Sarah would not miss a meeting unless she had something really important. He should try to connect with her in the next few days to discuss his visit with Juan, and just reconnect, professionally and personally.

Looking around the room for Sarah, Robert noticed Lindemann with David Butt and Dr. Aaron Solomon, sitting quietly in the back of the room. Solomon and Butt were chatting to each other, almost whispering, with an occasional comment to Lindemann, who mostly grunted his replies. Lindemann was sipping tea and looking grumpy, as usual. Probably lying in wait to pounce.

British Group Captain Bufton called the meeting to order and started things off.

"We first want to explain our rapidly evolving Pathfinder Bomber strategy. We think that our American friends might want to consider something similar. Starting several months ago, we started using Pathfinder aircraft. These are flown by our best pilots and crews, all tops in their ability to find targets at night. We also call this select group our Target Finding Force (TFF).

"They go in first and mark the targets with Target Indicators (TI's), usually colored Verey flares. The same system was used by the Germans in the Blitz. There is now growing support to make the TFF a permanent command. In the near future, this force would fly *Halifax, Lancaster, Stirling,* and *Wellington* bombers.

"The GEE system now guides the Pathfinders to the targets. The Pathfinders mark the targets. Then the first wave of bombers drops high explosives to do structural damage. The next wave of bombers drops incendiary bombs, creating widespread fire damage. We have discovered through trial and error that fires do far more damage to cities than explosives. This will be our strategy moving forward. Now, I will take questions."

A small group of squadron commanders were sitting together near the back of the room. Old enough to hold a little seniority, but young enough to be cocky and throw caution to the wind, they asked a few bold questions.

"Isn't this marker strategy just what the Luftwaffe has been doing?"

Answer: "Yes, we did say that, but we can do it better."

Question: "If we are not assigned to be Pathfinders, does that mean we are second string pilots?"

Answer: "Yes. Probably. Keep trying to improve!"

Much grumbling from the squadron commander, and laughter from others.

Air Marshall Harris stood to speak.

"Captain Bufton has been a bit too modest here today. To a large extent, he was the creator and the founder of the Pathfinders. It has been working very well. But I must tell you, my hope is one day the entire bomber force will be qualified as Pathfinders. Good job, Bufton. Hats off to you!"

Applause all around.

"Next, I have the very great honor to introduce to all of you Air Chief Marshall Sir Wilfrid Rhodes Freeman, Vice Chief of the Air Ministry, to tell us all about the *De Havilland DH 98 Mosquito*. Marshall Freeman has a long and distinguished career helping us develop some of our best aircraft."

Freeman stood up and moved to the front of the room. Robert watched Freeman move up to the podium. What an elegant man, he thought. Robert greatly admired Freeman because Freeman, even more than Lord Beaverbrook, had been largely responsible for ordering the *Hawker Hurricanes*, *Super-Marine Spitfires*, *Mosquitos*, and *Lancaster Bombers*. Which collectively saved Britain.

"Thank you, Marshall Harris, for your kind introduction. The *De Havilland DH 98 Mosquito* is an incredible aircraft. Period. The frame is mostly wood. It carries a crew of two. Its range is 1,300 with a ceiling of 37,000 feet and speeds of up to 415 miles per hour. It can carry up to 4,000 pounds of bombs. Both a bomber and a fighter, and an excellent Pathfinder."

Freeman continued at length and then answered many questions.

At the conclusion of this discussion, Harris turned to the American officers. "Any updates on American Operations which you are able to provide?"

General Ira Eaker stood up.

"Good morning. I am Ira Eaker, Commander of the U.S. Eighth Air Force Bomber Command. Many of you know me from the many meetings we have had over the past five months since I arrived in London.

"I do not have a great deal to add, but we are deep into the process of preparing twelve of our recently received *B-17s* for a daytime raid somewhere over Germany to attack military, transportation or fuel operations by the middle of August. We cannot match the incredible achievement of your Bomber Command putting one-thousand bombers in the sky, but give us time. We will catch up. In the meantime, at least we will have an oar in the water.

"As this planned August raid indicates, we continue to believe that daytime, precision bombing of military, transportation, and fuel operations are the best use of our bombers. We do not favor bombing German cities as a primary target. You all know our views on this subject. But, in the end, we are allies even if we don't always agree."

Robert could see that there was no meeting of the minds on the subject of precision bombing versus city bombing. Not even close. But the net result might be British bombings of German cities by night, and U.S. bombings of strategic targets by day. After a couple of years, there might not be much left of the Third Reich. He also wondered whether the Luftwaffe could assemble a roomful of military talent to match the group assembled here today. Probably not.

38

A Close Call

30 July 1942, London

After attending a late-day meeting at CCR, where Hannah expanded on her views concerning the treatment of European refugees, Hannah and Amanda slipped out for a light meal at a close-by pub. When they had finished, and said their farewells, Amanda grabbed a cab home. Hannah walked off to catch a bus.

By the time that Hannah sat down in her bus seat, it was twilight. When she arrived at the stop it was nighttime. The other two bus passengers had already reached their stops so Hannah was alone. The street was empty. It was a cloudy night. There were no other pedestrians, and no traffic whatsoever. Due to blackout rules, street lights were dark, and most houses were curtained. London followed blackout rules to make it harder for Nazi bombers to find city targets. Hannah set off to walk the four blocks to the Hawkins' house. They were always very nice and welcoming, but not as exciting, vibrant and engaged as Amanda and Alice and the mostly older Brits who were focusing on the European refugee crisis.

She walked along the narrow sidewalk, passing the quiet, small, neat houses that lined both sides of the street. It was a working-class neighborhood, so most of the neighbors had settled down for the night since they would be up early to get to work.

She could hear her own footsteps as she walked, and the wind. She stopped for a moment to listen for some activity. Nothing. Only quiet. The dark night closed in on her. Enveloped her. There were no cars parked on the street.

Just after she passed Stanton Street, Hannah heard an automobile engine start on one of the side streets behind her. The engine had a deep rumble sound, like a truck or a van. That seemed odd. She glanced back, but, as was customary during blackouts, the automobile had its headlamps turned off. Then she heard the up Doppler sound, an increase in frequency indicating that the vehicle was heading in her direction. That also seemed odd because the commercial area was in the opposite direction. If one of the local workmen was heading out to a late job, he should be driving in the opposite direction.

As the engine sound came closer, she heard the engine rev up to a higher speed. She was surprised because vehicles seldom accelerated on a blacked-out street with no headlamps due to the risk to pedestrians. Hannah turned toward the oncoming sound just in time to see the vehicle heading straight at her at a high rate of speed. With not an instant to spare, she threw herself to the left, hard and fast. Fortunately, at that very spot, there was a large rose bush hedge on her left, rather than the solid stone wall she had just passed.

The hedge was formidable but did have some give to it. She pushed just enough into the bushes to avoid the front of the vehicle. She quickly glanced at the driver and saw a middle-aged man, looking intently at her. He was wearing a pulled down cap and heavy glasses, so she could not make out his face.

She shouted out, "Stop! Watch out!"

The driver yelled something at her, then turned the wheel sharply to his right, so that his vehicle brushed by her with a powerful glancing blow, pushing her a little deeper into the thorny rose bush hedge. He then stepped on the gas again, and tore off down the street, first scraping the side of a stone post on the sidewalk, and then disappearing around the next corner.

Then all was quiet. Hannah fell from the hedge onto the sidewalk. She was hurt, badly scraped, and shaken up, but she felt that she had dodged a bullet. Barely.

She sat on the walk, rethinking her close call. What had just happened? Was that just an accident? There were many pedestrians struck by cars, trucks, buses, and cabs in London during the blackouts. Many were badly hurt or killed.

But this driver seemed intent on hitting her. And he never stopped to check on her. Is it possible that he didn't realize his vehicle had struck her? Not possible. The vehicle made a loud thump when it hit her. The driver had looked right at her. He yelled at her. This was no blackout accident.

A few minutes later two middle aged women came by, on their way home. They helped Hannah stand up, inquiring graciously about her condition, and then walked her to the Hawkins' home nearby.

"There are now so many of these nighttime accidents," said the younger woman named Mrs. Cargan. "So typical. And then the drivers just drive off."

Her friend Mildred Suffrin, an older spinster, scoffed. "No Brit would do this. I'll wager the driver was some foreign-born laborer who was too frightened to stop for fear of getting unwanted attention from the police."

When Hannah got home, the Hawkins' were extremely attentive and concerned. They examined her cuts and bruises, and thought she was probably okay. They also suspected an accidental hit and run by some thoughtless laborer. After all, no one would intentionally run into a young woman walking home alone on a quiet street.

Mrs. Hawkins cleaned Hannah's left side, which had cuts and puncture wounds from the hedge, and carefully examined her right thigh and hip where the side of the passing vehicle had brushed by her, forcefully shoving her into the hedge. It was a bad bruise.

The next morning, Hannah called Amanda to relate the story. Amanda was immediately suspicious. She was also concerned about Hannah's injuries. She asked Hannah to meet her at the hospital to have a look at her. Dr. Solomon would be on call and would want to check on her injuries. Hannah did not want to cause a big fuss about this, and felt embarrassed. But Amanda was insistent.

Hannah arrived at the entrance of Queen Victoria Hospital at 1:00 p.m. Mrs. Hawkins, concerned about Hannah's injuries, had accompanied her. Amanda met Hannah at the entrance.

"Hannah, you are clearly injured. Thank heaven you came here today!"

Alice ran out to meet them. "Hannah, you are limping. Let me help you."

After a hug from each sister, they all headed up to the women's ward. Hannah had a Haythornwaite daughter under each arm, mostly for moral support.

Amanda escorted Hannah to a small changing room to put on a hospital gown. She and Amanda then went into the small examination room, where Dr. Aaron Solomon was waiting. Amanda helped Hannah up onto the examination table. It was obvious that Hannah was in some pain. She winced a few times and muttered "ouch" twice. She had the look on her face that patients always wear when their doctors set out to probe and poke and push until the hapless patient evinces pain.

Aaron carefully pulled aside the gown, revealing her left side, and gently touched her wounds. He then ran his fingers over her right side to check on the contrast. At his request, Amanda did the same. Hannah was clearly embarrassed, but did her best to hide it.

"There are some deep wounds here from the rose bush, Amanda, and pieces of thorns and branches remain in the wounds. Could you please take Hannah into one of the small operating rooms, which have better lighting, and clean out these bits and pieces? That will speed the healing. Please also apply a little powder sulfanilamide to the wounded area. That will help to prevent infection. As you know, we use it for burn treatment here."

"Yes, doctor. I will do it. Right away."

"Dr. Solomon, will these wounds heal? Will there be much scarring?" said Hannah.

"They should heal just fine. Few if any scars, but you need to keep them clean and disinfected. Can you please turn onto your back? I want to take a look at the bruise on your right thigh."

He pulled up her gown on the right side just far enough to expose her thigh and carefully probed the dark bruise, asking her to report on her pain level from gentle finger pressure. Amanda did the same. Hannah was blushing from all the attention to portions of her anatomy not usually exposed to sight and touch. But again, nobody appeared to notice her embarrassment. It was, after all, a hospital.

"Amanda, after you clean these wounds, please take Hannah to the x-ray group, and get an x-ray of this right thigh and hip. I don't think there is a fracture there, but there might be."

Aaron looked at Hannah, now partially disrobed on the examination table. And Hannah looked up at him. No man had ever seen this much of her, so she blushed again. Amanda could see that Hannah was a little uncomfortable but appreciated Aaron's close attention to her.

"Hannah, these days there are literally tens of thousands of car accidents each year. Was this just an accident? Tell me what happened."

As Hannah related the story, Amanda took careful notes.

"Did you see the make and color of the car? Did you get a good look at the driver?"

"No. It was a small van but no business name was written on the side. The hood ornament looked like a spread wing butterfly. It was hard to see the driver's face. He wore a pulled-down cap, and thick black glasses. For some reason, the van's windows were heavily shaded. It was also too dark and too quick. The driver said three words. They sounded like, 'God Damn you!' He never stopped. His car scraped by a stone post, and then he sped away."

Aaron continued, "It has been my experience that wounds caused intentionally always seem worse than wounds caused accidentally. Your wounds are not insignificant. What you report sounds very odd. Amanda, please write up Hannah's accident report and give me a copy."

He then gently pulled down her gown to cover her.

"Don't worry, Hannah. Amanda and I will return you to good health. One-hundred percent. Please return next Thursday afternoon, and let us see how you are progressing."

Three hours later, Hannah had headed home with Mrs. Hawkins and Alice, who was holding onto Hannah's right arm to help support her right leg. Alice was focused on Hannah and had not noticed the concern and apprehension on the faces of Aaron and Amanda at the hospital.

Amanda stopped into Aaron's office. She found him staring at an x-ray of a hip and femur, and looking very unhappy. Not the usual calm, cool, and collected Dr. Aaron Solomon.

"Hannah's x-ray?" she asked.

"Yes, it is Hannah's x-ray. There is no break, but a very bad bruise. I find it hard to believe this was a traffic accident, but it seems almost unimaginable that anyone anywhere would want to hurt that fine, young woman. Or at least anyone besides those bloodthirsty Nazis lunatics!"

He thought for a moment.

"Amanda, you and Hannah seem very close. Can you shed any light on this mystery for me? The afternoon I first met Hannah, here at the hospital last Christmas, she expressed some very strong views—criticisms—of British policies towards Jewish refugees. Could there be some connection to those activities and the events of last night?

"Dr. Solomon, I must tell you, I have the greatest respect and admiration for this young woman."

She then related to Aaron the long story of the meetings, lectures, small conferences and sidebar discussions that the two of them had been attending in and around London on the Jewish refugee problems. She related how bravely and openly Hannah had spoken out.

"Your admiration is clear. She is a striking figure. But we cannot be blind to the facts. This so-called accident could be someone trying to silence her."

He thought for a moment.

"I had the great honor to meet your father, Captain Haythornwaite. I wonder if he might give us a little assistance enlisting Scotland Yard to look into these events? I don't have any police connections, but he might be able to make a few calls. We need a Scotland Yard detective to help us examine this accident scene. What do you think?"

"An excellent idea, Doctor. I will go directly to his office now to speak to him. He knows and admires Hannah. I am sure he will try to help us."

"We should try to examine the scene of this event soon, before rain washes away any evidence."

As a medical practitioner, she knew Dr. Solomon was reasonably comfortable with Hannah's medical condition, but the odd circumstances of this incident were worrisome. Amanda thought back to the meetings she had attended with Hannah, and some of the nasty animosity she had seen on some faces.

39

A Recap and a Nightcap for Sarah

1 August 1942, London

Sarah arrived at Robert's house promptly at 7:00 p.m. She gave him a big hug.

"You missed the big meeting last week at Bomber Command. That surprised me. I'm sure you were invited. Did you have a better offer?"

Robert opened a bottle of wine, and they sat down at the supper table. He had already queued up his gramophone, setting the mood for the evening with Vera Lynn's "White Cliffs of Dover." They started with wine, cheese and crackers.

"By the time I received the invitation, I already had a commitment I could not break." She paused. "I had to kiss a few Frogs."

Sarah watched Robert's reaction to gauge his interest

"Frogs? You mean Frenchmen?"

"Yes. Not my favorite pastime," she smiled. "Usually I prefer to kiss a Limey or better still, a Tommy!"

"If you ever have a few minutes to spare whilst kissing all these Angles, Saxons, Jutes, Goths, Vandals, and Franks, you might want to try kissing a Yank. It isn't too awful, if you first have a glass or two of wine."

"Let me see if you are telling the truth!"

Sarah walked around the table, took a big swallow of her wine, and gave Robert another kiss.

"You are right. That was not *too* awful," she laughed.

"So, you are hotly pursuing your French Connection with ties to the French Resistance?"

"Some success last week. Can you tell me about the Bomber Command meeting? What did I miss?"

Robert related the essence of the meeting. He noted all the big wigs in attendance, and also the attendance of Aaron Solomon, David Butt, Frederick Lindemann.

"Very interesting. Did they fill you in on Stalingrad? The Germans have launched a big push there. It seems strange to us. Hopeless. But they must know something we do not."

"I suspect that the Germans are putting heavy reliance on Luftwaffe support. It will be extremely effective in attacking Russian tanks and infantry, and interdicting Russian reinforcements in the opening days and weeks of the assault on Stalingrad, but probably unreliable in a month or two.

"U.S. Intelligence operations are now growing much closer to Russian military sources due to Lend Lease. They desperately need supplies from the U.S. and the U.K., so we are better able to see inside the Great Soviet Shroud. As we gain intelligence from them, we are learning that military decisions in Germany are being made by Hitler himself, for political objectives, rather than by the Wehrmacht, for military success. The Soviets believe that Hitler has made a terrible mistake in pushing his offense into Stalingrad, and in his heavy reliance on his Luftwaffe.

"Again, and again, the Luftwaffe has failed to deliver. The British evacuation of Dunkirk only succeeded because the Luftwaffe never really showed up in strength. Luftwaffe Commander Herman Goring is, in the view of U.S. Air Force Command, essentially incompetent. In any event, the power and impact of the Luftwaffe in the Russian Campaign will diminish by fall due to a number of factors. And their lost aircraft will be hard to replace."

He got up from the dinner table and pulled a map off his desk. Sarah moved around where she could see the map.

"A map of Russia—you come prepared," said Sarah with a wry smile.

Robert ignored her flirtation for the moment.

"I keep it handy for tracking repeated German assaults. Notice these factors. The Germans are laying siege at Leningrad. *And* 800 miles south of Leningrad they are attacking Kharkov. *And* more than 800 miles south of Kharkov they are laying siege of Sevastopol. *And* attacking Baku. Meanwhile, 800 miles east of Kharkov they are attacking the City of Stalingrad."

Sarah studied the map. Then she asked, "Why Stalingrad? It looks like a distraction from their principal targets."

"Stalingrad is the focus of U.K. and U.S. Land-Lease supplies from the Caspian Sea. Taking it could mean cutting off vital military supplies to the Soviets, including tanks, guns, planes and ammunition, coming via the Don and Volga Rivers on American and British boats. But the Germans don't have to take Stalingrad to cut off those supplies. And the German army supply lines to all those targets back to Germany are now very exposed.

"Like the invasion of Russia in 1941, the assault on Stalingrad is starting late in the summer. The Germans won't even be in position to assault Stalingrad until September. Winter starts early in Russia. October maybe. The Russians handle Winter battle conditions much better than the Germans. And the German Army's brutal and criminal mistreatment of Russian citizens and soldiers has now insured that the Russians *will* fight to the death. The Germans have foolishly placed their Hungarian units and their Romanian units on their flanks."

Sarah asked, "Why is that foolish?"

"Those units are generally poorly equipped and unreliable. There are other issues. Hitler should have learned his lesson from the idiocy of their first Russian invasion in '41. He still thinks of Russia as a traditional western country. But it is really an Asian empire, with vast reaches of land and enormous amounts of resources and human capital, stretching thousands of miles east from Moscow. He has again underestimated the Russian endless capacity to replace fallen troops. And the Russians now have Lend Lease, giving them huge amounts of armaments. No competent military commander would make all these strategic mistakes, which by my guess, is the reason senior military commanders in the Wehrmacht are seething."

Sarah looked at him. "Senior military commanders in the Wehrmacht are seething? Robert, you have picked up some intel. Can you share?"

Robert looked at her. He was always surprised and impressed, and maybe just a little annoyed, at Sarah's skill in picking up on words and then repeating them back verbatim in her constant pursuit of answers. But he knew that he should respond.

"Yes, I can share. It leads me to my next subject. Juan came to see me two weeks ago. He wants to introduce me to another messenger."

"Another high-ranking Nazis officer? They must be running out of deputy Fuhrers by now."

"Not a senior official. In fact, a junior officer."

Robert filled in all the details of his discussion with Juan.

"Another meeting, how do you feel about that?"

"I think I am really sticking my neck out and don't want to meet with this 'Gunther' person unless you get it authorized by MI5 or MI6."

"Agreed. It seems like such a long shot to achieve anything of value. But your summary of the German military blunders in Russia does help to put it all into perspective. Let me consult with my friends at MI5. They can give us some guidance."

Robert put the dishes in the kitchen, and they sat down in his favorite spot on the sofa. Sarah snuggled up to him.

Robert ran his hand up her right leg and thigh, under her dress. "I guess I better take a good look at that knee."

Sarah smiled, with Robert watching, she stood up, took off her dress, hung it carefully on the back of a chair, and sat back down. She swung her now bare legs onto Robert's lap.

"All right, Dr. Johnston, please take a very good look. And be sure to compare both knees, please!"

Robert checked carefully, but seemed to pay more attention to her thighs than her knees. He expressed some concern about the tightness of her inner thighs.

"Just as I expected and feared. You have some tightness in your inner upper thighs, which is putting stress on your knee tendons. Should I try a little deep muscle massage in that area?"

"Yes, please. That feels very good. A little higher please, and a little firmer please."

As things were beginning to progress, Sarah came up for air for a moment. Robert repeatedly marveled at the way Sarah could mix business with plea- sure. It almost seemed like maybe they were one and the same for her.

"Robert, when you were describing the big meeting, you mentioned that Lindemann, and that young Dr. Solomon, who you regard so highly, and David Butt all attended. I did want to tell you an interesting piece of news about Dr. Solomon. Apparently, he is an attending physician at the

RAF Burn Ward at Queen Victoria Hospital. One of his regular nurses, who is it seems very devoted to him in a professional way, is Amanda Haythornwaite. Her father, Navy Captain Spencer Haythornwaite, is a highly regarded British Naval aviator and a very old friend of my father, also a British Navy Captain. They were classmates at Dartmouth, the Britannia Royal Naval College."

Robert wasn't sure where this was going or why Sarah insisted on discussing it right now, but he hung in with her.

"I'm listening, Sarah. Continue."

"Amanda and your Dr. Solomon met a day or two ago with Amanda's father to request his help in getting Scotland Yard to look into an incident in which a young woman, a German Jewish refugee, was sideswiped and injured by a car or light truck at night while she was walking home. This injured young woman is a close friend of Amanda's and it appears the alleged 'accident' was suspicious. Dr. Solomon treated her, but they want Scotland Yard to look into the incident. My father filled me in on the details yesterday. I took the story to a section at MI5 which works with Scotland Yard to track cases of possible anti-Semitic attacks, and we did line up a very capable inspector to check into it."

"But aren't there hundreds of accidents in London every night due to the blackouts?"

"Very true, but this does not sound like an accident. Anyway, Inspector Dunbar will be looking into it with Dr. Solomon. I just thought you might be interested, since you know Dr. Solomon."

"Is there really that level of anti-Semitism here? That surprises me. Please keep me posted. My interest is complicated. I will explain all that to you at a future date."

Sarah turned playful once again. And Robert, once again, found himself scrambling to shift gears from weighty matters of British anti-Semitism to more enticing fleshy matters being "offered" by the attractive British woman currently sharing his space on the couch.

"Robert, you seem to have a keen interest in a number of subjects, including even leg injuries sustained by young British women."

"I came by my interest in the legs of young British women quite natu-rally. An interest I know I share with a great many American men who find themselves stranded here in London during this unfortunate war. Right now I need to turn my attention to healing that firm young body of yours!"

"All right, Dr. Johnston, I can see, or maybe feel, that I am in good hands. But you seem to have forgotten your gross anatomy course. My knee is way down there, not way up here!"

Sarah laughed, and then said, "But please, Doctor, do continue exploring my geography. If I may be so bold to ask, what exactly are you seeking?"

Robert smiled, and said, "I am seeking "The True Source of the Nile."

Sarah responded, "No man has ever discovered that!"

Robert said, "Really? No man ever?"

"Well," said Sarah, "No man who lived to tell the tale!"

"That is dreadful!" said Robert. "How did the unfortunate fellow die?"

"He died with a big smile on his face," responded Sarah.

40

Inspector Dunbar

3 August 1942, London

Aaron waited at the site where Hannah had been injured. Amanda had asked Alice to join Aaron because their father, Captain Haythornwaite, had initiated the request to MI5 to ask Scotland Yard to look into the accident.

Inspector Dunbar arrived in an unmarked car precisely on time. He wore civilian clothes. A brown suit, white shirt, and thin brown tie. He was a tall, thin man, with a very pleasant personality, but the air of a scholar or engineer. Very professional.

After greetings all around, he set out to examine the scene. He had studied the hospital accident and injury report, which had been sent the day before.

"We are very fortunate that it has not rained since the incident, and that it did rain two days before the incident. The site should still be fairly presentable."

Aaron and Alice followed behind Dunbar, listening very carefully to his running dissertation.

"Here is the heavy rose bush hedge into which Miss Hanauer was pushed by the weight of the vehicle. The bush is still showing clear signs of the impact. There seem to be a few bits and pieces of her clothing still entwined in these branches."

Dunbar picked off the small pieces and dropped them into a large envelope. He then walked back a few paces, following some dark vehicle tire marks on the street and the sidewalk. Using his Kodak Medalist Navy camera, one of the best cameras of the day, he took a number of photographs.

"Judging from these tire tracks, I believe that the vehicle was larger than a car, but smaller than a truck. A van, perhaps. Miss Hanauer said that she noticed a small butterfly emblem on the hood. That would suggest an Austin. But the Austin is one of the most widely used automobiles in London, so the hood ornament doesn't help us to identify the actual vehicle."

Dunbar pointed to the road.

"We can follow these tracks backward, to the point where the vehicle first came up upon the sidewalk. Deducing from the fact of the vehicle driving up on the sidewalk, which is elevated from the street, the driver might have fallen asleep or been drunk or distracted by something. Or the driver was intentionally trying to hit Miss Hanauer."

He pointed back to the sidewalk.

"The tracks come up onto the sidewalk right here, just before the bush, but we can also see from the tread marks that the vehicle had made an earlier attempt to drive up onto the sidewalk six feet back from that the point where it just missed her. The sidewalk curb is elevated at the spot six feet back by a drainage hole. That is fortunate for Miss Hanauer. At the earlier spot, she would have been pushed into a very unforgiving stone wall and her injuries would have been more serious. Perhaps fatal."

Alice gasped. Aaron looked grim. Dunbar continued.

"If the driver had been asleep, or drunk, or distracted, then running into the raised curb at the earlier spot would have alerted him to the fact that his vehicle was leaving the roadbed. The driver, roused to the problem, would have immediately turned the wheels to the right to return the vehicle to the roadbed. But the tire marks clearly show that instead he turned the wheels hard left again to put the vehicle up on the sidewalk again, driving directly and purposefully into Miss Hanauer. His act was clearly intentional and designed with malice to cause grievous injury. That drainage hole probably saved her life."

Alice was now crying. Aaron was glowering. Inspector Dunbar showed no emotion whatsoever. He was just looking for facts.

"Let's now follow the tracks forward. Here we can see that, just before the vehicle drove off of the sidewalk, it clipped the edge of this ornamental stone post. The post shows marks where the vehicle scraped by. There are some green paint marks. I can scrape them off and have them analyzed."

"Inspector, I noticed back by the drainage hole, on the curb where the vehicle tried to make contact, there were several clumps of dark brown mud," Alice said. "Could that tell us anything of value?"

"Maybe. Let's have a look."

They walked back to the drainage hole.

"Interesting. That mud looks too heavy and loamy to be from normal city street traffic, and it does appear to have come from the tires of this vehicle. I will take these for analysis, as well. Good catch, Miss Haythornwaite. I missed that."

"Inspector, your observations tell us how this happened, but not *why* it happened," said Aaron. "Do you have any thoughts why the driver would intentionally try to kill or injure this young woman?"

"No. Not from the evidence in the report and the site inspection. The next step will be to interview the victim, to see what clues we can pick up. Let's try to do that next week. In the meantime, I will report our findings to MI5. They will probably offer some lines of inquiry for us to pursue. They clearly have some suspicions."

41

Sarah Meets Juan

10 August 1942, London

Robert and Juan met at 2:00 p.m. at The Savoy. Robert could tell that Juan was nervous.

"You seem to be on edge, Juan. Am I reading you wrong?"

"As each month passes, I feel more and more like I am being watched. It's very uncomfortable."

"I would like to understand what is going on, but first, I need to raise an important issue with you."

"Please do so."

"Your request that I meet with Gunther puts me in a tight corner. I cannot afford to put myself on a British Intelligence list of suspicious persons—or worse. I met with people at MI5 to get clearance to meet with this Gunther fellow. They have agreed, but *only* on the condition that a member of MI5 also attends the meeting. That is advantageous for Gunther because it will markedly improve the chances that the British Government will give serious consideration to his overture."

Juan frowned. "This constitutes a very high risk to Gunther, and maybe to me as well. We could both be arrested as spies. Gunther is a German army officer, who will be meeting with you here in London in civilian clothes. He could literally be shot at dawn."

"Yes, he could, but it is safer for him if he has cover. By meeting with MI5, he also has some measure of protection. He would not be the first, nor the last, German agent to come over here to talk about aspects of the war. The tradeoff is that MI5 will be hoping to learn a great deal from him. As I suspect you know, this is how this business works."

"So, Robert," Juan said. "Do you recommend this involvement with MI5? Gunther will want to know if you recommend it."

"I absolutely do."

"And can I meet the MI5 person first? A woman, you said?"

"You absolutely can. She is in the lobby. I'll ask her to come up right now."

"So, it is a 'she'?"

"This agent is most definitely a 'she.' You will be able to judge that for yourself. She is very impressive."

Juan nodded.

Robert called down to Sarah, who was waiting by the lobby phone, and invited her up.

"Juan. A warning for you. This young woman is very good. She will make every effort to turn you into a British double agent. She can be very persuasive."

A few minutes later, there was a knock at the door.

Robert opened the door to Sarah, dressed to kill, looking like a million pounds Sterling. He was taken aback. He had thought she would show up in her Navy uniform. Instead, she was outfitted in a chic, civilian summer dress with a sweater and a scarf. She had her light brown hair in a bob. And she was wearing high heel shoes. Robert had never before seen her in heels. They certainly accentuate her shapely legs. Robert glanced over at Juan, who looked quite surprised and impressed. This was not the "stiff upper lip" British MI5 Agent that Juan had imagined. Far from it. Both men required a minute or two to collect themselves.

After taking his "pause" to digest the vision of Sarah, Robert introduced them.

"Juan, this is Lt. Sarah Leach, a Special Agent for MI5."

Juan happily extended his hand. Sarah diplomatically shook it.

"Pleased to meet you, Agent Leach."

"Hello Juan. My pleasure. Please, call me Sarah."

The men sat down at the small conference table. Sarah made a beeline for the elegant sofa by the window, sat down with a big smile and crossed her legs.

Robert noticed the dress that Sarah was wearing was short for the present-day styles of London. He had never seen her in a skirt that short. And sitting down on the sofa in the short dress revealed her very shapely legs, which were further highlighted by the very fashionable high heels.

Robert saw right away that Juan had noticed and seemed pleased. The room brightened markedly.

"Juan, you have just arrived from Spain? I do love it there. Are you from Madrid?"

"I have lived in Madrid for the past ten years. It is a charming, beautiful and exciting city. But at this time of the year, it is always pleasant to find an excuse to visit London. Much cooler here."

They went on for twenty or thirty minutes, discussing the culture and history of Spain, and its rocky relations with England. Particularly in the days of Elizabeth I and Phillip II.

"Juan, your accent. Not Madrid. I'm picking up a Catalan flavor."

"You are good. I was born and raised in Barcelona. I am Catalan through and through."

Robert could see lights going on in Sarah's incisive mind. He watched Juan carefully to see if he was picking up on this. He was. But he was going along for the ride, curious where Sarah was headed. Both Sarah and Robert were well aware that General Francisco Franco, the current ruler of the Spanish state, had been brutal to the Catalan and the Basque people after the Spanish Civil War.

The Basque and the Catalan had sided with the Republicans, loyal to the Popular Front and Communists, who were defeated in 1939 by the Nationalists. The Nationalists, led by General Francisco Franco, were allied with The Fascists and Nazi Germany. How is it that Juan, a Catalan, is now living in Madrid, under the nose of Franco and his Nazi-leaning Government? Sarah wondered. She switched gears and moved onto the subject of Gunther. She probed for all the details. Juan seemed very forthcoming.

After a long discussion about Gunther, the talks meandered into the subject of Germany and the Third Reich.

Juan interrupted. "I was about to tell Robert this before you arrived, Sarah. I can now tell you both. The Gestapo people were very suspicious of my allegiance and my motives last year when I applied to visit London. But my boss in Berlin, Dr. Christian von Buckholtz, has many friends. So now the Gestapo has put on a guise of trusting me. And because of that, I have more windows into their methods, thoughts and objectives. These are very nasty and unpleasant people."

They both nodded in agreement.

"Dr. Christian von Buckholtz?" Sarah made a mental note of the name.

"Yes. That is his name."

"Please continue."

"The Nazis made some effort to appear reasonable in the early years of the Third Reich. Hitler was even named 'Person of the Year' by Time Magazine in 1938. But their true colors have become more evident in the past few years. Hitler and his inner circle have been brutal towards the Soviet people, the Polish people, and the Greek people to name a few. Their treatment of Jews everywhere is an international disgrace. They butter up the short-sighted French, both because they need their support at the moment, and because a high percentage of French people would prefer to be governed by the Nazis than by the Communists.

"But I also have experience with the German people. This evil pale that has befallen them has deep roots in the Fuhrer and his Nazi Party. If he could be pushed aside, and more sensible and decent people brought to power, I do believe that the future of Germany, and most of the world, would improve immeasurably. A sensible and decent Germany would and should be the driving force behind a thriving unified European community."

Robert and Sarah looked at each other and fell silent. Their thoughts blended.

Sarah broke the silence. "This is why you are willing to assist this German officer and his German superiors in pursuing a separate plan with the Allies to allow Germany to succeed in defeating the Soviets? Not a sound strategy for the Allies—to facilitate a divide and conquer strategy for Germany. Why would the Allies ever agree? There is nothing in that for them. Recent history has clearly shown that the Nazis are never to be trusted. None of them."

She paused and glared slightly at Juan.

"And probably not you, either."

Juan stiffened. He knew that he had to take this punch without flinching. He looked straight at Sarah, showing no emotion.

"I urge you both to focus on the simple truth that there are two sorts of Germans. They are not all of one mind. Some Germans revere and follow the Fuhrer. But plenty of Germans fear and loathe him. Take your pick. The elements in the Wehrmacht and other departments of the German Government who are pursuing the particular strategy are one-hundred-percent certain that the German army and its puppet allies, such as Italy, Hungry and Romania, will never defeat the Soviets, even if there were to be a separate détente with the Allies. The Soviet army, now swollen with hundreds of thousands of Asian troops, and increasingly well-armed by the U.S. and U.K. and supported by large numbers of new aircraft from the Allies, will overwhelm and destroy the German Army. The Soviets are already well on their way, and the Allies have not yet even opened a western front.

"Unless and until this absolute mad man, Adolf Hitler, is moved aside, there never will be a real Allied victory. Germany will be defeated, but the cost will be unimaginable. All sides will be losers. Maybe the U.S. will suffer less. Tens of millions of people will die horrible deaths, most of Europe will be devastated, and the entire western world will take generations to recover. It seems highly improbable that the effort to push Hitler aside can ever succeed without some meaningful assistance from the Allies."

Silence all around.

Juan and Sarah looked to Robert for his reaction.

"I am virtually certain that this effort cannot succeed, but we have little to lose by a meeting with Gunther, and possibly much to learn."

Juan nodded, and looked at Sarah.

"I suppose that is right, Robert. I will talk to others at MI5 to seek their advice and concurrence."

Juan wanted to smile, but knew it would be a big mistake. He froze his countenance with a silent frown.

As the meeting was beginning to unwind, Sarah asked Juan how well acquainted he was with the French Resistance. Robert understood as this was the lynchpin of her new assignment for MI6.

"I do not know very much about the French Resistance," Juan said. "I hear comments from Gestapo agents that there is no French Resistance worthy of their concern. The German soldiers occupying non-Vichy France devote a lot more time taking young French women to dinner and to bed than worrying about any so-called resisters.

"There certainly are some young resistance people in Vichy France. Quite a few of them are Jews. Mostly from Paris. Unlike their Christian countrymen, these French Jews know all too well that the German forces occupying half of France will most assuredly soon occupy the other half and pose a mortal threat to all Jews. Many sources tell me the Germans are determined to eliminate all of the Jews in Vichy. The Vichy government is already rounding up Jews. If you seek assistance from the French, French Jews are a likely source."

"Interesting idea. I will need to find an entrée into that group. Perhaps through one of the Jewish groups here in London."

Sarah stood up for a minute to stretch her legs, or maybe to show off her legs, brush off the one or two cookie crumbs, all to pull down her short skirt just a bit, and ensure that she was the focal point of Juan's attention (and Robert's). Somehow, when she sat back down, her legs crossed again, her skirt was even higher. She looked down at her exposed legs (as did Juan and Robert), thought for a moment, then continued.

"Juan, this has been an amazing meeting. Thank you for opening up to Robert and me. I am pleased that this unfolding encounter with Gunther will give us a chance to work together. But you have not told us very much about yourself. Your Catalan background? Your history? Your family? I sense there is a fascinating story there."

Robert noticed that Juan winced at the probe. He understood why Sarah was probing. She needed to know Juan's background to better ascertain his possible value to MI5 and MI6, but Robert also sensed that Sarah might kill the goose now laying some golden eggs.

Juan took the bullet head on.

"I live and work in Francoist Spain. I also travel frequently into Nazi Germany for business meetings. I am originally from Catalan country. For these reasons and a few others, I never discuss my Catalan background, my history, or my family. Never. It is known that I come from Catalan country. That is all they know. I can assure you, it is better that way."

Robert and Sarah locked eyes for a moment.

"Understood. Your discretion makes perfect sense." Sarah smiled at Juan.

Robert looked on with skepticism. Being Catalan put Juan even one step further from his alleged Wehrmacht contacts. Sarah was making her point. The Nazis must have some reasons to trust Juan. Some very good reasons.

"Interesting," Robert said.

Juan picked up on Robert's suspicions.

Sarah shook Juan's hand warmly, taking his hand in both of her hands. She looked into his eyes for a moment or two.

"Juan, have you been able to visit your family in Barcelona?"

She was still holding his hand. Juan was almost too mesmerized to respond. Robert watched this scene play out in awe of Sarah. He knew this was a trick question. If Juan said, "Yes," then that would show he was cozy with the Franco Regime and the Nazis, otherwise they would never allow a man with his anti-Nationalist history to make frequent trips into hostile Catalan Barcelona. But Juan, not thinking as he held Sarah's warm hand, responded, "Yes. Every other week."

Juan then said his farewells, and headed off into the night, leaving Sarah and Robert alone to ponder the meeting.

Sarah now took Robert's hand. She knew that she had been a little "unfaithful" with her warm and inviting overtures to Juan. But she also knew that Robert shared her mission. Business is business. And Spy Business is Spy Business. Body language opens doors. Juan is an exciting fellow, Sarah mused to herself.

"Robert, you are so amazing. Juan is a diamond! What a prize! MI5 will be very supportive. MI6 will be drooling!"

Robert looked down into Sarah's face. The meeting had taught him ten times more about Sarah than he and Sarah had learned from Juan. It seemed clear that Juan was playing for both sides. Robert wondered whether this "Gunther" person was aware of that. But Juan's playing both sides didn't come as a surprise. Double agents, by definition, are always working both sides. More surprising was Sarah. It is one thing to be attractive and charming and very bright. But quite another to be so quick and wily and focused as Sarah. She sliced and diced Juan like pickled relish. So, what does that make Robert? Chopped liver? Probably.

"You are very welcome, Sarah. It was fascinating and enlightening to see a very slick British agent in action. A Lady Sherlock Holmes. And those high heel shoes. A *brilliant* touch. Where did you get them? Shoes are so carefully rationed in Britain these days—and even in the US."

Sarah smiled. "Not mine, unfortunately. My mother borrowed these very beautiful black satin Spanish heel pumps from one of her well-to-do lady friends. They actually belong to the lady's daughter, who wore them to Queen Charlotte's debutante ball a few years ago. I thought they might get Juan's attention. Was I right?"

Robert frowned, but with a hint of a smile. "Oh yes. He too was 'drooling.' Just like your boys at MI6. Speaking of 'drooling,' how about some dinner at The Old Bell Tower?"

Sarah put on her pouty face. "Robert, why can't I ever make *you* drool?"

Robert put on his lawyer face. "Because Princeton men are well trained to *never* drool. Drooling is a sad affliction of Yale Bulldogs!"

Sharing a good laugh, they headed off together into the night.

42

Hannah Meets Inspector Dunbar

10 August 1942, London

When Inspector Dunbar arrived at the entrance of Queen Victoria hospital, Amanda was there to meet him. She escorted him to a small administrative conference room, where Hannah and Alice were waiting.

Amanda headed out of the office to find Aaron. Alice stood up to greet Dunbar. Hannah grimaced as she slowly rose out of her seat.

"Miss Hanauer. Sorry about your encounter. You still seem to be in pain from your injuries."

"Yes. The injuries from the bush seem to be healing well. I hope Dr. Solomon will have another look today. My problem now is with my right hip and thigh, when the car sideswiped me. Nothing broken, but painful bruises."

Aaron and Amanda arrived, and they all sat down at the small conference table.

Inspector Dunbar pulled out his notes and reports. He then proceeded to ask Hannah questions.

"Might be possible for you to stand up and let me look at the bruises on your hip and thigh? Discreetly of course."

"Yes, Inspector," Hannah responded.

Amanda helped Hannah pull up her skirt just enough to expose the thigh and hip bruises. They were surprised when the inspector pulled out a tape measure and measured the size and location of the bruises, and their distance from the floor. He then asked them to sit back down.

"I need to identify the vehicle that struck you. First let me show you some photos of hood ornaments. You said, 'a butterfly.' Did it look like this?"

Dunbar showed Hannah a photo of the hood ornament of an Austin.

"Yes, Inspector. That is it. I'm sure."

"An Austin. There are hundreds in London. Sizing up these bruises, it was at least a full-sized car, or more likely a van. Did it perhaps look like this?"

He held up a photo of an Austin 7 Ruby van.

"I think so."

"Based on the paint I scraped off the post, and my subsequent checks with an Austin dealer friend, was it the green and black model?"

He showed Hannah a photo of a green and black model Ruby 7 van with a commercial name on the side panel, "Edward Greg, Electrician."

"Yes. Yes. But I don't remember seeing a name or any writing on the panel."

"That is typical. Many buyers do not paint the name of their business on the side panel. Unfortunately, there are quite a few of these green and black Austin Ruby 7 Vans in London. Do you recall if it was damaged, or dirty, or personalized in any way?"

"There was some dirt, caked mud maybe, on the side that struck me. I say that because there was some caked mud on my dress where the van hit me."

"Do you still have the dress? Have you cleaned it?"

"I have it, but I am embarrassed to admit that I haven't cleaned it, mostly because it is now unwearable from the tears and dirt. I was keeping it to try to repair it, or at least reuse the buttons and some of the fabric."

"At your first opportunity, please bring it to me at the station." Hannah nodded her acquiescence, but was not thrilled to be giving up one of her very few dresses.

"Did you see the driver? Could you identify him or her? Did he or she say anything?"

"It was a man. Middle-aged. It was difficult to see his face. He wore a hat, pulled down, and thick dark glasses. The windows of the van seemed to have been shaded, or somehow darkened. There was so much commotion and distraction. I thought at the time that maybe he said, 'God damn you!' Something like that."

"And he did not stop? He just drove off? Was it clear to you that he knew that he had hit you?"

"He knew very well that he hit me. There was a loud thud, and the car bolted, and he glared right at me. And he just drove off."

For the others in the room watching and listening, Hannah recounted the events of her accident as though she had been a spectator, rather than the intended victim. Hannah just wanted to put it all behind her and move on. Being emotional would not help.

Dunbar was rapidly taking notes.

"This was certainly not an accident. The driver was lying in wait for you, so he must have known where you live. Then he intentionally tried to drive into you. Twice, actually. All that is very evident. What is not evident is *why*. When they asked me to look into this, MI5 speculated on the possibility that the driver was pursuing some anti-Semitic objective, which, if true, would be very embarrassing to the British Government."

This observation came as a shock to Hannah. It has never crossed her mind that this incident could be the result of fervent anti-Semitism. How could anyone possibly know her well enough to make that connection?

"Miss Hanauer, do a many people know that you are Jewish? Are you involved somehow in Jewish activities that might have aroused animosity or anger—vengeance at this level? Even if the driver is totally deranged, it all seems incomprehensible."

Amanda, Alice, and Hannah all looked at each other.

"It is possible," said Amanda.

Aaron looked dismayed. He had already heard some of this story from Amanda.

Amanda then spent the next hour analyzing and describing their activities over the past two years. Everyone in the room, most particularly Aaron, was now focused on the fact that Hannah had been stirring up a hornet's nest in London.

"Miss Hanauer, your activity could fill in the missing pieces of this puzzle. Nothing stirs righteous indignation like the arrival of foreign immigrants, particularly immigrants who look and talk a bit different from a country that is a mortal enemy, and especially those who come to criticize. Even King George 1 of Hanover, Brunswick-Luneburg, Germany, was not popular when he arrived in London in 1714 to become King of England upon the death of Queen Anne.

"You seem like a very nice young person, Miss Hanauer, and it is not my place to comment, but it would be best for you to maintain a low profile for some period until people and things calm down."

Hannah hung her head for a few minutes.

"Thank you, Inspector Dunbar, for your help in sorting this out. You are absolutely right. My unrelenting pursuit of the European and Jewish refugee problem is creating enemies, and clearly some of them are telling me to sit down and be quiet. I should follow their advice and your advice and do exactly that."

Amanda and Alice were sitting on either side of her, and each of them took one of her hands.

"However, Inspector, here is my dilemma. The British people have been very forthcoming in their efforts to provide wide ranging aid and assistance to the refugees now flooding Europe, and they have my deep gratitude, but there remains an ocean of effort to be done to make a meaningful impact on the enormous refugee problem.

"There are now probably over 3 million European refugees, and this number probably includes 600,000 Jewish refugees from Germany and Austria. Their suffering and dislocation, starvation and sickness are almost beyond comprehension. And my own family may be among them, if they are even still alive.

"I am a very small voice. But I must continue to speak out. This enraged and deranged driver had one bite at the apple. He missed. Now I will be watching for him. I won't be such an easy target the next time.

"I have been thinking more about what that driver said to me. I am now so accustomed to speaking and hearing English that my ear was tuned to hear his words in English. But now I am virtually certain that he spoke in German, not in English. And I think he actually said, "Gottverdammt Judin!"

These words, spoken by Hannah in harsh German, hit Aaron, Amanda, and Alice like an electrical shock. They all looked at Hannah.

"What?" they said in unison.

Dunbar's earlier observation about an anti-Semitic attack hit home. It also registered with Hannah. This was no accident.

43

A Visit from Big Bill

25 August 1942, London

A few weeks after the meeting with Juan, Robert was sitting in his office, perspiring. It was a very warm day, and he was wearing a woolen suit, a vest, a white shirt and a tie. But it was not just the heat. He was nervously awaiting an important visitor from the U.S. A visitor who was always welcome, always charming, and always a very big challenge.

Kathleen Scott tapped at the office door and stuck her head in with a big smile. She knew she was bringing news that would make her boss happy.

"Your guest is here, sir. If you don't let him into your office right away, I think he might break down the door!"

"I'm quite sure that he would do just that. Please show him in."

Kathleen showed Big Bill Donovan into Robert's office, and then couldn't resist chatting with him. Most people found Bill Donovan magnetic. While they spoke, Robert took a long look at him. A tall, ruggedly handsome man about to turn sixty, Donovan was truly bigger than life. A heavily decorated veteran of the Fighting 69th Irish Division from the Great War, a former U.S. Assistant Attorney General for Civil Rights, an unsuccessful candidate for the Governor of New York and a very trusted confidant of FDR. And now Donovan was heading the OSS. He was a man with many talents, a man with many friends and many enemies. But Robert greatly admired him.

"Big Bill. In person, no less. To what do I owe this great honor of a personal visit?" They shared a big handshake, and Donovan gave Robert a hug.

Donovan laughed. "Well," he said. "I do have some good reasons to be here. My *first* reason for being here is that they are trying to arrange another lunch for me with King George VI. Me. Irish Bill Donovan. This just shows that these Brits will do anything to strengthen their ties with my now-famous Columbia Law School classmate, FDR. My *third* reason to be here, is to have dinner with the Prime Minister. My *second* reason to be here, right after lunch at Buckingham Palace, and right before dinner at Checkers, is to have tea with Attorney Robert Johnston. In *fourth* place, by the way, is my hope to visit with my son David who is on active duty in the Mediterranean."

"I don't want to disappoint you." Robert picked up the phone. "Kathleen, could you please bring in some tea? Make it high tea, please. My guest is a big, thirsty and hungry fellow."

Robert smiled and looked at Donovan. "Want some wine, or maybe whiskey?"

"No. Thanks. I am still an Irish teetotaler. Robert, I am very sure that you have some interesting news for me. But I have some interesting news for you, so let me start. You know that Churchill flew to Moscow on 12 August to meet with Joe Stalin. Let me give you some color. You know already that they each hate each other, and they both know that they hate each other, but the Mad Hatter German Fuhrer has now brought them together."

"Long story short, Churchill had to tell Joseph Vissarionovich Stalin, The Secretary General of the Communist Party and Prime Minister of the Soviet Union, that the Allies were not going to launch an invasion of France in 1942. Joe claimed to be highly surprised and upset with that news, but that is nonsense. Joe knew very well there would be no Allied invasion of France this year. August would be much too late. Any invasion of France must be launched in the spring. So, all these half-baked schemes in England to prepare for a '42 invasion should stop."

"I hear you, Bill, but there do appear to be serious invasion preparations underway."

"I know. I know. But it is nonsense. A lot of talk. Mostly from us Americans. Maybe in the spring of 1943. That is a remote possibility, but most likely not happening either. We just do not have the men and equipment in place. Nor do we have the training and the command experience yet. We need more time. More troops. More plans. More equipment. More training. And the Germans have not yet suffered sufficient losses on their Eastern Front to make the invasion achievable. Maybe spring of 1944."

Robert broke in again. "Can the Russians hold on that long?"

"Stalin cannot surrender, so he won't. If he were to surrender, he wouldn't survive a week. The Germans have now launched their full on frontal attack on Stalingrad. It began with a massive Luftwaffe assault on the city on 23 August. By all reports, it was horrific. Incredible loss of life—mostly civilians. But our Russian friends tell us that Stalin had and has no intention whatsoever of pulling civilians out of the city. He believes the Germans mean to take Stalingrad block by block, house by house, person by person. The loss of civilians, who Stalin intends to arm, will be catastrophic, but so too will be the losses to the German army.

"The Germans are going to have to pull divisions and logistical support from other theatres of their eastern front to bolster the Stalingrad effort, but their chances of success at Stalingrad are slim. Very slim. In order to further cripple the Axis forever, the Allies will soon open a second front, but *not* in France. Not yet."

Robert asked, "Where? Italy?"

Donovan thought for a minute. "Most likely Italy because its fate is tied to North Africa. Let me fill you in on the North African campaign, which have some very encouraging developments for us."

"Bill, before we leave the subject of the German invasion of Russia, there is a related issue on which I would definitely appreciate your guidance. From our days in Berlin before the war, and from our many discussions of global issues in The Room, you and I both still have contacts there. One of my major clients was Gleiss GmbH. Their chairman, Dr. Christian von Buckholtz, became a good friend. We are still in some contact.

"Last year, in mid-November 1941, von Buckholtz contacted me through one of his Spanish employees. A fellow named Juan Frederico. Frederico came to see me to alert me—and hopefully to alert the right channels in England—that a very high-ranking Nazi would be coming to England in hopes of connecting with George VI to seek his assistance in pursuing a separate détente agreement with the British. His story sounded incredible but just two months later it turned out to be true. The high-ranking Nazi turned out to be Rudolph Hess, the Deputy Fuhrer of Germany. And Hess did want to meet with King George to present a separate peace deal with Great Britain.

"The Hess mission failed miserably, but now according to Frederico, there do appear to be a number of senior officers in the Wehrmacht who are convinced that the Russian campaign will surely fail and they apparently want to move Hitler aside to allow for a new German Government to make sensible peace agreements.

"They seek British support for their effort. Frederico now wants me to meet with a young German officer who supposedly represents these dissident channels."

"I'll tell you, Robert, that story is very interesting. We are picking up the same signals from other German officers who connect with us in Switzerland. In my personal view, some sensible peace discussions are much to be desired. But the president and the prime minister want nothing but vengeance on Adolf Hitler and on Emperor Hirohito. I must warn you, Robert. You could put yourself into considerable jeopardy meeting with this Nazi officer in London unless you have cover from some official British agency here."

"Agreed. I have been working with MI5 on this. They are not particularly interested in any separate peace negotiations, but they believe that they can glean a great deal of very useful information from both Frederico and the officer. They had previously assigned an MI5 agent, who is also an MI6 agent, to work with me in order to help develop a U.S. Intelligence capability. She was then assigned to join me for the August 8th meeting with Frederico. It became clear that she was more interested in digging into Frederico than she was in training me. Maybe these intelligence people are not all that intelligent!"

Donovan laughed. "She? This MI5 and MI6 agent…is she *Delilah*?"

"No. Her name is Sarah. WRNS Lt. Sarah Leach. I actually know her pretty well."

"Do you, Robert? Is Lt. Leach the daughter of British Royal Navy Captain Benjamin Leach, highly regarded in British Naval Intelligence? And is she a favorite of my nemesis, Major General Sir Stewart Graham Menzies, Chief of MI6?"

"Yes. That is the lady. Lt. Sarah Leach."

"Well, my Princeton Tiger friend, that lady is Delilah. Her MI6 *code name* Is Delilah. I am told that Menzies himself picked that name for her. The Brits are not always keen on female agents, but Menzies seems plenty keen on this one. I think they are wrong to be lukewarm on female agents. I plan to employ a number of female agents. If you didn't know her code name, maybe you do not know her as well as you think you do."

"Probably not," Robert smiled sheepishly. "She certainly has her dark passages and mysterious alleyways, but she is a gifted intelligence officer. Smart as a red fox and quick as Caithness rabbit. I regard her highly. Perhaps your 'frenemy' Menzies is more clever than we thought. Delilah is a delicious code name for her."

"I would like to meet her one day, Robert, if you would be willing to share. I am told that Menzies assigned her to connect with French Resistance, and I intend to do that myself."

"She would relish meeting you," Robert said but thought to himself, *no way is Donovan going to meet Sarah.* His extra marital affairs were no secret.

Donovan paused. He was thinking about something. He poured himself a little more tea.

"Run with this Gunther meeting. It might bear some fruit for us. I am a little confused on one point. This Sarah Leach is assigned to the Gunther meeting by MI5? What about MI6? If the Gunther meeting is important, why not MI6? Menzies could easily bring the Gunther message to the prime minister."

"I guess because Gunther will be in England, that puts the meeting under MI5's domain. Lt. Leach seems more comfortable dealing with MI5 Chief Petrie than she does dealing with MI6 Chief Menzies. But you are right, Menzies definitely has more swat with the PM. No one really knows why, but I have a theory. It all seems to be top secret, so I do not want to surface my theory just yet, not until I gather additional evidence."

"Good, Robert. All very interesting. Keep me plugged in. And let me know when I can connect with WRNS Lt. Delilah. In the meantime, let me return to the pressing subject of the North African campaign. There's one Top Secret I can share with you today. It was a good move for the British War Council to replace General Auchinleck with General Montgomery. The British must now hold the line in Egypt at Alam

El-Halfa, some little unknown place about twenty miles west of Alexandria. Monty is digging in there to defend Egypt at all costs. And we know that Rommel is on his way. What Rommel *does not* know is that we Americans, having lost patience with watching others fight our battles, have now resolved to enter the fray in North Africa in a major way, through the back door.

"The U.S. operation, called Torch, is very hush-hush, but likely to take place in a month or two. It will probably be under the command of Dwight Eisenhower. His star is rising very fast. I don't expect rapid success because our troops are as green as broccoli. But this North African strategy will put heavy pressure on Spain and Portugal, and eventually Vichy France, and Italy. It is a *big deal.* Anyway, keep it to yourself."

"Interesting news. Very interesting news." Robert pressed Donovan for more information on Operation Torch.

"Before you head off," said Robert. "I was wondering if you or Ruth have seen or heard from Ellen? I try to talk to her every other week or so, but the conversations are a bit strained."

"Ruth did have a lunch with Ellen several weeks ago. She seemed okay, for the most part. Ruth does like her a lot. Any chance that you two might get back together?"

"Probably not while this war is still raging. Unless I pull out of London and return to the U.S. She did not approve of my German contacts in Berlin before the war, nor does she approve of my continuing involvement in this shroud of military intelligence secrecy and intrigue. It is antithetical to her nature. I feel my work here is valuable in helping to end the war. She feels that I should return to sea duty on a destroyer somewhere. Maybe someday she will relent and forgive me."

"Most Americans disapprove of this nasty spy business."

Donovan sat quiet for a moment, looking at Robert, then spoke again.

"Maybe Ellen has a point here. It was fine before the war when you and I were members of our little club of international lawyers or businessmen sharing foreign intelligence and picking up on clues in our so-called Room Meetings. But these days London is crawling with military brass from the four corners of the globe. Are you now feeling somewhat out of place as a New York lawyer in a fancy suit?"

Robert said, "I hadn't really thought much about it, but I guess I have become something of a fish out of water."

"Robert, I would like to offer you a commission as a full Commander in the United States Navy. Not on a destroyer, but here in London. Given the nature of your work here, it could be a useful cover for you."

Robert considered the offer. "I do like the idea, but I would need to continue my work for my law firm on the side. The house I'm living in and the office I work in is owned by my firm."

"You can do that on the side. We all keep one hand in our professional connections. The Commander rank would be essentially a brevet—a recognition of your invaluable military service in your current work. A Navy Commander serving in Naval Intelligence can be as valuable to his country as a Navy Commander commanding a U.S. Destroyer. Think about it. No rush."

"Would I report to you?"

"Indirectly, but formally you would probably report to Eaker. Robert, I need to run. I am off to a dinner. Great to see you again."

Bill extended his hand and they had a warm handshake.

After Donovan departed, Robert sat thinking about the repercussions of becoming a U.S. Navy Commander. It might help to resolve Ellen's strong adverse reaction to him staying in Britain. And he would feel more a part of the Military team, which he did love and admire. He also wondered what Sarah would think of it. All in all, it was a very welcome offer. Donovan had read Robert very well.

44

The Battle of Alam El-Halfa

30 August - 16 September 1942,
South of El Alamein, Italian Libya

On the night of 30 August, British Army Captain Thomas Leach was in his M3 General Grant tank surrounded by his small regiment of forty-six cruisers and eight close support tanks, part of the British 7th Armored Division. They were all watching as the German 15th and 21st Panzer divisions began their penetration of the British VIII Army southern flank. Rommel's grand objective was no secret. Rommel planned to envelope the British VIII Army before the arrival of substantial Allied reinforcements, and then proceed rapidly into Egypt and take control of the vital Suez Canal.

Sitting on his tank perch, where he could see the action under a bright moon, Tom reported down to his tank crew.

"This is quite a sight. Just as General Montgomery anticipated, the Germans and the Italians are attacking in our Southern sector, which Monty intentionally left weakly defended so that the enemy tanks would fall into his trap. Which they did. Now our RAF *Fairey Albacores* are illuminating the German tanks, and our *Vickers Wellington* medium bombers are blasting the hell out of them. Their tanks will be in our range in about twenty meters. We will weigh into the battle ourselves, and then we will fall back to pull the Germans into our heavy defenses on Alam El-Halfa. I think they will pay a heavy price once they get there."

Shortly thereafter, the 7th Armored Division moved in, inflicted heavy casualties on the Axis Forces, and then withdrew to allow the Axis forces to become overextended.

Midday the next day, the 15th and 21st Panzer divisions, with a total of almost 200 tanks, and reinforced by 250 tanks from the Italian armored division, ran smack into over 700 British tanks defending the ridge. On 1 September, the German tanks found themselves without fuel as the Royal

Navy had somehow located, and then sunk, the Axis tanker bringing in fuel from Sicily.

The next day, 2 September, Rommel, lacking fuel and air defense, elected to withdraw. Tom and his brigade attacked again. Meanwhile, the more powerful 5th New Zealand Brigade advanced in force until they were stopped by a staunch Axis defense. The New Zealanders withdrew on 4 September. The Axis forces, now completely unsuccessful in their initial attacks, all returned to their original base. The battle of Alam El-Halfa was over. Egypt was saved.

On 6 September, James drove his armored vehicle up to Tom's tank. Tom climbed down and sat next to James in the front seat.

James said, "Casualties and losses in this "Seven Day War" were high on both sides, but for the first time in the North African Campaign, our tank losses were not disproportional compared to the Axis. We lost about seventy tanks and they lost about fifty. Thanks to the RAF, the Axis suffered a loss of four hundred transport vehicles."

"James, we are fueled and full up on ammo. Ready to go. The Krauts seem to be in disarray. Why are we not being ordered to attack? Seems like the time is ripe to push them back. Way back."

"Monty doesn't see it that way. He intends to hold our forces right here, for now."

"What? Really? Why?"

"His reasoning is sound. Our assignment at Alam El-Halfa was to defend Egypt and the Suez Canal from a massive German assault. Against high odds, that is what we did. At relatively low cost to us, and very high cost to the Germans and the Italians. We were in a good position to hold a defensive position. Monty seemed to have a sixth sense for Rommel's tactics, which enabled us to thwart Rommel's attacks. We also had a significant advantage in air forces. And as you could see from your tank positions, the Panzer divisions are short on supplies, particularly fuel."

"James, Monty is wrong. Dead wrong. He will spend years defending this lame decision. We could end the North Africa Campaign here and now."

"No, Tom. If we send out our tanks now to pursue him, we will run into Rommel's anti-tank screen. The RAF can see their defenses. In the past, that has cost us dearly in tank losses. One of those lost tanks might be yours. We have many new units and new equipment and lots more on the way here. But right now we are nowhere near ready for a major offensive. We need some time to regroup."

Tom was getting red in the face. "This is *not* the British military tradition. We should be pushing our advantage by attacking."

James was very calm. "Tom, settle down. Look at the big picture. The Germans had their one big chance to take Egypt and the Suez Canal. They failed. The chance of them ever being in a position to do so again are nil, particularly because their sea and air superiority over the Eastern Mediterranean is in sharp decline. Rommel has not gone very far. He is digging in again at El Alamein. Our best guess is that he would really prefer to dig in even further west, to shorten his supply lines from Sicily, and get closer to his Axis air bases. But probably the Fuhrer and Mussolini overruled that move, again for political motives. So, you can tell your tank crews to stand down, and rest up. We will go for Rommel once we build up our forces."

Tom was unconvinced. He looked very unhappy. "I don't see it that way at all. But I am just a lowly lieutenant so I will have to follow orders. Our tank crews will be disappointed to be put on a leash. We have not forgotten the licking we took at Gazala."

"I know, Tom. But you just need to hold on. We'll get our chance."

"I'm not so sure. But one more question, James. We all participated to varying degrees and from different vantage points in the firefights over the past seven days. Some of us wondered how it was that Montgomery seemed to be aware of every Rommel tactic in time to plan a specific and well-coordinated defense and counterattack. Have we now been kicked in the pants so many times by the Desert Fox that we can read his mind? It is almost creepy."

"I agree with you. It is creepy. But I cannot answer your question. I do have some suspicions. We'll talk later. I have to get back for a staff meeting."

The division medical officer drove up next to them.

"Colonel. I just stopped by to check up on Lt. Leach."

"Check up on him? Tom, were you wounded? I didn't know you were hit."

"We were helping out the 5th Indian Infantry Division. I picked up some shrapnel from an exploding anti-tank shell. But is hasn't slowed me down."

"Tom, you did not report this. I would have seen the report. "

"I did not. I did not want to miss the great British fox hunt."

"The fox hunt is postponed. The Fox is scurrying off to El Alamain to lick his wounds." James turned to the army medic, "How severe are these wounds?"

"I cleaned them yesterday and removed all shell fragments, but I asked him to check into the field hospital to keep an eye out for any infection. Several of the fragments were deep, and the fragments took some shirt shreds into the wounds, which are hard to remove. Why we like to watch these wounds for a few days. He refuses to go, as he just told you."

"Tom, go spend a few days in the field hospital. You won't miss any action here. We are not going anywhere this month, and Rommel is sure as hell not coming back here."

Tom felt let down, but he figured that in view Montgomery's decision to Stand Down, he could take a few days off. So, he glumly nodded his agreement.

James smiled. "If anything were to happen to you, your big sister would kill me. And unlike the delicate big sisters of the vast majority of all you spoiled little Cambridge University boys, *your* big sister is fully capable of killing me and might even relish the opportunity because I haven't written to her in a month. So, please, go take care of those wounds. That's an order, Tom. Your sturdy Grant tank will be here waiting for you."

Tom got out of the Grant and watched as James drove off to his meeting.

Then Tom slowly climbed into the jeep with the medic, and they headed off to the field hospital. As they drove off, Tom thought that he was very lucky to have a cool head like "Big Brother James" keeping an eye on him. And he felt very proud that his small tank regiment had a role to play in the historic Battle of Alam El-Halfa, the Battle of the Empire, which saved two of its Empire Crown Jewels—Egypt and the vital Suez Canal.

45

Aaron Takes on Hannah

18 September 1942, London

Hannah returned again to Queen Victoria hospital for a checkup with Dr. Solomon. With Amanda at his side, the doctor carefully probed the skin wounds, now almost entirely healed, and the hip and thigh bruises, which were better, but still a little tender to his touch.

Hannah still felt self-conscious about Dr. Solomon touching and probing her skin and parts of her body that no man had ever seen and certainly never touched. She was also conscious of the fact that this man touching and probing her was a handsome young Jewish doctor, who she found interesting in a number of dimensions. So perhaps she regretted just a little that her wounds were healing.

"You are healing well, Hannah. You can get dressed now. Come back here after you've dressed, please. There are a few things I would like to discuss with you. Amanda, please join us if you can."

"Of course, Doctor."

Hannah and Amanda returned and Aaron escorted them to one of the small conference rooms to talk.

"Hannah, I do not want to overstep my boundaries. I am only your attending physician. But as your attending physician, I must have your physical wellbeing as my foremost concern. I do agree most strongly with the advice that Inspector Dunbar gave you. You are putting your personal safety at risk by being so outspoken on these refugee resettlement issues. I sympathize fully with your deeply felt concerns. And as a Jew, I stand with you.

"As a Jew living in England, where I was born and raised and trained as physician, I should also confess that I have a deep love and respect for the British people. I believe that these people have reached out to European refugees in general and Jewish refugees from Germany and Austria in particular with much more concern and sympathy than most of the rest of the world. I think that we should give credit where credit is due. The British people have their own country to defend, and their own people to protect. And the pressing needs of this brutal war to consider.

"They did reach out to take you in, and take care of you and thousands of other German Jewish children. So, Hannah, if some aspect of your activities here in London has set off such a strong reaction that someone now seems determined to cause you grievous bodily harm, it is time to step back and assess the situation."

Hannah was listening intently. Respectfully. She remained silent. Aaron was scoring some points, but she had no intention of withdrawing from the game. Aaron turned his attention to Amanda.

"I'm very sorry to bring you into this discussion, Amanda. But it does seem that the two of you, and Alice, and now me, are well intertwined with this situation. If we three are not part of the solution, then we are part of the problem. And the welfare of this very fine young woman is the price we might pay if we are not part of the solution. There are strong anti-Semitic undercurrents in this country.

"To further complicate the situation, Hannah is not British by birth. She does speak very elegant English, but people do know that she is German, which can only further influence the reactions of Brits to her comments. A toxic brew.

"I am sure you have heard about incidents where German Jewish refugees have been ushered out of London bomb shelters. I do not know if there is any truth to such stories, but they do paint a picture."

Hannah looked thoughtfully at Aaron, and then responded carefully, "Dr. Solomon, I have personally experienced being ushered out of a London bomb shelter. It was very unpleasant. But in that process, I did meet a very nice American lawyer, who personally led us all to a safe place. A very impressive gentleman. He took charge with the air of a military officer, and the perception of a senior barrister. That was two years ago, during the Blitz. I am quite sure that he has long since forgotten the incident, but I shall never forget it and him. I do hope that our paths cross again.

"More importantly, do you have any specific suggestions for us to ameliorate the negative effects that I am generating? As I told the inspector, this mission is too important to me to just abandon it."

After listening thoughtfully to Aaron and Hannah discuss the situation, Amanda spoke up.

"Doctor, your observations are accurate and your advice is sound. But I have seen Hannah in action many times. It is unlikely that she will ever withdraw from the field entirely. Maybe we can convince her to back down for a while. I have noticed that when I am with her, the adverse reaction seems more constrained, and that when both Alice and I are present the attitude is much improved. Maybe there is strength in numbers? For the next meeting, let's all four of us attend."

"All four of us?" Aaron asked. "Who is the fourth?"

Amanda looked right at Aaron.

"You, Dr. Solomon. You should be our fourth. The presence of a man, and a Brit, and a medical doctor, would help to verify our *bona fides*. Will you join us? Please?"

Aaron considered Amanda's suggestion. He did not smile and appeared to deep in thought. Then he took a long, hard look at Hannah. Her face softened, just a little, and then offered a hint of a smile. That in turn triggered a smile from Aaron.

"*Yes*. The Three Musketeers, plus one new Musketeer. But let's also agree, Hannah, that you will tone it down. At least try not to criticize the British people or government. Focus your wrath and frustration on the refugee problem itself and seek solutions."

He smiled at Hannah and offered his hand to shake on a deal. Hannah looked back at Aaron, took his hand, and shook it.

"I agree. Doctor's orders!"

They all laughed.

Amanda noticed that Hannah and Aaron were not shaking hands. They were now holding hands.

46

Arctic Convoy PQ 19

26 September 1942, London

Robert arrived at MI5 Headquarters early for his meeting with Sir David Petrie, the Director General (DG), in hopes of catching a few moments with Sarah before the meeting. Robert laughed to himself upon seeing the MI5 headquarters in the old MGM building on St. Jones Street. Instead of a "MI5" sign on the front door, the only identification of the top-secret organization so widely feared and respected, and so critical to the war effort, was a large sign announcing "To Let." A clever ruse.

Once admitted, Robert was pleased, but also a little surprised, to find Sarah sitting serenely at her desk.

"Sarah. I expected you would be out kissing frogs on your new assignment."

"Hello, Robert," Sarah said with a big smile for Robert. It was clear that she was eager to see him and to have him come straight to her office before the meeting. A nice compliment.

"My sweet mother told me that kissing frogs can cause facial warts. So, I broke the habit. I got a call last night from DG Petrie, asking me to be in my office this afternoon for a possible meeting with you and him. Has he told you the purpose of our meeting? He did not tell me."

"Nothing. And he did not tell me that you would be joining us."

"My sense is that he intends to talk with you first."

"He's the boss. If he does not call you into our meeting, I will stop back and tell you what I can."

Robert headed on down the hall to Petrie's office.

"Robert, thank you for coming on such short notice to our stately and elegant London headquarters."

Petrie laughed. He came across as a quiet and thoughtful man. Probably more focused on organization than sleuthing. Genial. Somewhat the opposite in many ways from Menzies at MI6.

Robert laughed too. "Happy to be back at MGM. Hoping to be cast in the sequel to *The Wizard of Oz*. I'm a good fit for the Cowardly Lion."

"Not far from it, actually. But not the Cowardly Lion. We are in need of the Wizard himself, a role you often fill so well!"

"I do my best."

"Here is the issue. Convoy PQ 19. Code for the 19th Convoy from Iceland to Russia. Today's crisis involves this Convoy which is currently scheduled to sail from Iceland to Russia, carrying a significant supply of armaments to the USSR. '*Is it to Be or Not to Be, That is the Question.*' The President of the United States and Joseph Stalin insist that it "Be" but the British Admiralty and British Prime Minister insist that it 'Not be!' The PM's office has asked MI5 to see if we can work through U.S. Military Intelligence to make Great Britain's grave concerns clearly understood in Washington. I'm afraid that the situation has become a very sticky wicket.

"Before I can get into the details, which you will require to succeed in this request, I do first need your thoughts on a related internal political British intelligence wrinkle. This request came directly to MI5 from several members of Churchill's staff. No problem with that. This is a creative department.

"But the ever-mercurial Chief of MI6, Stewart Menzies, will not be happy to hear that this request came to MI5 rather than MI6. He is very 'turf conscious' and tries to spend time with the PM every day. That is another story for another day. Anyway, it would be helpful if we could bring Menzies into the loop, in a low-key way, to avoid 'a dust up!' He does not like your Bill Donovan, as I'm sure you know, but I suspect that you will need Donovan to get the right message to the president. I was thinking that the easiest way for us to get Menzies on our side is to bring in Lt. Sarah Leach. Nobody can handle Menzies like Lt. Leach. He thinks she walks on water. Would that be alright with you? She is here today, just down the hall."

"I am always happy to have Lt. Leach assigned to work with me. Unlike Menzies, I do not think she walks on water. I have actually seen her do it!"

Petrie laughed.

Sarah was then invited into the meeting. Petrie brought her into the loop.

"We received a request from the PM's office, and we need you to bring Menzies onto the playing field in a way cleverly designed to keep him out of the ball game."

Sarah smiled and nodded. Robert and Petrie looked at her for confirmation.

"Understood," she said. She knew that her feet were about to get wet from the water she was about to walk upon.

Petrie continued.

"Last October, about four months after the Germans launched their 'surprise' invasion of the USSR, the PM promised Stalin that we would send a convoy every ten days to the Soviet Arctic ports to deliver 1,200 tanks a month in this year, and 2,000 tanks a month next year, plus an additional 3,600 aircraft. Most would be sent from Iceland. But our most recent convoy, PQ 18, sustained heavy losses. The next scheduled Convoy, No. 19, will need substantial protection by the Royal Navy. Well enough. But, as you are both aware, the Americans are in the final planning stages of a major amphibious assault on French Morocco in about one month. That means that a major portion of the British fleet will have to sail south to defend the enormous U.S. invasion fleet which will be sailing from the U.S. to Morocco. To make matters worse, our critical intelligence capability to track and determine the location of enemy aircraft and U-boats operating in the North Atlantic seems to have diminished in recent months, which only further increases the need for British warships to defend these convoys. Do not press me for further details on that particular point. That particular intelligence capability falls into Menzie's Shire, not mine. In any event, that piece of the puzzle is somewhat irrelevant to your current assignment.

"The Soviets are fighting off a major German offensive at Stalingrad, the outcome of which will surely have a major impact on the outcome of the war. President Roosevelt is adamant the PQ19 be sent to the Arctic as promised, but we cannot send our ships to protect that convoy whilst at the same time send our ships to protect over 500 Allied ships required for the invasion of Morocco. We simply do not have enough warships. Roosevelt and Stalin are both furious, and Churchill is stuck in the middle of a huge mess."

Robert and Sarah looked at each other with that "why me?" expression.

"Robert, our reliable Wizard, we need your help. We need to get our message through to the White House loud and clear and now. Can you help us?"

Sarah and Robert glanced at each other, which did not escape Petrie.

"Sir David," Robert said. "I understand what you require. I will make some calls as soon as I get back to my office to set up some consultations with the administration in Washington."

"It seems we can always count on you to handle things. Before you begin those consultations with Washington, I suggest that you get more and better details and specifics on our fleet logistics, so you can persuade your people why it is absolutely impossible for us to both escort QP19 and the U.S. Fleet during the next thirty to forty-five days.

"Lt. Leach, is your father the right man for Robert to contact on this?'

"Probably. Ironically, my father did tell me that he had a very long conversation last month with his old Navy friend, Captain Spencer Haythornwaite, when Haythornwaite was asking our assistance in investigating that possible anti-Semitic attack on a young German Jewish lady immigrant. My father said that they spoke for almost two hours, during which time Captain Haythornwaite gave my father precise details of fleet dispositions, all the while expressing amazement and also grave concern about how thin our fleet are being stretched. Maybe Robert could talk to both of them?"

"That will work. See if your father can set it up. Haythornwaite is a naval aviator. He is very solid. Please be sure that they both know that this matter is 'Top Secret.' It would be a huge problem if this disagreement between London and Washington were to leak. Can you also plan to meet with Menzies sometime this week? It is 'double urgent.' I checked. He is in London this week."

Petrie was now looking at Sarah for some feedback on "The Menzies Problem," which he wasn't getting. So, he pushed her button again. "Sarah, handle Menzies as you see fit. You are much better at that than I have ever been. You are free to tell Menzies I received a visit from Jock Colville and Eric Seal, Churchill's secretaries who are known to Menzies, to request that both MI5 *and* MI6 try to set up a back-channel line to the

White House to better convey the Prime Minister's concern on this messy dispute. Jock and Eric know me better, so they came here first. I assured them that MI5 could consult with MI6."

"I understand, sir."

"You might also suggest to Menzies that maybe our mutual friend Robert Johnston could be very useful in this. Let it be Menzie's idea to use Robert, and then ask him to tell the PM personally. However you choose to handle Menzies, be sure that he agrees to our Robert Johnston back channel plan because we have already set it in motion!"

They all laughed at that.

"Good plan," agreed Sarah. "I will execute it today."

On the way out of Petrie's office, Robert and Sarah stopped into Sarah's office. She closed the door. She looked at Robert.

"The Chief just told us, 'Our critical intelligence capability to track and determine the location of enemy aircraft at U-Boats operating in the North Atlantic falls into Menzie's Shire.' Guess what else falls into Menzie's Shire?"

Robert smiled. "Bletchley Park! The Center of British Code Breaking activities."

"And the 'recent loss of our capability?'"

Robert frowned. "The Germans switched codes!"

Sarah smiled. "Bingo! Robert, you are a fast learner!"

Robert smiled. "I have such a *good* teacher. Do you now have 'Need to Know' regarding British code breaking efforts at Bletchley Park?"

"Absolutely not. Not even close.

But I can connect the dots!"

47

Two Royal Navy Captains

1 October 1942, London

Robert and Sarah arrived in separate cabs at the Haythornwaite home. They both made a mental note that the stately home was beyond the realm of affordability for a captain in the Royal Navy. Spencer Haythornwaite had married well, as was often the case with British naval officers.

They were greeted at the front door by Pamela Haythornwaite with Amanda and Alice. The two young women sensed that this was an important meeting – very hush, hush—and so these two attractive guests now at their front door must be persons of importance. Robert looked distinguished in his navy blue suit, crisp white shirt, and blue-and-white striped tie, every bit the well-heeled and well-connected American lawyer and U.S. Navy veteran.

Sarah was in her blue WRNS uniform. She looked like she had walked out of a poster advertising for young British women to join the WRNS. Although their fathers were old friends, the three daughters had never met.

Sarah observed Alice and Amanda, wondering which of these classic British beauties would be the best fit for her little brother, Tom, if and when he ever returned from pitching the horrible Huns off of the Barbary Coast.

The three Haythornwaite ladies escorted their guests into the study, where Captain Haythornwaite and Captain Leach, both in civies, awaited them. The Haythornwaite's impressively large gramophone aptly suited the well-decorated room. The lively song "It Don't Mean a Thing (If It Ain't Got that Swing)" by Duke Ellington was playing at a low volume, foreshadowing the meeting that was to follow.

Captain Leach gave his daughter a big hug. It was evident that he was immensely proud of her. If Captain Leach was aware of the very close relationship between Robert and Sarah, he did not give a clue.

These were two very impressive, knowledgeable and warm spirited gentlemen and Robert was very glad to have an opportunity to meet with them together privately.

While Leach was visiting with his daughter, Robert spoke to Haythornwaite.

"An honor to meet you, sir."

"Hello to you, counselor. This honor is mine."

Robert was most keen to meet Captain Leach, Sarah's illustrious father. Sharing a warm handshake, Leach spoke first.

"Mr. Johnston. Good to meet you at last. My daughter sings your praises, and she is very hard to impress."

"Everyone in London sings your praises, Captain Leach, but your daughter is the Mezzo Soprano!"

After a few minutes of chatting, the three Haythornwaite ladies excused themselves and then Captain Haythornwaite opened several large navigation charts, showing channel and sea areas around Britain, and also around the western Mediterranean Sea.

"I will try to give you a quick overview. Digging deeply into the weeds on the subject of British Navy deployments would take us six months.

"The British Royal Navy is probably the largest and strongest navy in the world. I say 'probably' because the U.S. will overtake us soon. The Royal Navy has fifteen battleships and battle cruisers, seven aircraft carriers, sixty-six cruisers, one hundred and sixty-four destroyers, and sixty-six submarines.

"These charts show approximately where the ships and subs are deployed today. Spread very thin over a large area. And, of course, there are many more of our ships and subs deployed to the eastern Mediterranean Sea and in the Far East."

They spent the next hour and a half getting into details.

Haythornwaite continued. "Part of our problem is that the Royal Navy, at the start of the war, was very well equipped to fight conventional surface engagements with enemy combatants as we've been doing that for hundreds of years. But these days conventional warfare is now only part of what we need to be doing with our Navy. We are not especially well equipped to deal with U-boats. We are holding our ground, but barely.

And we are not especially well equipped to extend our airpower with our carriers. Our ability to successfully land and support our troops on enemy shores is also very limited. And of course, since the war began, our losses have been very heavy."

Robert then spoke. "I can certainly see now the extent of the overstretched and over-extended Royal Navy problem from the UK perspective. Ironically, what I am lacking here is the US perspective. Is this proposed Operation Torch so large in size and scope as to require substantial Royal Navy protection?"

Haythornwaite responded. "Oh yes. Operation Torch in North Africa is proving to be an enormous endeavor. It will require very significant protection from the Royal Navy to succeed. We are told that the Americans had first planned to invade North Africa somewhere east of Gibraltar, probably near Tunis. But that involved a risk that Franco might then be pressured by Hitler to allow German troops to cross Spain to invade Gibraltar. Our guess now is that the Americans will instead attempt to land at Casablanca, Morocco. Right here." He put his finger on Casablanca on his chart. "We do know that their landings will use three battleships, *Texas*, *New York*, and *Massachusetts*, plus twenty or more cruisers and destroyers, and many troop ships.

"Casablanca, itself, is formidable. But no one knows how determined the French defenders will be. The French are still plenty upset about the British, attacking and sinking portions of the French fleet in Mers-el-Kabir at Oran, in Algeria, and Dekar. But we had to keep those ships out of the hands of the Axis.

"Fortunately, there are no German troops in Morocco, as far as we know. But you can be sure that the Germans will arrive promptly. It will be a hard slog for the Americans to fight their way east from Morocco to Tunis with so many unseasoned troops and unseasoned commanders. We shall see."

"I take the point," said Robert. "We can ill afford to have the first major US foray into this war be a failure."

The three Haythornwaite ladies brought in some tea and biscuits. Pamela said, with a big smile, "Oh my. Just look at all these huge crinkly charts. This study is starting to look like Ye Olde Map Shoppe down on Wilbury Street."

Amanda laughed. "Pease don't criticize, Mother. Father is planning our next family cruise!"

Alice added, "We had better take our life jackets. There might be a few German U-Boats lying in wait!"

Another laugh. They stayed for ten minutes and then all left the room.

Watching the Haythornwaite daughters, and admiring them, Sarah began to think that Alice might be a good match for Tom. She had so much sparkle. After further discussion of Royal Navy deployments, Captain Leach broke into the discussion.

"Robert, for you to be truly prepared to venture into this debate with your colleagues in Washington, it is only fair to give you the rest of the story. The major debate between London and Washington on this issue is both timely and appropriate. The British Government is clearly correct, as you now plainly see, that the Royal Navy does not have the resources to provide an adequate defense for Operation Torch *and* this Arctic Convoy at the same time. But let's look at the overall war situation from the global perspective.

"The outcome of the war with Germany will probably hinge on the outcome of The Battle of Stalingrad, which is now well underway. The combined strength of Germany, Romania, Italy, Hungary and Croatia at Stalingrad will, we estimate, total over 1,000,000 men, 700 to 800 tanks and maybe 1,500 aircraft. All of their finest units. Ranged against those Axis forces will be well over 1,000,000 Russians, over 1,000 tanks and probably over 2,000 aircraft.

"By comparison, Operation Torch will involve maybe 120,000 U.S. troops and probably zero Germans for the initial stages. If Operation Torch fails, it will be a painful black eye for you Yanks, but far from a mortal blow. If the Germans win Stalingrad, it could free up the bulk of the German army to turn its attention once again towards England.

"We know that last year, 30 or 40 percent of the tanks used by the Soviet army were supplied by Allied convoys. We did give them almost 500 tanks last year alone. Our *Matilda MKII* and *Valentine* tanks were not as good as the Soviet *T-34* tanks, but they were pretty darn good, and they were there. This year we believe that the Soviets now have over 10,000 tanks, and that probably a quarter of that number was provided by Allied convoys.

"Last year we provided them with 700 aircraft. Mostly *Hurricanes* and *Tomahawks*. This year we are increasing our supply. The Soviets claim otherwise for their own internal political purposes, but they are heavily dependent on these Allied convoys to defeat the Germans. So, we abandon these convoys at our peril. That is the dilemma we all face."

Everyone sat in silence, digesting their biscuits and these weighty considerations.

Robert broke the ice. "Thank you, gentlemen, for this stirring and troubling explanation. It now seems that I have my marching orders. Hopefully, the Royal Navy can take a quick respite from the grind they encounter while escorting critical convoys, in order to help Operation Torch, and then turn their attention once again to assisting our Russian allies. Convoy PQ 19 is vitally important, but it is only one of many convoys. Operation Torch is one of a kind, and if successful, it will open an entirely new chapter of the war. It cannot be allowed to fail. I will head back to my office to make some urgent phone calls to Washington."

They all stood up to shake hands and say farewell. Sarah held her handshake with Robert just a little longer than necessary. And she looked at him. Silently.

Captain Leach walked over to Sarah.

"I do love seeing my widely admired daughter in that crisp Women's Royal Naval Service uniform. But I hope that my wonderful daughter is *not* planning to marry the Royal Navy! Your Mother and I do not want our grandsons to be little destroyers!" he laughed.

Sarah looked just slightly annoyed.

Captain Leach pressed on. "I can see why your favorite tank corps Lt. Colonel persists in calling you, "Our Little Brown WREN in Navy Blue!"

A hearty laugh by the two Navy captains. Robert knew that he had better not laugh at that remark.

"Thank you, Father, for reminding me that Lt. Colonel James does sometimes have a very annoying sense of humor. Let's hope that he leaves that not-very-clever term of endearment back in Egypt on his next visit to London."

She gave her Father another big hug. He knew he was forgiven for 'crossing the line.'

Sarah and Robert soon stood outside the Haythornwaite home, alone together after Captain Leach climbed into his car and headed home.

"I am going to my office, to make those calls. Do you want to come with me, in case I need someone to help me remember all of the facts that I am still processing?"

"I will join you on the condition that you buy me a nice dinner afterwards."

"That would be both an honor and a pleasure!"

As soon as they arrived, Robert placed a radio telephone call to Bill Donovan. He had prearranged the call yesterday.

"The government here is very concerned that the views of the British Admiralty, the British War Cabinet and the British prime minister, all on the subject of Royal Navy support to both Operation Torch and PQ 19 at the same time, are not being adequately conveyed to the White House. They are hoping you can clear the fog. I am sitting here with Lt. Sarah Leach, who was assigned by MI5 to help me get the facts straight. Lt. Leach says that it is all male ego head butting."

"Yes, Robert," replied Donovan. "I am well aware of the difference of opinion on this. Give me what you can, but first give my regards to 'Delilah' and tell her that I do hope to meet her in the next visit to London."

Robert conveyed the message to Sarah, and then rolled his eyes and shook his head, to convey "No way!" Sarah smiled. Robert then spent the next two hours summarizing deployment issues regarding the British fleets. Sarah piped in from time to time.

When they finished, Donovan said, "Leave it with me. Lt. Leach is correct. This entire contretemps sounds more like a clash of aroused male egos than a well-considered difference of opinion. The answer is obvious. We are sure as hell not going to jeopardize our troops and our fleet just to deliver more tanks to Grumpy Joe. Lt. Leach, thank you for helping us to sort this out. You women always seem so capable of discerning and managing male ego problems."

Sarah smiled. "Probably because we women had to spend 100,000 years negotiating with you men for a few scraps of meat around primordial Homo sapiens campfires!"

Big Bill laughed and they finally hung up.

It was almost 8:00 p.m.

"Robert, am I going to get that dinner you promised me? I am a hungry cavegirl!"

"Yes, *if* after dinner you come to my home and take off that annoying WRNS uniform, which reportedly excites all those lonely British tank commanders, so that I don't feel like you are spending time with me just because it is one of your MI6 official assignments."

Sarah thought quietly for a moment, to be sure she had Robert's attention. Then she said, slowly, "I will gladly come to your home after dinner and take off my uniform, which actually excites only one particular British tank commander, who is, by the way, easily excited. And I will gladly take off even more if you wish. But at the moment of truth, when our passions run deep, I still reserve the right to whisper into your ear, "For God and My Country!""

48

The Association of Jewish Refugees

15 October 1942, London

Hannah, Amanda, and Alice were seated towards the back of the room, waiting for the meeting to begin. None of them were members. The Association of Jewish Refugees in Great Britain (AJR) was a relatively new group. The audience did include a number of AJR members, primarily older Jewish men, all dressed in dark heavy woolen suits. Some others in the audience, including a smattering of women, seemed to be there out of curiosity about this new organization. Hannah, Amanda, and Alice found themselves staring at the door, looking anxiously for Dr. Solomon. They were holding a seat for him.

When Aaron did walk in, all three stood up and waved their arms. He saw them, looked around the room and nodded at a few familiar faces. He sat down in his seat with a broad smile. It was clear he felt comfortable in the room and with his little group of attending young ladies. Others noticed them. The four were twenty years younger than most attendees. Two of the young women, Amanda and Alice, appeared to be Knightsbridge or Kensington Londoners, dignified and well-dressed in the fashion of the day. The third young woman, Hannah, was striking in the severity of her Continental attire. Dr. Solomon had his usual dignified air and professional bearing, notwithstanding his relatively young age. The other attendees seemed very pleased to have this impressive foursome in attendance.

The meeting got underway, addressing the usual problems. The large number of European Jewish refugees. The sad state of affairs of most refugees. The origins of the refugees. The problems entailed in finding a country to admit the refugees. The need for concerted government efforts to address their many problems. The need for money for assistance. The widespread lack of such efforts.

Hannah and her three supporters were very impressed with the AJR. Its efforts were focused on representing German and Austrian Jews by addressing the reality that most of the refugees would never return home. War or no war. Their best hope for a future would be in English speaking countries. Therefore, all AJR meetings were always conducted in English.

There were a number of speakers. Their focus was a disturbing litany of events since the beginning of the war.

Ernst Gottfried Lowenthal was the main speaker and moderator. This tall, handsome young German Jew was born in Cologne. Trained as an economist, he was now becoming a journalist and author in London, working to aid German Jewish refugees.

"We have grave concerns that the British government and press are blind to the fact that Nazis atrocities are *targeting* Jews. We note that the British Government White Paper published two years ago was entitled, *Concerning the Treatment of German Nationals.* The title excluded the Jews. The treatment of German Nationals? Ridiculous! Most 'German nationals' are treated just fine, thank you very much. It is the German Jewish nationals who are being mistreated. Why isn't the paper entitled "The Mistreatment of German Jews"? I am a journalist. How would it be if I were to write an article on the horrible bombing of Coventry with the headline, "Falling Objects Damage some British Property!" One has to wonder why there was no specific reference to the Jews when they have been the principal target of the Nazis. But in fairness to the British Government, they probably do not want to support German propaganda, which now promulgates lies that Britain is fighting the war just to save the Jews. The British Government also fears more foreign pressure on Britain to admit more Jews into Palestine."

A number of other current topics were discussed by a panel of speakers. A lengthy question and answer session followed. Toward the end of that session, Hannah raised her hand.

As Hannah stood up to speak, Amanda and Alice both looked at Aaron, their eyes pleading, *Can you stop her?*

Aaron was looking at Hannah with a proud smile on his face. He had no intention of stopping Hannah. He was anxious to see her in action. He subtly nodded his head to her as if to say, "Go get 'em!" She picked up on the signal and gave him a quick smile in return. Then she turned very serious and spoke—slowly and deliberately.

"What each speaker has said here today is enormously enlightening. The work of the AJR in this past year has been encouraging. But I have heard some recent reports which are disturbing. I wonder if it is possible to bring more pressure on the British Government to take greater action regarding Jewish refugees and the Jews *still* in Germany and Austria and in Nazi occupied areas? This group of refugees is enormous. They are in an impossible predicament. They have no way out. Their living conditions are generally miserable. There are a great many women and children. Small children. Hungry children. And as each day passes, they have less and less hope. We are their hope. You. You are their hope.

"Earlier this year we heard reports from Russia, Germany, Poland, the Netherlands and Belgium of mass murders of Jews. This February we heard from the Jewish Agency that millions of Jews would soon be killed. This summer, the World Jewish Congress reported that the Nazis plan to 'exterminate' all Jews under their control. And now there are many reports that France is also turning on its Jews, even in Vichy France.

"Just last week we learned that British Lord Chancellor, Lord Sim, reported to the British House of Lords on the Nazis persecution of Jews. He called for the establishment of a United Nations Commission for the Investigation of War Crimes. That is a noble effort, but that process will take many years and will not save many lives. For hundreds of thousands of these Jews, maybe for millions, time is running out. Or has already run out. And my parents and my brother are among them. According to some reports, the Nazis are gassing thousands of Jews to death! If we are unwilling, or unable, to rescue these people very soon, there will be none of them left to rescue!"

As was so often the case when Hannah spoke, some members of the audience loudly applauded. Some quietly applauded. Some sat in silence, glaring at her, as if to say, *This is not our problem. We are doing all we can do. And who are you to be lecturing us?*

Aaron observed that the diversity of their reactions largely reflected the British public reaction to the refugee problem. Some felt annoyed that yet another German generated problem was being dropped on Britain. Others felt that people who are suffering need help, no matter the cause. But Aaron was also deeply moved at seeing this young Jewish woman speak out so forcefully to defend her people. His people. He could plainly see that Hannah was making enemies, mortal enemies, in this very room, on this very day. But she was right. Dead right.

After Hannah sat down, Aaron took her right hand. He held on tightly. She was shaking a bit. Almost crying. He said, quietly, "Hannah, you dropped a bombshell here today. Thank you for having the courage to speak out. You have certainly enlightened us. The entire world is ignoring this enormous problem. The enormity of the horror is too big to grasp."

Hannah then put her left hand on top of Aaron's hand. She looked at him, and said, "It is so nice to have you with us here today. Thank you!"

After the meeting ended, as people trailed out the door, many said thank you to Hannah or waved. Others appeared ready to approach Hannah with a word of criticism. But seeing four handsome young people standing closely together scared them off.

Hannah and Aaron stood spellbound, their hands still together. It did not escape the notice of Amanda and Alice. They could see and feel the electricity between them. A strong, personal bond rapidly grew. If the foursome was hoping to sneak out quietly, that strategy did not work. The main speaker and moderator, Ernst Lowenthal, made a beeline to meet them.

He turned first to Hannah. "Young lady, a pleasure to say 'hello.' May I have your name?"

Hannah smiled just slightly. "Yes, Hannah Hanauer."

Then Lowenthal introduced himself to Aaron, Hannah, Amanda, and Alice.

"And, please also allow me to introduce one of the founding members of AJR, Adolf Schoyer, a Berliner by birth and a recent arrival into London."

Aaron was aware that Schoyer was an immensely important German industrialist before the war and an Orthodox Jewish leader.

After the introductions, Schoyer cleared his throat. It was his signal that he wanted to speak. Everyone was silent, awaiting his words. Schoyer looked at Hannah and Aaron, still holding hands. Then he spoke, quietly, with considerable authority.

"Aaron, you said. And Hannah. Your close bond and your message here today do bear historical Biblical overtones. Aaron, for whom you were aptly named, was the founder and head of the Israelite priesthood, and with his brother Moses, led the Hebrew people out of Egypt. And Hannah, after whom you were wisely named, the seemingly barren wife of Elkonah, who, after her prayers and vows to Yahweh, the God of the Israelites, then bore Elkonah six children. Together, you two make quite a team. Clearly fate had a hand in bringing you together, and in bringing you to us. We're living in unprecedented times, therefore the insight from younger generations can give us better answers than we could provide ourselves. Ernst, we had better note well their message today. As we have seen throughout history, fools who fail to note the somber warnings of Biblical prophets are doomed to suffer Biblical retribution."

49

The Battle of El Alamein – Setting the Stage

20 October 1942, Egypt

James drove up and spotted Tom as he and his tank crew were removing tons of waste material from under camouflage netting. It was twilight and as the sun was setting in the west, the golden red sands of the desert stretched out as far as the eye could see. Long shadows highlighted the height of the dunes. It was an ocean. An ocean of sand. James gave a shout out to Tom. Tom smiled and jumped in the front seat of his Jeep.

"Tom, if I weren't your biggest fan, I would put you on report for being out of uniform. No shirt, in shorts, dripping with sweat. You might be mistaken for a Berber day worker."

"Before you turn me in, please tell me what we have been doing out here in the burning desert heat for the past three weeks? Three weeks ago, we all spent days placing empty crates and cans in the camouflaged storage sites, and now we are spending many more days removing all the trash and empty cans we put in. The rest of our unit has been building flimsy pipelines, which will blow sky high if we ever actually use them to transport fuel, disguising our tanks as supply trucks and nailing up plywood covers on our Jeeps. This is crazy making! Does Montgomery want to kill off half of his Tank Corp from heat exhaustion before the battle even begins?"

"Hopefully not. This is all part of Operation Bertram. Monty is taking some pages from Rommel's playbook. We want Rommel to believe our attack will come in the south in late November. In fact, we plan to attack very soon, in October, at his northern flank. Your wish has been granted! We're attacking! Monty thinks we have a real chance at El Alamein to deal Rommel a mortal blow.

"For the first time, we outnumber Rommel two-to-one in troop strength, tanks and anti-tank guns. We also have air superiority. But the Germans and Italians are very well-dug in, behind extensive mine fields.

Maybe our most significant advantages are their severe lack of fuel and ammunition. And also maybe the astute intelligence we are somehow picking up on their strengths, weaknesses and strategies from sources I can only guess at. We also have a great advantage in field artillery pieces, coupled with Montgomery's field artillery expertise, and the RAF. Nothing knocks out tanks in the open desert like aircraft. If all else fails, this time their 500 tanks will be sitting ducks."

Tom broke in. "We had air superiority in spades at the Battle of Alam El-Halfa, but they backed off from fear of the Luftwaffe. My guess is that the Luftwaffe haven't flown home to Berlin."

James looked at him. "There will be Luftwaffe aircraft over the battlefields, but for reasons we do not entirely understand, their planes always tend to focus on aerial combat, rather than trying to knock out our tanks and gun emplacements. We expect to begin our attack in two or three days, which will surprise the Germans and Italians. Rommel's last hope is that the Germans win a swift victory at Stalingrad to free up troops, planes and supplies to send south through Transcaucasia to threaten Iran and the Middle East. That would force us to move our troops north to protect Iran. Very unlikely, but possible, I suppose."

James stopped talking. He could see that his comments had struck a chord with Tom, and that Tom was deep in thought with a bit of a scowl on his face.

"You sound optimistic for once, James. I hope you are right. Britain has suffered defeat, after defeat, after defeat. The fall of France. The retreat from Dunkirk. The loss of Singapore. High losses in the Atlantic. Barely holding on in North Africa. We need a victory. We need a victory right now. At El-Alamein."

Then it was James' turn to dig deep into his own thoughts.

"Yes, Tom. You are correct. We need to turn the tide. Right here. For once, the odds are in our favor. If I don't see you before the attack, jolly good luck. Keep your head down if you can. Casualties on both sides will be brutal, but we desperately need a British Army victory over the Axis forces. My bet is that it happens right here, and very soon!"

50

The Battle of El Alamein –
Operation "Supercharge"

2-11 November 1942, El Alamein, Egypt

Tom was sitting next to his tank, talking to his crew. It was 1:00 a.m. on 2 November. A clear night, plenty of starlight illuminating the desert sky.

"It is very hard to believe that this battle, which began with our massive attack on the German-Italian positions back on 23 October, is still far from resolved ten days later. The German defense has been very tough. And Rommel wasn't even here. He has been ill. When they did fly him in, their defenses got even tougher. Five days ago, on 28 October, Rommel made his first counterattack, using the 15th and 21st Panzer Divisions. It failed. We finally got some good news. Three nights ago, the 20th and 26th Australian Infantry Brigades launched a major attack intended to break through the German and Italian line, reach the coast road, and cut off elements of the enemy forces. The night before last they finally did break through. The Germans and Italians are now forced to withdraw, opening an opportunity for us to break through all of their defensive positions, in force, which we have been unable to do for the past ten days."

"What's our next move, sir?" asked one of his crew.

"The 1st and 9th British Armored Brigades will lead the charge. In about thirty minutes, Monty will open up with over three-hundred field artillery guns, and then we move out with British and New Zealand infantry units. Our initial target is Tel el Aggier. Good luck to all of you, and to all of us!"

Forty-eight hours later, Tom and his brigade were still in their tanks, pushing forward very slowly. Early on 3 November, the 5th Indian Infantry Brigade launched a major attack. By the time the Indians broke through to Tel el Aggier, the Germans had turned tail and suddenly began a major withdrawal. The Axis tank force was by then reduced to 30 tanks. The desert was littered with the burnt-out remains of the rest of the Axis tanks. Overhead, the RAF had complete control of the skies. In the week that followed, the Axis forces perfected their full retreat, while the British Army floundered, unable to effectively attack and destroy the depleted Axis forces.

Early on the evening of 11 November, James was able to reconnect with Tom.

"Tom! You appear to be alive and well. Are you and your crew ready for a little rest and relaxation?"

"Not exactly. We rearmed and refueled, and we were hoping to mop up the remaining fragments of Germans and Italians. Why were our orders changed?"

"Rommel lost The Battle of El Alamein. In dramatic fashion. Perhaps even a loss of Shakespearean or Wagnerian proportions. All in all, the Germans and Italians probably suffered more than 60,000 casualties and lost virtually all of their tanks. The RAF had its finest moment since the Battle of Britain. And you and your tank brigade scored a resounding victory! Congratulations!"

"There are droves of shattered German and Italian tanks strewn for miles all over the desert," said Tom. "And plenty of dead bodies. And we have taken thousands of mostly Italian prisoners. But we missed our golden opportunity to close the trap and finish the job."

"We did. You are absolutely correct. Rommel saved his best for last, pulling off an absolutely stunning retreat. We know from captured Germans and Italians that both Hitler and Mussolini ordered Rommel to remain in place and fight to the end. He did just the opposite. Using all of his remaining fuel and tanks and motor transport, he and his troops are heading west at maximum speed. Amazingly, he abandoned the Italian infantry, most of whom we captured. According to the information gleaned from the captured Italian officers, Rommel and the remnants of his army are now headed in the direction of Tunisia. Almost 1,500 miles to the west of this battlefield. I suspect that Rommel will not go that far. Mussolini will not let him abandon Libya, so he will be ordered to dig in there first."

"Has there been any accounting of our losses? From what I could see myself, we lost hundreds of tanks, and thousands killed, wounded and captured. It was our first major victory of the war, but it was a costly victory."

James got up out of his jeep, straightened his sunglasses, and pulled a small piece of paper out of his pocket. He looked at it, with a sour look on his face. Then he spoke, nodding his head in agreement.

"It was costly to us. Very costly. Ironically, it was like a huge chess match on a great desert chess board. We traded pieces for pieces, but we had many more pieces to trade. So, we won. And there is another irony. Just three days ago, about 120,000 US troops invaded Casablanca, and they are in the process of wiping up the Vichy French units there. Those flaky French never seem to know what side they are on. The Americans will soon be heading east from Casablanca to Tunisia. Not all good news. Tunisia is a German fortress with 50,000 troops there now. More are coming through Italy. Rommel and his remaining forces will soon join them. Rough terrain and German and Italian airfields nearby. Sicily is very close. The American troops and their commanders are inexperienced, and the Yanks gave their best tanks to us, the new Sherman and M4 Grant tanks. Their remaining tanks, the old General Lee and General Stuart tanks, are inferior. So, The Battle for Tunisia will be a real challenge."

"A *real* challenge," agreed Tom. "The old M3 General Grant and General Lee tanks have very adequate seventy-five millimeter guns, but the way in which they are mounted limits the gun swivel to about fifteen degrees. A big disadvantage in a tank battle. The new M4 tanks are much faster and more mobile. The Sherman tanks are even better but we are only now receiving them. Our old Stuart tanks have only the smaller thirty-seven millimeter guns, and relatively light armor. We do need to replace them."

James weighed in again. "Our tanks are able to hold their own against most of the Panzers here, and they are generally much better than the old Italian tanks. And we are now receiving more and more M4 Grants and Shermans. Anyway, the Battle of El-Alamein is now over, with a happy ending.

"It could have been a much happier ending. The simple truth is that our Generals Alexander and Montgomery were caught totally unprepared and surprised by the speed, efficiency and scope of Rommel's retreat. We had his army in a deadly trap, and he eluded us. Again. He is indeed a Desert Fox. Very unfortunate. Our usually fearless RAF Desert Air Force suddenly became very cautious, fearing the expected appearance of strong counterattacks by the Luftwaffe that have yet to appear. We've gone into a defensive mode again, and Rommel has bought time for the Germans. Many, many months of time. And the time will be used to take many, many Allied lives. Including, perhaps, yours and mine. Not good. This Rommel Escape reminds me of General George Washington's midnight escape in August 1776 from the British Army under our General Cornwallis, with Generals Howe and Clinton, at The Battle of Long Island. That British military fiasco, which Generals Alexander and Montgomery, and all of the rest of us, studied in War College probably caused England to lose the American Revolutionary War. After being defeated by the British, General Washington ferried his 9,000 remaining troops with their wagons, horses and cannons, across the East River into Manhattan under the dark of night.

"But Washington and the Americans escaped the British with only those 9,000 Colonial rag-tag troops. Rommel has escaped with 80,000 elite highly experienced German soldiers, and will eventually take them all the way to Tunisia, where they will make life miserable for the inexperienced US forces. But for Rommel, the Battle of El Alamein is now in the books! Done. Recorded in history. The Nazis' absolute worst army defeat ever. We can only hope that an even worse army defeat awaits them in the Battle of Stalingrad."

Tom and James stood quietly together. Side by side. Both in their khaki uniforms, looking off to the west, towards Tunisia and their personal future rendezvous with their American allies, and their forthcoming battle with the Germans and the Italians. Both wet with perspiration and dusty from the sand and wind. Both smiling as they felt the warm glow of a much-relished victory over the Desert Fox. They watched the sunset over El-Alamein.

On hearing of the British victory in the desert at El-Alamein, Churchill said, "Now this is not the end, it is not even the beginning of the end. But it is, perhaps, the end of the beginning."

51

Two Vichy France Generals

15 November 1942, Casablanca, Morocco

French Brigadier General Marie-Emil Antoine Bethouart and Major General Maurice-Marie Salbert_stood on the roof of the French Army headquarters in Casablanca, assessing the events of the past week and the extent of damage to the city. Standing with them were five young French army lieutenants, listening respectfully.

General Salbert was not a tall man, but at age fifty-six, he was wiry and muscular. He spoke rapidly, and was not hesitant to display his impatience and skepticism for the rapidly changing situation in Morocco.

"It strikes me as almost inconceivable that this huge US fleet of over 300 warships and at least 500 transport ships with well over 100,000 troops sailed all the way from the US, across the entire North Atlantic Ocean, all the way to Western North Africa, unseen and unbeknownst to the mighty German Kriegsmarine, which has several hundred U-Boats on patrol in North Atlantic, day and night, and the Luftwaffe which has hundreds of flights over the area. Those facts are very disconcerting and not particularly reassuring for the future success of Nazi Germany. Control of the North Atlantic and the Mediterranean is critical for the Axis.

"The Allies overwhelmed our Vichy French forces here in Casablanca in two days. Once again, the French Army suffered a major defeat in short order. Where is Joan d'Arc now that we need her again!"

General Bethouart, a tall, elegant man, with a serious bearing, was a Great War veteran and light infantry commander. He spoke with authority. His style was more deliberate than Salbert, more measured. More cerebral.

"It is also suspicious and disturbing that our own Admiral of the Fleet Francois Darlan, the Supreme Commander of all French Armed forces, was in Algiers exactly at the time of the Allied invasion. Then he is conveniently captured by French Resistance fighters in our own ranks and promptly turned over to the Americans. Darlan is now issuing orders to the Vichy French forces here to join the Allies, contradicting Petain's Orders from Vichy France to fight on the side of the Axis. A set of facts simply too incredible to believe. It is as though our German *allies* intentionally set us up for this defeat. They have never trusted us. They have *never* given us up-to-date armaments and supplies. We are still using WWI tanks. We *never* get adequate training. We have *very little* air support.

"Now the Germans will have to send their own precious troops to defend North Africa, the same second-rate German soldiers who are now occupying Vichy France. The French Army and Navy have to make some tough decisions. Where to throw our support? To *which* side? And *how*? And *when*?"

Salbert listened thoughtfully, with a very unhappy facial expression. Then he looked at the ground, shifted from leg to leg as though impatient to leave.

"Antoine, I have to leave for a meeting. Please meet me in my office at 4 o'clock. There is someone you will want to meet."

Salbert made his departure and walked briskly down the stairs. Bethouart remained, gazing out at the still smoldering city.

Later that afternoon, Bethouart walked into Salbert's office and was surprised to find Henri d'Astier de La Vizerie there. Henri d'Astier was a tall, thin, young French resistance fighter. His appearance was more academic than military, but he spoke with great intensity and confidence.

"Henri, what a pleasant surprise to find you here in Morocco. We have been hearing wild stories about your adventures in Algiers. Did you and Jose Aboulker really arrest General Alphonse Juive, the Commander of all Vichy troops in North Africa, and Admiral Francois Darlan, the Commander-in-Chief of the Vichy Military in Algiers? The stories are so incredible."

Henri, hands on his hips, gave a hearty laugh.

"We did, part of our plan to use the Vichy French resistance to support the Allied invasion in Algiers. Our small force of 400 French resistance soldiers took command of a number of key facilities in Algiers, as well as seizing Juive and Darlan. And it worked. The Allied forces found very little resistance from the Vichy soldiers. Darlan and Juive were released to the Americans the next day, and Darlan struck a deal with General Eisenhower to negotiate a surrender. The very same devious Darlan who just three days earlier surrendered our Vichy French forces to alllow the occupation of Vichy France by the Germans and the Italians.

"Darlan has now put all Vichy French officers, including the two of you, in the position of deciding which side you will fight for. It was a pleasure to arrest Darlan. I personally know that he is a fascist-sympathizing, political weasel. British and American public opinion will be outraged to hear that General Eisenhower struck a deal with Darlan. But I suppose the Allies had no choice. It is clearly counterproductive to the Allied cause to be fighting with and killing Frenchmen when the only way for the Allies to get to Germany is through France. Suffice it to say, the French people have now seen for themselves two glaring facts: the German invaders are very nasty people, and the Axis Powers are now destined to fail."

Salbert, with his usual impatience, spoke first.

"How can you be confident of a German defeat? Aside from some setbacks in Egypt, they have enjoyed an impressive string of military victories."

Listening closely, d'Astier considered his response. Before he could respond, Bethouart, more deliberate and thoughtful than Salbert, said, "I am not sure what you mean by 'destined to fail.' They may well fail here in Morocco, but their position on the continent of Europe seem very secure. So, I must ask, what do you know that we do not know?"

Henri responded, "My two brothers, Emmanuel d'Astier de La Vizerie, the former head of intelligence for the French Navy, who you probably do not know, and Francois d'Astier de La Vizerie, the French Army General who you probably do know, have been keeping me well informed and up-to-date on the military situation on the German eastern front. Both of my brothers have reliable ties into the British MI6.

"They tell me the German Army is in a perilous situation. After a long summer of fighting, the three objectives of the entire German campaign, the Caucasus, Stalingrad and Leningrad, are all still held by the Russians. Hitler's chief of staff, Halder, was dismissed. The German Armies are now stretched thin over hundreds of miles. The German Sixth Army is barely holding on at Stalingrad. And winter is coming.

"You are both very smart and savvy Generals, so pick your poison. The Allies or the Axis. But I assure you of this: Vichy France military officers who choose to fight for the Axis will live to rue the day, if they live at all."

General Salbert was the first to respond.

"I have every reason to believe that the Vichy France forces in Morocco and Algiers will join the Allied cause. But the Vichy France forces in Tunisia are in a terrible squeeze. The Germans are moving in considerable forces from Sicily. And the Italians are remaining in their positions in Libya. My guess is that the Vichy France forces in Tunisia have no alternative other than to ally themselves with the Germans and Italians. At least for a while."

At that point, d'Astier said his farewell and headed out into the afternoon heat. Salbert and Bethouart looked at each other, and sat down. Salbert waited to hear Bethouart's reaction.

"Even if we accept that the German Sixth Army will suffer a major defeat at Stalingrad," Bethouart began, "the war is far from over. And France itself is locked in the death grip of Nazi Germany."

"Antoine, you are correct. As usual. But we are just two relatively minor Vichy France officers stuck in Casablanca which is now occupied and controlled by the Allies. At this point in time, in this location of the globe, we really have to join the Allies. We have no other option."

Bethouart nodded in agreement.

52

The Battle of Stalingrad – Operation Uranus

27 November 1942, London

The meeting was held in the Department of Operations Research in the Admiralty offices in London. Principal Invitees were Jacob Bronowski, Patrick Blackett, Director of Coastal Command's Operational Research Section of the Admiralty, Fredrick Lindemann, David Petrie, Stewart Menzies, Arthur Harris, Ira Eaker, Spencer Haythornwaite, and Benjamin Leach. Many members of the military branches, both UK and US, were also invited, as was US Military Intelligence liaison Robert Johnston. Sitting in the back of the room were Aaron Solomon, David Butt and Sarah Leach.

The men had self-selected their sitting buddies. Bronowski and Blackett were studying a recent research paper on bomb trajectories. Petrie and Menzies were quietly discussing some intelligence reports from North Africa. Harris and Eaker were looking at photos of the modified B-17 bomber. Robert was asking Haythornwaite and Leach about the U.S. and British Navy operations in the Allied landings in Morocco. Sarah was entertaining Aaron and David Butts with current gossip, first about Menzies and then about Lindemann. Her little audience was eating it up.

Then Lindemann opened the meeting.

"The War Cabinet wanted to ensure that the many diverse elements of the Allied military and intelligence communities present here today will hear the current news, and the War Cabinets' views, regarding the events now erupting on the German eastern front, particularly at Stalingrad, and also current operations in North Africa. Operations Research will provide the overview. For those who don't know, Operations Research is an interdisciplinary science focusing on mathematical modeling and analysis. Its director is Patrick Blackett. Director Blackett, please get us started."

Blackett was young, having just celebrated his forty-fifth birthday with his wife, Constanza Bayon, and his two children. Tall and very lanky, with a full head of black hair, Blackett seemed to never stand up straight. But in this room of extraordinary people, Blackett was second to none. Born in Kensington, educated at Dartmouth Naval College where he was usually first in his class, and he then joined the Royal Navy in the Great War. After the war, he studied math and physics at Cambridge and became heavily involved in physics.

"Thank you, Professor Lindemann. I am aware that the collected wisdom, talent, and experience in this room far exceeds anything that I will be able to impart today. But like our celebrated colleague, Jacob Bronowski, I do have a couple of unique vantage points. First, as a mathematician and a physicist, I tend to look at things from a strictly empirical point of view, largely devoid of emotions. Secondly, I receive a lot of research on these subjects, and so I have up-to-date intelligence to share with you.

"The Battle of Stalingrad is monumental. In many ways, a lynchpin for the entire German eastern front of this war and quite possibly the war itself. Germany threw everything it had into this battle, but recent events show clearly that the they have lost that battle. As a result, they will also lose the entire eastern front. And from those two colossal failures there follows a high probability that they will lose the entire war.

"You will see this play out. But it will take a few years. Probably three. The Germans are enormously over extended. Their Sixth Army is in extremis. Foolishly, they allowed the Romanian 4th Army Corps and several Italian and Hungarian units to protect their flanks. All of these units were poorly equipped. The Russians crushed them. The Russians have now encircled the entire German Sixth Army. General Paulus, Commander of the German Sixth, should have retreated. It seems clear that Hitler ordered him to remain at Stalingrad for political reasons, hoping, no doubt, that the Sixth could be supplied by the Luftwaffe and then relieved by other German divisions. Neither came to pass.

"By 19th November, German Army Group South was itself in full retreat from the Caucasus. Hitler is not likely to do anything to change the equation at Stalingrad. A pull out of the German Sixth would significantly increase Soviet Army pressure on the German Army units retreating from the Caucuses. It would force the greatest admission of failure by the Third Reich ever. Not politically palatable for Hitler.

"But the Sixth Army is there. If it remains, the Germans will try to supply it using the Luftwaffe. Not feasible. To supply the German Sixth Army, now reduced to 300,000 men, will require about 700 tons of supplies per day. That requires 350 *JU52* flights per day. According to our Russian sources, the Germans are bringing in only about 100 tons per day with about 120 flights per day. The Soviets are taking down an increasing number of German transport flights and attacking an increasing number of German airfields recently developed on Russian soil. And *winter is coming*. The Germans can probably hold on for another month or two, but the end will be cataclysmic for General Paulus and the entire remaining German Sixth Army.

"At the beginning of this month, the Germans and Italians suffered a disastrous military defeat at El-Alamein. That defeat, while very significant in several respects, will pale in comparison to their defeat at Stalingrad later this winter."

"Thank you gentlemen." He paused and smiled. "And lady!" He looked at Sarah. She smiled.

Blackett sat back down. There was loud chatter in the room. It had been a long time since the Brits had received such good news. Many walked up to shake Blackett's hand. Lindemann appeared a little disgruntled at Blackett's popularity.

"Thank you, Director Blackett," grumbled Lindemann and turned to his right. "Now our good friend Professor Jacob Bronowski would like to add a few words."

Bronowski got up. Bronowski following Blackett was a sharp contrast in styles. Bronowski was short, heavy set, always a bit rumpled and frumpled, and spoke with a heavy Polish accent. But everyone knew who he was. He too was widely admired and very popular.

"Hello friends. From a strategic viewpoint, we continue to see the strong tendency of the Third Reich to overextend in their eternal hope, and dare I say their eternal expectation, that such bold initiatives will thereby produce dramatic results. That strategy worked in 1938, 1939, and 1940. It began to wear thin last year. This year, such tendencies have left them hyper-exposed and hyper-vulnerable. One example of this strategy failure is now playing out in Tunisia. The Germans are moving rapidly to transport paratroops, infantry, tanks and supplies into their defense of Tunisia.

"They can and they will supply Tunisia from Sicily, but then what? Montgomery and the heavily armored British Eighth Army are approaching Tunisia from the east. Eisenhower and the Allied Forces from Operation Torch are approaching Tunisia from the west. The sea and air supply routes on and near the Mediterranean Sea are increasingly controlled by Allied sea and air forces.

"The German and Italian forces defending Tunisia will make life miserable for the Allies for several months. But there is no future for the German-Italian military defense of Tunisia. The Germans and Italians are doomed to failure there. Vital troops and resources which they need elsewhere will be wasted.

"The loss of the German Eastern Front means enormous German casualties and very substantial loss of equipment and supplies. More importantly, it means the likely loss of German allies, captured territories, resources, and defensive geography. And the Russian Army will now push farther and farther west. The loss of North Africa, and the loss of sea and air control of the Mediterranean Sea, puts southern Italy and soon thereafter all of Italy in jeopardy. The Italians have been losing their best units both on the Eastern Front and in the western deserts of North Africa. The remaining reliable units are now in Tunisia and will probably be lost there.

"Operation Torch has, thus far, not been a great success. The landings went well, and the operation was a very useful training exercise for American troops and commanders, but the Americans are advancing very slowly. Nevertheless, time and geography are on their side. Their fighting skills, once learned, will prove useful in Italy soon and in France later.

"The continuing destruction of the Axis military forces is great news for all of us here, but the attendant loss of millions of lives throughout Europe is a human tragedy of unimaginable proportions. All of us in this room are so proud of our scientific breakthroughs. But, Science Be Not Proud, for those same scientific breakthroughs are in the process of destroying the human race. And a warning to you all. There are even more far reaching scientific breakthroughs on the horizon which are capable of killing much larger segments of our population.

"Lest we forget, dear colleagues, the continuing and increasing military attacks on civilian populations on all sides of this war are adding hundreds of thousands to the toll of dead and wounded. This mutual and shared inhumanity of the war, on all sides, will be remembered long after the war itself has drawn to a sad end."

When Bronowski concluded his remarks, everyone in the room was on the edge of their seats. Bronowski's final words were profound and deeply disturbing to all. Harris and Lindemann, the proponents of blanket bombing, sat silent and solemn. Then Lindemann rose to speak.

"It is always enlightening to listen to Blackett and Bronowski, two of our eminent Cambridge mathematicians, because they can extrapolate their mathematical analysis to both human and political repercussions. As some of you here know, they and I are not always in agreement, but all sides of these issues do require frank and open discussions. Thank you, gentlemen. Let me now share further thoughts on the human and political repercussions of this war.

"I suppose almost every military operation has both military and political objectives. But the Battle of Stalingrad falls heavily on the political side of the equation. It is doubtful that Hitler would have been so keen on taking the city itself if Stalingrad had retained its historical name – Tsaritsyn. But seizing a city named for Stalin himself was too juicy a "plum" for Hitler to pass over.

"However, the primary military target of the Russian invasion was the oil fields in the Caucasus, not Stalingrad, a big city with minimal military significance. By dividing his forces between these two objectives—one military and the other political—Hitler is losing both.

"If you choose to fight a major military battle to achieve a political objective, what then happens if you lose? Your enemy, in this case the Soviets, wins a major political windfall. We must all watch for further fallout. Over the next two years, countries caught between Hitler and

Stalin—Hungary, Romania, Croatia, Bulgaria, and even the Fickle French—will have to rethink their 'alliances' with Germany.

"At the same time, the British successes in Egypt and Libya, and the pressure of the American forces arriving in Morocco via Operation Torch, plus the growing strength of the British Eighth Army in Eastern North Africa, will eventually flip both North Africa and control of the Mediterranean Sea to the Allies. That, in turn, puts enormous pressure on Spain to remain neutral. Italy, now clearly threatened with a possible Allied invasion of Sicily, will be pressured to change sides.

"From the earliest days of the Roman Empire, most of southern Italy has been inextricably entwined with the Mediterranean Sea and North Africa. Italy cannot be divorced from them. If they both fall into the hands of the Allies, all of Italy is threatened. The Italians will struggle to resist the pull of that suction force, which means the Germans themselves will have to defend Northern Italy. The Germans will then be fighting the Americans and the British, and probably large numbers of Southern Italians as well, to defend their position in Italy.

"1942 is drawing to a close. Allied military operations in 1943 will soon be able to focus on Southern Italy. Remember that Italy is essentially two countries. Southern Italy is closely tied into the Mediterranean Sea. Northern Italy has strong ties to Austria, France, Switzerland and Germany. My best guess is that Southern Italy will welcome the Allies with open arms, but Northern Italy will resist until the Germans themselves surrender.

"If there is a battle for Italy, it will be neither quick, nor easy, but control of air or sea will give the Allies a huge advantage. Interesting times, indeed.

"And finally, the heavy bombing of Germany will continue and intensify by the rapidly growing British and American air forces operating out of the U.K. We will get their attention, and they will pay for the enormous loss of life they have caused!"

Lindemann called for questions. Well aware of his tendency to never suffer fools lightly, few dared raise their hands. But Captain Leach did.

"Professor, your observations on Italy were very interesting. Is there clear evidence that the Allies are now gaining control of the Mediterranean?"

"Yes. Our control of Malta and Egypt and now most of North Africa means it's virtually impossible for the Axis to block us there, except around Sicily. And we have them boxed in there!"

After more questions, Blackett raised his hand. Lindemann did not look thrilled to see that hand go up. He suspected that he was about to get a difficult question about the British bombing strategy, knowing that Blackett opposed it. Blackett stood, and spoke.

"Professor, it seems that all the successes we are beginning to see on battlefields and at sea indicate that we should be supporting our land and sea forces rather than RAF Bomber Command. Don't you agree?"

Blackett sat down with a hint of a smile on his face.

Lindemann frowned and responded, "No. No. I do not agree!"

The room showed no more hands, so Lindemann brought the meeting to a close.

"Gentleman, we will reconvene soon. To our American friends and now Allies, Happy Thanksgiving."

53

The Walpole Bay Hotel

28-29 November 1942, Margate, England

The actual date for the much anticipated first meeting with Juan and Gunther was arranged during several long telephone calls between Juan and Robert. They agreed to meet on Sunday, 29 November. Robert suggested a Sunday because Sundays are usually quiet, family days in England, even during the war. Sarah agreed to Sunday afternoon but then added a wrinkle of her own.

During a quiet dinner at The Old Bell Tavern in mid-November, about a week before the meeting, Robert noticed that Sarah seemed restless.

"Is everything okay, Sarah? You seem tense. Problems at the office?"

"No. Not really. I am just so sick of London I could scream. I expect to be heading off to a few 'invisible' meetings in occupied France in the next few months, so I will get a break then, but I was thinking that maybe you and I could use the meeting with Gunther to get out of town. My family likes to stay at the old Walpole Bay Hotel in Margate, down on the English Channel coast. Almost an hour and a half drive from London. Margate is busy in summer months because of the beaches there, but in the winter months it is an absolute tomb. I have known the place for many years.

"I can tell the hotel that I'm planning a quiet dinner meeting with some old family friends. You and I can book two rooms, not too far apart, where we could spend an interesting Saturday night."

She put her hand on Robert's knee under the table, out of sight. Robert jumped just a little, hitting the table and almost knocking over the bottle of wine. He was not expecting a hand on his knee out in public.

Sarah couldn't help but laugh. "Oh my! Somebody has very sensitive knees."

Robert laughed. "Yes, I do know that lady very well. In fact, her knees are the most sensitive part of her." Robert smiled.

Sarah put on a playful frown. "I think that I do know that lady you are describing, but I have heard reports from others who say that lady actually does have more sensitive body parts. Certain body parts that she saves for certain people."

Robert said, "Certain people?"

Sarah smiled, "Well, certain men!"

Robert said, "I guess I should seek their advice."

As they settled down, Sarah became serious again.

"Do you think that Juan and Gunther would be uncomfortable moving the meeting to Margate? It is easy to get lost in the London hubbub, but in Margate they might be more visible."

"Actually, I think an old hotel in Margate on a Sunday afternoon in November is the perfect setting. Quiet. Remote. Isolated. And user-friendly. I will tell them. Consider it done. Here's to Margate. And maybe I can find those "certain body parts" of that little blue hen."

Sarah smiled. "Maybe. But that little blue hen is getting peckish. Can we please order some dinner?"

A week later, on Saturday, 28 November, Robert and Sarah pulled up to the Walpole Bay Hotel and checked into their separate rooms close by each other. They had dinner at the hotel at 7:00 pm. Enjoying some mutton stew with a nice bottle of cabernet. There were two other tables having dinner in the small dining room. Four RAF officers at one table and two mothers with their young children at another. Being British, none of them spoke to the people at the other tables.

Eventually the other two tables paid their bills and departed. Robert and Sarah savored the last of the cabernet alone in the dining room, discussing the recent heady events of the war. Then they both walked upstairs to their separate rooms.

About thirty minutes later, Robert went quietly into Sarah's room. He found her already in bed, in her pajamas, and asleep. Undeterred, he climbed under the blanket next to her. After a few minutes of respectful inactivity, he slowly untied and pulled down her pajama pants. She smiled and pulled close to him. Then he proceeded to unbutton her pajama top. He did admire her breasts. They were not large, but firm and well-proportioned to her figure. But Robert's hands on her bare breasts were cold.

"Oh, Robert. It is so cold in this room and you are taking off my nice warm woolen pajamas. How am I going to stay warm?"

Sarah pressed her now naked body into Robert, and with a little laugh, she unbuttoned his pajama top.

"Oh, my warm-blooded friend. If I am to be the plucked goose, then you must be the plucked gander. Or half plucked, anyway!"

Sarah had made a point to Robert a year ago during the first night they spent together that a pregnant Sarah was not "on offer."

At this time she had said to him, "Robert, these are the most important years of our lives, both yours and mine. In my current assignments, I am fulfilling the role for which I am well trained. An important role at a critical time. I cannot do my job if I turn up pregnant. And both of us have other pre-existing commitments to other special people and special relationships. There still might be an Ellen out there for you—and a James out there for me—at the end of the rainbow. So, for now, let's plan to postpone the usual finale of these performances."

Robert fully understood, and of course he agreed.

So, tonight, as usual he did not take off his pajama pants.

As they lay together, keeping each other warm, Robert ran his hands up the back of Sarah's thighs, then her buttocks, then her back. Her body was smooth and soft, but strong. Then he ran his right hand down her abdomen and into her now warm crotch. Knowing her love of Shakespeare, he whispered into her ear, "*My hand doth stray lower, where the pleasant fountain lie.*" He held his hand there, moving his fingers until she gave the soft moan that he loved to hear. At last his hand felt warm, and Sarah finally stopped complaining about being cold.

Then Sarah slowly slipped her hand down inside his pajama pants. She playfully groped around his lower abdomen until she "accidentally" discovered that he had become excited by the cuddling and caressing. She took his phallus in her hand, slowly, but firmly, and then mimicked his own earlier reference to Shakespeare. She whispered into his ear, "*This thorn, doth to your rose of beauty right belong.*" While doing this with her right hand, she wound her left arm around his back, pulled his body tight to her, and kissed him fervently, so that he couldn't speak, even if he had wanted to. Soon she felt him pulsate in her hand. In a few short minutes, he was spent, and in a few more minutes, he was sound asleep.

Sarah smiled. After putting on her warm pajamas, and making a quick stop in the loo, she returned to the now very warm bed, and fell sound asleep herself, more or less entangled with Robert.

The next morning was bright and cold. Robert and Sarah enjoyed a welcome breakfast of eggs, toast, a little ham and a lot of coffee for Robert and some tea for Sarah in the hotel dining room. Several other guests were there, as well, but no one spoke to other tables.

After breakfast, they took a long and bracing walk through the quiet town of Margate. They stopped at water's edge to take a long look out at the cold English Channel.

As she looked across toward France, Sarah wondered about her future clandestine and dangerous visits to meet with local French resistance fighters. Would she succeed? Her thoughts then turned to her recently injured brother, Tom, and her lifelong friend and sometimes paramour, James, off somewhere in North Africa. Her family, and James' family, always just assumed that Sarah and James would get married and settle down some day. And before the war, so did she. But the war changed everything. And now she was enjoying her time with Robert. A fine man. A fine "assignment." And maybe much more. But then, there was Ellen. Far away. But still very present. Perhaps because the Christmas Season was approaching, she suddenly thought of Ellen as The Ghost of Christmases to come.

Robert walked away from Sarah and looked out at the water. He had his own thoughts. His quieter days working in Berlin, before the war madness, coming home each night to have dinner with Ellen, Nancy, and Mark. Very peaceful. Would he ever have that back? And Robert had to wonder. Did he even want that back? He thought of his college days. Perhaps the best days of his life. College football games. Parties with Ellen always holding his hand. The challenge of law school. Practicing law in New York City. The birth of Nancy. And then Mark. But everything seemed to come unglued in Berlin. Robert had greatly admired Germany and the Germans. He saw the rise of the Third Reich as an all-consuming and evil perversion and deviation. He knew that someday, somehow, the

German people would rid themselves of these Nazi criminals. But Ellen was convinced that the Third Reich did actually reflect the true nature of Germany and the German people. She wanted to leave Germany. As soon as possible, and turn her back on the entire mess.

Robert felt strongly that ignoring the problem would not make it go away. That it would take a monumental effort to erase the Nazis. And he wanted to be part of the effort. These were painful thoughts.

Then he looked over at Sarah, as she stood gazing toward France across the Channel. She was a thing of beauty in so many ways. And he did enjoy looking at her. He thought to himself, "I know that she has been assigned to stay close to me, but I also suspect that she has a true affection for me. Not even Delilah could sustain such a complete pretense of true affection. He dismissed the notion of pretense. But what he could not dismiss was the fog of war which pushed aside all reality. He sensed that the War had pushed them together, and that the War, or the end of the War, would pull them apart. It was both a mystical and a fleeting relationship.

During his time in Berlin, while browsing one rainy afternoon through a small bookstore, he came upon a dusty old book of German legends. In it he read an 1860 story by Fredrich Gerstacher called *Germelshausen*. It was the story of a cursed village called Germelshausen that would appear once every century for just one day, and then disappear until the next century, when it would once again appear for just one day. A young artist, Arnold, comes upon the village on that one day, and falls in love with a beautiful young resident, Gertrud. At the end of that one day of romance, both Gertrud and Germelshausen disappear into the mist and Arnold is left alone and forlorn.

And so, Robert thought to himself, this major war, like every major war, is a time bubble. Just like the once every one-hundred-year appearance of the village of Germelshausen. When the village appears, time goes into a bubble, where it remains until the village evaporates once again. While the village exists, the entire surrounding countryside is transformed. It is now a microcosm. A microcosmos. All previous life is pushed aside. All current life is encapsulated. The village is now the center of all the surrounding existence. Up until the moment it disappears again. And so it is with this war. When this war is over, the bubble will burst. The now vibrant and vital and vigorous City of London will disappear. Just like the mist shrouded village of Germelshausen. And so too, will this beautiful and mystical Delilah disappear. Just like the beautiful and mystical Gertrud. Treasure it while you have it, he thought, just like youth and good health. Once gone, they are gone forever.

Then they walked back together to the Walpole Hotel, holding hands, each now beset by haunting fairy tales.

54

The First Meeting with "Gunther"

29 November 1942, Margate, England

Robert and Sarah sat waiting quietly in the small private conference room at the Walpole Hotel the next afternoon. Sarah wore civilian attire, warm clothes for the weather. Sunday had turned even chillier than the day before. The curtains on the windows were pulled back, but the sun had just set, so the room was illuminated by electric lamps that were too small to provide much light. It gave the room a warm and friendly feeling.

Juan Frederico walked in and right behind him was Gunther.

"Hello, Robert." Juan had a big smile and a warm handshake. He looked Robert in the eye to convey his sincerity and trustworthiness.

"And Sarah. Lovely to see you." Juan took Sarah's hand in both of his. A two-handed handshake. She sensed he was about to hug her hello, so she backed up a step. Juan glanced at her eyes, but then ran his gaze down her outfit. If he was trying to compliment her appearance by looking her up and down, she did not appreciate it.

Gunther stood apart from Juan. Robert and Sarah approached to greet him. He firmly shook Robert's hand, and then Sarah's.

"Hello," he said.

All eyes were on Gunther.

He was a striking figure. Tall, blond, erect, slim but well-built, handsome with deep and piercing blue eyes, very much the German-publicized Aryan prototype. Gunther wore well-pressed dark-blue trousers, a white open-collared shirt, a blue woolen sweater, leather zip-up jacket, and elegant brown leather shoes; well-dressed in resort casual to avoid attention in a quiet, sleepy resort town in the off season. This was no common soldier. He radiated class, status, military bearing, and most of all, deep and serious purpose.

"This is Gunther," Juan began. "Not his real name, as you know. He will explain the details surrounding the purpose of his visit. Beforehand,

I want to make clear he is an officer in the German Army, serving on active duty, but he is not here on official Army business. His current Command is unaware of this visit, the purpose of this visit, and Gunther's general mission. I should say, his Command is not 'officially' aware. With that, I will turn this over to him."

Robert pointed to the sitting area in the conference room. "Shall we all sit down?"

Everyone looked around the room for a place to sit. Juan walked to the small dinner table, pulled out a chair for Gunther, and then joined him at the table. Robert took a cushioned chair by the window. Sarah spied a nice perch on the small sofa, sat down there, and crossed her long legs, and her Spanish pumps, with the usual effect. Juan looked and smiled. Gunther didn't appear to notice.

Gunther spoke in very crisp, clear English, but with his distinctive clipped German accent.

"Thank you for agreeing to meet with me. I realize this meeting entails grave danger for all of us, notwithstanding the presence of this Special Agent from MI5 here to monitor our discussion. The danger to Mr. Johnston and Agent Leach comes from the British Government. But at least they are somewhat reliable and predictable. Unfortunately, the real danger to me and Juan comes from the Gestapo, who are neither reliable nor predictable. If they learn of this meeting, the repercussions for Juan and me will be very unpleasant.

"Although I am *not* here to represent my current commander, I do represent an impressive group of senior officers in the Wehrmacht. For obvious reasons, they cannot be here themselves. My relatively junior rank and deep family ties in the German military establishment give me more latitude to pursue this tricky mission.

"I am here to seek some secret dialogue and assistance from the Allies, in order to create an opening for more reasonable, responsible and rational elements within Germany to curtail our mutual mass suicide and return all of us to a normal world. Such dialogue and assistance could help to facilitate a change in current leadership of the Third Reich. The search for a mechanism to effect these changes is complicated enough, but ironically, beginning the search is even more challenging. If we could effect such a change, we would most certainly save tens of millions of lives, including many British and American lives. So, it is worth the huge risk we are all taking.

"The current British Government seems to have little or no interest in pursuing a separate detente. Rudolf Hess was treated very harshly when he was arrested. The Americans might be more reasonable and more open to seeking a mechanism. That is why we continue to involve Mr. Johnston."

Gunther turned to Robert. "Can you give me any thoughts or advice on potential American interest in what I am proposing?"

"I agree that the U.S. would be a more likely prospect for your proposal than would the current British Government, but I have no idea whatsoever if the White House would be interested. And even if they were, the full cooperation and participation of Britain would be a prerequisite. I can make some soundings. I do agree that the prospect of ending this endless and bottomless loss of life deserves all of our attention. We have been hearing proposals along those lines from Germany for years, dating back to the late 1930s. Those proposals were sponsored by the Fuhrer, of course, so this proposal is quite different. But the objective being pursued now by your people in the Wehrmacht, to avoid the complete and utter destruction of Germany, is of course diametrically opposed to the current fervent objective of the Allies, who are now determined to carry out the complete and utter destruction of Germany."

Sarah, hoping to break the growing tension in the meeting, spoke up.

"To be clear. Your group is not contemplating an assassination of the Fuhrer?"

Gunther, who had not looked at Sarah once during the meeting, now turned toward her.

"Correct. Absolutely not. He is enormously popular in Germany. Even an assassination *attempt* would be quite counterproductive. What we are suggesting would be more akin to a peaceful military coup. In fact, we would eventually need the Fuhrer's cooperation to bring German popular opinion to our side. He would be 'moved aside,' but carefully protected. His inner circle would be replaced with reliable military officers. The clique now surrounding the Fuhrer are, with a few exceptions, complete buffoons."

The foursome spent the next hour discussing the ramifications, problems, and perceptions surrounding Gunther's proposal until Robert sensed the need for a break.

"We now have an understanding of your mission and some preliminary thoughts on how to explore it. Let's have some dinner. We should restrict our conversations when the wait staff is in the room, please."

"Of course," Gunther responded.

Robert picked up the phone and called for room service, where the pre-ordered dinner was being prepared. While they were waiting, Juan spoke quietly with Gunther, Sarah went to the WC, and Robert stood looking out the window, deep in thought. The meal arrived with a knock at the door, the wait staff laid the table, set out the meal and the pre-ordered wine, and then left the room.

They all quietly sat down at the small round table to begin the meal. It was Sarah who had wisely pre-ordered a bottle of fine claret. Robert suspected she wanted to loosen up Gunther. He had noticed during the meeting that Gunther had never looked at Sarah, or even in her direction. A sharp contrast to Juan, who looked at her frequently. Sarah was dressed demurely, either for warmth or to be unobtrusive. But Robert did take note of her eyes. She was wearing dark eyeliner, which made her eyes look larger, and gave her a certain air of mystery. Very exotic, he thought. *I like it.*

Gunther did not seem to notice Sarah's eyes.

Once everyone was settled into eating, Robert turned to Gunther again.

"If the White House has any interest in pursuing this idea, Gunther, they will want to know a great deal more about you to prove your *bona fides*. We don't even know your real name. Can you put a little flesh on these bare bones?"

"A little, perhaps. My family name is fairly well known in my home area of Saxony. A very old Saxon family line. The family has been very careful to maintain respectful ties with the Nazi Party, while keeping our distance, a necessity to survive at all in Germany today. If my name were to be connected to this unsanctioned mission, my entire family and many of my friends would suffer terribly. And my name doesn't really matter anyway. If we three, or we four assuming that Special Agent Leach might be supportive, can breathe some life into this project, highly clandestine meetings with several officers on both sides would have to be arranged.

"The members of our group who know and work with the Fuhrer have assured us that he will never openly and officially condone, support, or tolerate a negotiated settlement unless it is presented to him on 'bended knee' from one or more of the Allies. So, when these piecemeal ceasefire discussions with senior military offices do occur, and of course they will sooner or later, they will have to be done without his knowledge. As long as he is in charge, that will be difficult. Maybe impossible. His Gestapo is watching our every move. That is why we now believe that he must be moved aside.

"I can tell you that I am on active duty. Obviously, and thank God, I am not on the Eastern Front. If I were, there is no way I could be here today. I am currently serving in North Africa, under one of Germany's best and most admired military officers, General Erwin Rommel. The Fuhrer regards him highly, in spite of the fact that Hitler and Rommel often disagree on military strategies. And as you can tell, I am very proud to serve under his command."

"Were you involved in the second Battle of El Alamein?"

"I was. Heavily involved. I sustained a minor injury in the Battle of Gazala, just last June which took me out of commission for two months, but I was back in action at El-Alamein. That was not a good week for Afrika Corps."

Sarah turned slightly to look at Robert. He narrowed his eyes just a bit, sending her the message that he, and not she, should press Gunther on this sensitive topic. She got the message.

Robert continued. "Gunther, on the subject of El Alamein, General Rommel suffered one of his worst defeats. Since you were there, can you shed any light on the result? I don't want you to tell us anything *confidential* or *secret*, and I'm sure you wouldn't anyway, but if you can give us some insight it would enhance your credibility with those to whom we report and make them understand that future contacts with an assistance to you and your group could be worthwhile."

Gunther looked straight at Robert. He did not even pause for a moment.

"We take great pride in General Rommel's many desert victories. He is a brilliant tank combat tactician. But, at El-Alamein, all of the cards were stacked against us. I cannot tell you what you do not know. That would violate the oath I have taken to the Fatherland. But I can tell you what you do know, or should know, and that will confirm that I am who and what I say I am. General Rommel did not want to attack Montgomery at Alam El-Halfa on 31 August. He was under orders to do so. And he did not want to retreat only so far as El Alamein. He was ordered to do so. Both positions were beyond the far reaches of German-Italian logistical support and air cover. In both battles, the British had significant air supremacy, as well as control of the sea supply lines. The Luftwaffe and the Italians promised us fuel, ammunition, heavy armor, and sea and air cover. None ever reached us. We were outmanned and out gunned and out tanked by a ratio of two-to-one or more. We had meager fuel supplies. Rommel himself was quite ill in a hospital bed. But the Fuhrer ordered him back to the battle front. His specialty is tank maneuver battles, but there was no opportunity for maneuvers at El Alamein. We were in a tight box. Our losses were significant. He wanted an early and orderly retreat, but the Fuhrer ordered him to stay.

"Finally, acting against orders, he ordered a massive and high-speed retreat, all the way back into Libya in order to save and protect our dwindling army. In this he achieved a magnificent victory. Montgomery was left behind in a cloud of sand dust while Rommel moved his entire army to safety. We will eventually head for Tunisia. There we will have excellent air cover from Sicily, and reinforcements from Italy and Germany. The Americans are coming at us from Morocco. Let them come. They will pay a high price—of that you can be sure. They will pay a very high price. They are sending very green troops and very green commanders, and some very unreliable French troops, against battle-hardened German and Italian units. We will have more and better tanks, equal troop numbers, air superiority, ample fuel, and, hopefully, General Rommel. Over these remaining winter months, your White House will be given ample reason to consider negotiations."

Sarah sensed that Gunther was becoming combative, which was not helpful in achieving the goal of the meeting. She rose from the table, knowing her movement would catch the attention of 'the boys' and stop their squabbling, and she stuck her head out the door to order a second bottle of Claret. Juan had genially consumed a goodly portion of the first bottle himself. Before sitting back down, Sarah poured a full glass for Gunther, while touching his shoulder for just an instant as an act of friendship. Robert watched her in awe. She always seemed to manage things so well. But he also noticed that Gunther did look at her when she rose from the table, and when she sat back down. Sarah, too, noticed that she had caught Gunther's attention. So, she spoke.

"I am very impressed that you speak English almost as well as a native-born Englishman. Were you, by chance, born in England?"

"No. Born and bred in Saxony. A pure-bred German. But my parents and a small group of their professional friends saw fit to hire an excellent English language tutor and formed a small group of young boys, and a few young girls, into an intensive private English-speaking class. This was during the inter-war period when relations between our two countries was pretty cordial. My parents and this small group thought that having their young children master English would expand and improve their future careers. Both of my parents were rather fluent in English themselves.

"As it turned out, these lessons, which I undertook very seriously, surely saved my life. As a young tank commander in 1941, I received orders to join a tank unit on the Eastern Front. But one of my superior officers had become impressed by my knowledge of English. He believed that I would be of much greater value to the war effort in North Africa, fighting against the British, in an area where English was the official second language. And that superior officer was exactly correct. In addition to my combat duties, which were extensive, I was able to liaise with much of the local population, using my English fluency.

"The local people gave me a great deal of useful intelligence. As I am quite sure some of you know, only too well, the North Africa Muslim population is very unhappy with the British Government about the Jews now settling in Palestine. They see the future of Jewish dominated Palestine as a dark cloud on their horizon. My English fluency has also allowed me to be very close to General Rommel, notwithstanding my junior rank.

A great honor for me. '*Once more unto the breach, dear friends, once more, or close the wall up with our English dead.*'"

Sarah was visibly impressed. She found it hard not to like and admire this courageous young man. "Well done, Gunther. *Henry V*, Act 3, Scene 1. This is turning into a Shakespearean weekend!" She glanced at Robert who smiled at the pleasant memory. "Are you also a Shakespeare buff?"

"I am. I interrupted my military studies with a year at Oxford to study English, and I focused on Shakespeare. *Henry V* is my favorite. This bit of knowledge might make it easier for you to track down my real name at Oxford, but please do not do so. It could be fatal for me. And, by the way, I must confess to you that I do prefer Friedrich von Schiller."

"You have my word. We will not attempt to chase down your identity on the rolls at Oxford. We share your concern. And it would be counterproductive to our efforts here today. '*That's a valiant flea that dare eat his breakfast on the lip of a lion.*'"

"Thank you for the compliment, Agent Leach. We four are in this together. As you are so found of William Shakespeare, please allow me to quote Prince Hal himself:

'*This story shall the good man teach his son, and Crispir Crispian shall ne'er go by, from this day to the ending of the world, but we in it shall be remembered:*

We few, we happy few, we band of brothers.

For he to-day that sheds his blood with me shall be my brother!'

They all sat silent for a few minutes. It felt like a prayer or maybe an obituary. With her head bowed, and her hands in front of her, Sarah spoke,

"*The game's afoot:*

Follow your spirit, and upon this charge

Cry 'God for Harry, England, and Saint George!'"

"Amen," said Gunther. Then he pulled a small sheet of paper out of his pocket and unfolded it.

"In anticipation of our meeting today, I wrote down some very important numbers. Not because I need help remembering these numbers. I do not. But because people always take numbers more seriously if they are in writing."

He held up the paper. "This is a list of the anticipated casualties in Europe if the war continues at its current pace until one side or the other prevails. I obtained these numbers from a Wehrmacht source in our group who I deem to be reliable. This source carefully researched detailed records and projections compiled for the German army and provided the following estimates:

"By the end of 1942, after four years of a global war, at least 100,000,000 men and women have been mobilized by over 30 countries. Every one of these countries has mobilized all of their economic, industrial, and scientific capabilities into a concerted effort to kill, injure, or maim as many human beings on the other side as possible. And the distinctions between killing, injuring, and maiming *civilian populations* versus strictly *military personnel,* and the identification of 'sides,' have now all but vanished. We are already well over 30,000,000 fatalities, with civilian deaths exceeding military deaths. Meanwhile, each 'side' kills and maims many thousands of their own people in an effort to kill or maim as many people as possible on the other side. The war has unleashed genocides, rampant starvation and disease. The weapons of mass destruction have gotten bigger and more deadly every year and the war is nowhere near over. It is destined to go on for years.

"The longer it has continued, the more frenzied it has become, and the more frenzied it will become. Just look at what you know too well. British Bomber Command is sending several hundred heavy bombers each night to shatter and burn large, populated areas of Germany, civilian populations. Who do they cremate on those deadly nights? Not German soldiers, who are off fighting far away in Russia or the Mediterranean, but German women, and children, and old people, by the thousands, most of whom have no desire whatsoever for this war. They did not vote Hitler into office, and they have no say whatsoever on how much longer Hitler will stay in office. Bomber Command justifies its actions on the fact that the British are unable to open a front in France to kill German soldiers. So, instead, they kill their German wives, and their children, and their parents.

"These were the tactics employed by the American Indians when they attacked white colonies, while the white men were off at war. And by the white soldiers when they attacked the Indian villages, while the Indian braves were off at war. Each side always says, 'They started it! They did it first!' It was those people 'on the other side.' But, in the end, what difference does that really matter what side they are on? It is a vicious circle!

"According to Wehrmacht internal estimates, perhaps 30,000 to 40,000 British civilians perished from German bombing raids, mostly in London, during the Blitz from September 1940 through May 1941. Perhaps 1,000,000 houses were bombed. This is inexcusable. Indefensible. And, as a result the British seek revenge and retribution. Pay back. But the retaliation bombings by the British over Germany have already far surpassed those numbers. At the current accelerating rate of the British and American bombings, the resulting German civilian deaths will be catastrophic, and these civilian deaths of German women and children will only intensify the desire of German soldiers to pursue revenge and retribution. Payback. It all goes 'round and 'round and round again. And it will set the pattern for the conduct of war well into the future. We are legitimizing the execution of women and children and elderly people living peacefully in their homes as a perfectly acceptable method of conducting war. We Germans stand guilty. But so do you. So, do we all.

"These numbers show only war casualties. But we cannot forget the millions of refugees and displaced persons throughout Europe. This is also a huge problem for every country in Europe and elsewhere. We should note again the horrible repercussions of genocide not just in Germany, but many other countries. This global war is providing a pretext, a rationale, a cover, and an opportunity for so many of these countries to rid themselves of elements of their population which are unpopular minorities. Millions of Jews will perish, and so too will millions of other population groups who find themselves in the wrong place, at the wrong time, and with the wrong ancestry. Would the British and Americans really prefer to fight their way through Tunisia, then Sicily, then all the way up the boot of Italy, with hundreds of thousands of casualties on all sides? And then invade France and fight their way all through Europe and all across Germany, with millions of casualties on all sides? Doesn't anyone see that this sheer madness could be solved by Germans themselves in Germany, by getting directly at the root of the problem?

"The man who has made himself the epicenter of this enormous cyclone of mayhem, death, and destruction must be pushed aside.

The German women and children and grandparents in Cologne, and Hamburg, and Frankfurt, and Karlsruhe, most certainly cannot do that, no matter how many of them you cremate with your bombing raids. The only element of German society with any chance at all of doing this is the German military. For them to take this enormous personal risk to themselves and their families and their friends, they must have some assurance from the Allies that a peaceful settlement and an intact Germany is the reward. That is what they seek. It is the height of folly for the Allies to refuse to assist them."

As he spoke, Gunther increasingly looked directly at Sarah, now zeroing in on her as his intended audience. He knew that it was very unlikely that the Americans would ever provide support and assistance to German army officers to replace Hitler without the full backing of the British Government. Perhaps, he thought, this very mysterious MI5 Agent could deliver the message to her government.

They all stood up to say goodbye. The men shook hands, but Sarah took care not to. She was no longer comfortable shaking hands with a German Army officer who might personally kill Tom or James in the Battle of Tunisia. Gunther did not offer his hand. He read her negative vibe.

As Robert and Sarah drove back to London alone, Sarah chose her words carefully.

"Robert, you have been quiet. What do you think?"

The night was dark, so Robert kept his eyes on the road. Sarah had her hand on his knee.

"I am still digesting Gunther's words. You are always more insightful than me. What did you think?"

"I thought that this Gunther, so very young, so very German, so very bright, so very dedicated, scored a number of points," said Sarah. "What he described was analogous to the situation faced by our Crusader ancestors, one-thousand years ago. They followed the call of Pope Urban ll to drive all the Muslims out of Jerusalem, no matter what the collateral damage to the residents, the Middle East and the world order. Their sole focus was to wage war. After taking Jerusalem in 1099, they killed all the residents, including all Muslims, Christians, and Jews. Men, women, and children.

"And so today, the sole focus of the Allies is to wage war. We, too, kill men, women, and children. We have become so consumed with our own righteous crusade to kill the Nazis, we are overlooking a grim reality. Probably over 90 percent of the people being killed in this war are not Nazis. In fact, most of the people being killed actually detest the Nazis as much as we do. If there might be a better way, we should search for it. I think Gunther is a very valuable source for us. Well worth cultivating."

Robert listened intently, then spoke.

"I agree with all of your points. And I also agree that Gunther is well worth cultivating. But I am skeptical. Very skeptical that this 'mission' will bear fruit. I lived in Germany for several years. They have their internal divisions, of course, some pro-Hitler, some anti-Hitler, many just ambivalent. But Hitler looms large in their collective German aspirations and collective Germanic Lore psyche. There is no question about it. Hitler has been and remains very popular with the German people. So, I agree with Gunther that assassinating Hitler would be a monumental mistake, converting that deviant into a martyr. Moving him aside is the right answer. But those senior Wehrmacht officers, and particularly senior line officers, like Rommel, wield enormous power. If many of them want to do this, then they should try. My guess is that a few of them will try, but most of them will not join the plot. The US and the UK could certainly help them, but probably will not do so. The few German officers who do try, like this passionate young Gunther, will in fact fail and then pay a terrible price. And we cannot and should not forget or forgive the fact that these Nazis leaders are truly monsters. They have been unleashed on the world by Germany. The Nazis and their beloved Germany do have to pay the piper! But I will carry his message to the White House. It is worth a try. Please see what you can do with MI5 and MI6 as their support would be very helpful."

Sarah nodded. They drove on in silence, each lost in thoughts of this intense weekend in quiet, little Margate.

55

Rommel Retreat from El-Agheila

13 December 1942, El-Agheila, Italian Libya

Tom was in his Sherman tank with the rest of his unit, 4th British Light Armored Brigade, "The Black Rats," operating in support of 2nd New Zealand Division, under the Command of Major General Sir Bernard Freyberg. The overall Commander of the British Eighth Army, General Montgomery, was hoping to cut off the retreating German-Italian Panzer Army.

Tom's column was ordered to hold fast, awaiting further orders. James pulled up next to Tom's tank.

"James, why are we stopping? I thought the whole purpose of this maneuver was to cut them off?"

"That is the purpose. But we have been spotted by Axis aircraft north of the Maradoh Oasis. Our aircraft can see that Rommel is preparing to make his own armored attack. The 2nd New Zealand will have to wheel right and defend our flank. I do not understand Rommel's reasoning here at El Agheila. He is in a very defensible position, and we know he would need substantial supplies of new tanks, artillery, ammunition, fuel, and reinforcements to attack us successfully. None of which he has received. My guess is that Mussolini ordered him to defend Tripolatania. But clearly Rommel cannot hold the retreat line here because the Germans and the Italians are diverting supplies from Rommel in order to strengthen their forces in Tunisia. I very much doubt Rommel can launch a counterattack. So, I expect Rommel to continue his overall retreat to the relative safety of Tunisia and leave his Italian units here to protect his general retreat. We will know very soon."

By late morning, Tom and his New Zealand compatriots were ordered to launch their attack with almost eighty tanks. The Italian Ariste Division defended the Italian-German flank very well, damaging twenty British-NZ tanks, including Tom's tank, and several armored cars, including James' car. Both of them survived. Tom was not injured. James did suffer shrapnel wounds.

Several nights later, under cover of darkness, just as James had surmised, Rommel and his remaining Panzer army escaped once again, heading out in small units racing towards Tunisia.

Tom heard that James had been injured, so he went in search for him and found him resting in a field hospital tent.

"You don't look too bad, except for those bandages hiding your handsome face and left shoulder. How are you?"

"Not great. I was very fortunate that the shell landed on the left side of my vehicle. I was seated on the right and suffered some bad burn wounds. Several others in the car suffered worse wounds. The doctors have some concerns. All four of us here have been ordered to return to England for treatment at the Special Burn Unit at Queen Victoria Hospital which treats many of our injured RAF pilots and crew."

Tom was momentarily stunned. "Well, good for you. I do know a particular young WREN officer who will be very happy to see you back in London, and very much looking forward to your full recovery."

"Tom, I am not going back. WREN or no WREN. I am contesting the order to return to London for treatment. I have an official right to demand active combat status. These wounds will heal soon enough. It would be grand, of course, to spend some time with your delightful sister, if she even had time for me, but we have chased the Desert Fox and his band of elusive rats over 1,000 miles, and I want to be there in Tunisia when we and the Yanks push him out of North Africa. You can bet I will be there. You recently expressed the *very same* sentiments to me."

"Well enough. I do not cherish going into these major campaigns without my honorary Big Brother hovering over me like a fussy nanny."

"Future brother-in-law, if I get lucky someday. Tom, I do need a favor. In order to speed up the healing process, they want me to try to move around as little as possible for a week or two. But I do owe a big thank you to fellows from 28th Maori Battalion, 2nd New Zealand, who risked their lives to pull us out of that burning armored car. I never got their names. Please check over in the New Zealand section of the field hospital for Lt.

Keith Elliot from the 2nd, who was wounded a couple of months ago. He is a great fellow, and he can track them down."

Tom located the New Zealand section and had a long discussion with Lt. Elliot. He then went over to the headquarters of 28th Maori Battalion where he was given the names of the two Maori soldiers who rescued James and his mates, Second Lieutenant Moani-Nui-a-Kiwa Ngarima, and Lance Sargeant Haane Manahi. Tom found both of them, and all three of them went to see James, still confined to his bed.

"Thanks to both of you for pulling us out of the burning car under enemy fire. We owe our lives to you. Very few soldiers would have had the courage to pull us out at risk to yourselves, and many fewer would have the strength and ability to succeed."

"You are very welcome, Colonel," responded Lt. Ngarima. "We have had considerable practice pulling injured soldiers out of burned-out tanks and armored cars, so we are pretty good at it. But in this particular situation, there was considerable added incentive. You are very well known to us as one of the senior officers who is always out in front, leading the charge, with little regard for your own safety. This courage is much admired, but it often shortens one's life expectancy! We did hear that you were a tough rugger in college, so we thought of inviting you to join the All Blacks, but Lt. Elliot told us that you are now too old!"

He laughed and so did James.

"Lt. Elliot will have to answer for that later," James said, smiling.

"Just joking! Anyway, we noticed you had pulled well ahead of the British tank units, and so you encountered those Italian tanks before our tanks could provide you with cover. Good luck that we were able to get to you in time. But bad luck for all of us that Rommel and his Desert Rats were able to slip the noose again. Maybe next time. 28th Maori Battalion is looking forward to a return match in Tunisia."

Tom, the two Lieutenants and James all nodded in hearty agreement.

56

Disturbing News from Wild Bill

15-16 December 1942, London

Robert sat in his office with Kathleen, waiting for a secure radio telephone call from OSS Chief Bill Donovan. The call came in promptly at 4:00 pm. Kathleen took the call then quietly stepped out and closed the door.

Donovan asked, "Robert. How are you?"

"A lot of activity here in London. And a few rays of sunlight in the horizon. How are you?"

"I wanted to touch base. These sensitive discussions you mentioned after the meeting in Margate with 'Gunther.' There is some interest here in developing lines of communication, but this Gunther fellow is too junior to carry much weight. The timing is premature and the British Government is adamantly opposed. They think Stalin would go ballistic and might pursue a separate peace himself, thereby unleashing the German army on the west. Frankly the momentum for war here in the States and the fervent hatred for the Nazis is now unstoppable. Public opinion frowned on Eisenhower's deal with Admiral Darlan to bring the Vichy French Army and Navy over to our side in North Africa. Nobody likes or trusts Darlan."

"I'm not surprised to hear this. What now?" Robert said.

I'm pretty darn sure that there *will be* discussions, along the lines that Gunther proposes, between senior Allied and senior German military commanders in the field, but probably not for a couple more years. Once we push the Nazis out of North Africa and Italy, and the Russians push them out of Russia, and we are able to engage the German ground forces in France, then we foresee many more senior German army officers making overtures. I wouldn't be surprised to see Rommel's boss General Albert Kesselring himself get involved. He is a very respected and well-liked field marshal in the Wehrmacht with a steady hand, and he has considerable stature with Hitler. Time will tell. But please stay in contact with your German source. He has opened a line of communication that could be very useful."

"Understood," said Robert.

"More urgently, our Eighth Air Force officers in London are hearing of upcoming plans over at Bomber Command to commence area bombing of operational U-Boat bases on the west coast of France—Loriert, St. Nazaire, Brest and La Pallise. Intentional and deliberate area bombing of French towns at night. Robert, this makes no sense at all. The German U-Boat pens in that area are heavily armored and most of the U-Boat structures have been moved into the countryside. But the resulting damage to our relations with the French will be grave. We are hoping to invade the west coast of France, maybe as early as this summer. We will desperately need strong support from the French people living there."

"I hear you, Bill, but they are determined."

"Well get over to RAF Bomber Command to head off this folly. Try to talk to your friend Captain Bennett. He's an Australian, so he's not drunk on the rich wine of RAF legend. He is a brilliant technical airman and a straight shooter. If your young friend Delilah plans to fly into occupied France to start lining up our French friends, it will be helpful for her if the Allies still have a few French friends on the west coast of France to line up. But if we continue to bomb them, they might conclude that we are actually worse than the Bosch."

"I'll meet with Bennett as soon as I can get on his calendar. I do know him pretty well, but he is a very busy man. A taciturn fellow, and he does not suffer fools gladly, and he is not always the most-friendly of RAF officers. Bomber Harris regards him highly and Harris will listen to Bennett."

"Good, good. Make sure that he does. Anything else, Robert?"

"Have you heard any news of Ellen and my family? It has been difficult to reach them due to all the holiday call traffic."

"Ellen stopped by to see Ruth a few days after Thanksgiving with your daughter and son. Ruth said they all looked terrific. She suspected that Ellen's visit was more official than personal. Ellen took Ruth aside and started to probe her on whether she was aware of any plans that you and I might have to make clandestine visits into Germany or Occupied France. Ruth told Ellen that she was unaware of any such plans, any such trips would worry her too.

"She also confided to Ruth that you had said in a call to her on 2 December that you were getting signals from 'old friends' in Germany that this war might end sooner rather than later. That signaled to Ellen that you, or I, or both of us, might be in private negotiations with the Germans. Not an unreasonable deduction. I also suspect that Ellen is better at connecting dots than you and me put together."

"I did say that," said Robert. "I was primarily referring to growing angst in German military circles over major impending defeats of German armies in North Africa and Russia, not to our very low-level conversations in London. I am keenly and painfully aware that Ellen wants the war to end, so that I will come home and revisit with her the difficult subject of our broken marriage. Perhaps because she is so darn incisive, she always maintains that wars do not solve political problems, they only make such problems worse, and kill millions of innocent people in the process."

"She's not wrong about that, but we do what is necessary."

"Ellen hates the Nazis. While I was based in Berlin during the mid-'30s for my law firm, she developed an intense hatred first for them and then all German people. She did not want to be there, she did not want our children to be there, and of course her parents did not want her to be there. But like you, I saw that apocalyptic world events were coming, coming fast, and I wanted to play a role in heading them off."

"And we need you to keep doing that, Robert."

"I hear you, Bill. Ellen is the one who left with our children. I doubt that this can be patched up until the war ends. Maybe not even then. And she is spending far too much time with her dopey friend Tolliver, who shares her intellectual aversion to the war. Anyway, enough of that."

Donovan was silent for a minute.

"Robert, it's an impossible situation for you. But life as we know it is on hold for the duration of this war. We will all have to pick up the pieces and try to move on with our lives if and when the war ever ends."

"Good advice, Bill. Thanks for letting me know about Ellen's concerns. I will meet with Group Captain Bennett and get back to you.

First I need to speak with General Eaker to see what he knows. He is close to Harris, which can be helpful."

The next day Robert was in Group Captain Donald Bennett's office at RAF Bomber Command headquarters. Bennett was a striking figure. Tall, erect and severe in his appearance. Australian, yet very British at the same time. Robert thought him a bit aloof for American tastes.

He was surprised to learn from his earlier conversation with General Eaker, who in turn learned from Harris, that the *Pathfinder* bombers might soon be promoted to Group status and then placed under Bennett, who would be promoted to the rank of Air Commander. A huge step up for the *Pathfinders* and for Bennett.

"Trust me, Robert. You're gonna like this guy Bennett. When I asked Harris about him, he said, 'Bennett is a brilliant technical airman, an outstanding pilot, and fully capable of overhauling his own aircraft engine or radio.'"

Robert knew Bennett was impressive, but would he listen?

Bennet greeted Robert with a warm handshake. "Very nice to see you, Robert. I hear your message today is urgent. So please tell me, how can I help?"

"Congratulations on your promotion, Captain. Well deserved. I do bring urgent concerns from the US intelligence community about the plans of Bomber Command to bomb German U-Boat facilities on the west coast of France."

Robert spent the next forty minutes going over the concerns in great detail.

"I concur with the US assessment, Robert. But you are barking up the wrong tree. This new directive is not coming from Arthur Harris. He agrees with the US assessment. In point of fact, this new directive, which we are told is now being finalized, is straight from the British War Cabinet. If you and your colleagues could turn them around on this, it would be good news for the RAF and all concerned."

"Do you have any information to help me succeed?"

"Good news first. After struggling during '39, '40, '41 and most of '42, Bomber Command has moved into a much higher operational level. We can now do serious bombing. As you know from earlier meetings here, we have come a long way with our ground-based bomb targeting signal device, Oboe. Just this week, the first squadron of our Oboe equipped *Mosquitoes* will be ready for operations. These light weight bombers can fly at 30,000 feet, much faster and higher than our *Wellingtons* and other heavy bombers, considerably extending the range of Oboe signals emanating from England. The device has greatly improved our target accuracy. The system uses pulsating radar signals to keep the bombers on line to the target, and then measures the time it takes for the pulse signals to return to the base to calculate when the bomber is over the target. Very precise. We also have two other important navigation devices to employ, H2S radar and the Mandrel jamming system, but I am not at liberty to discuss them yet. And we now have many more four engine bombers. We are now regularly receiving *Lancasters, Stirlings,* new *Halifax* types, and even some *Mitchell* bombers. We are finally in a position to do real damage to the Hun, but we have been called off, same as we were back during the '41 Naval Diversion to attack U-Boats. Tell those people who issued their misguided directive to allow us to focus on bombing Germans now that we have the equipment to do so!

"There is Bad News. We had our chance to hit those U-Boat bases before they were hardened a year ago. Now it is too late. We won't be able to do any real damage to these now-hardened pens, but we certainly will injure and kill a lot of French civilians. I always get a lot of criticism for being too outspoken, but maybe the British Brass will listen to you Americans! Good luck to you, Robert, and thank you for always being there for us beleaguered Brits."

"Thanks, Captain. I will do my best."

Robert knew this was a huge challenge. The British War Cabinet was not about to change its directive because of concerns by the still fledgling U.S. Intelligence Service. Robert decided that he had better alert Sarah that her MI6 assignment into Occupied France was about to become a lot more difficult. Anyway, it was a good excuse for a private meeting with her.

57

More Dark Clouds for Jewish Refugees

18 December 1942, London

In the two months since the AJR meeting, Hannah's wounds had healed, and she had stopped focusing on her accident. Still wondering what, if anything really, the attack meant. She and her group continued to attend refugee meetings and speak out. She and Aaron were seeing more of each other.

Hannah, Amanda, Alice and Aaron made plans to attend the next meeting of the Jewish Refugee Committee. They each arrived separately but then congregated in the back as was their custom.

The Chairman of the Committee, Otto Schiff, presided. In addition to the usual attendees, Mr. Schiff had invited two young government officials, one from the British Home Secretary Office and one from the British Foreign Office.

Otto Schiff, age sixty-seven, had spent a great many years aiding Jewish refugees. He enjoyed enormous respect for his work. When he spoke, everyone listened.

"We are here today to ask for help, yes, even more help, from our good friends in the British Home and Foreign Offices. For the past six months, we have received here in London a steady stream of bad news from Vichy France. That 'government' has started handing over thousands of Jews to the Germans, who in turn have been shipping these Jews to concentration camps in Poland. More Jews have been deported from Paris. You may or may not be aware that Pierre Laval, the current 'head of government' in the Vichy Regime, has specifically vowed to 'cleanse France of its foreign Jews.' But there is simply no place for these Jews to go. Switzerland has now closed its border to them.

"In fact, Poland and the Nazi occupied portions of France are a case in point. The news there is really too awful, too grim to share, but we have no choice. We need to share this information if we have any hope of stopping this travesty. We know from very reliable sources in Germany that Hitler ordered the Nazi Einsatzgruppen murder squads to kill virtually all Jews in those extensive areas. And they did. Our best estimates are that 1.5 million Jews were killed there over the past year.

"Everyone in this room is well aware of statements made on 17 December in the British House of Commons by British Foreign Secretary Sir Anthony Eden confirming the mass murders of Jews by Nazi authorities in Poland. Eden promised eventual war crimes retribution against those responsible. All very helpful and encouraging to our cause, but this will not save the lives of the massive number of Jews, and others, now trapped in this hellish maelstrom.

"Neither Great Britain nor the other ten Allied governments has offered any concrete solutions. So, these senseless killings go on and on unabated."

Schiff opened the meeting to address comments and questions from the audience. The first comment came from a middle-aged man, seated up front. His strong accent intimated that he was not British born. He sounded Polish.

"On the painful subject of Poland, I am well aware there is now, and probably has always been, rampant anti-Semitism in Poland. Long before the Nazis. But now Britain has welcomed large numbers of Polish troops who are stationed in this country. They are spreading their own brand of Polish anti-Semitism here in Britain. They accuse the Jews of being unwilling to serve in the Polish Army in exile, and of being cowardly. Nothing could be further from the truth. Great numbers of Jews are currently serving in the British Army, Navy, and Air Force, and in the Army of the United States, and in the Armies of the Soviet Union. They won't serve in the Polish Army because the Polish Army treats Jews like dogs. I, myself, served in the Polish Army, in my youth. It is true. They make the Jews feel very unwelcome. I do wish that the British Government would put a collar, or a muzzle, on these visiting Poles. It is bad enough to have Poles killing thousands of Jews in Poland, but these particular anti-Semites are our guests right here in our host country!"

There was supportive applause from the audience. The officials from the British Home Office then assured everyone that the matter was being addressed with the Polish Government in Exile.

Then followed a lengthy discussion of anti-Semitism in other segments of Britain. A very real concern, but there was an understanding that the British Government, and clearly the prime minister, were trying their best, under the circumstances, to be a beacon of hope for the Jews of Europe.

As the energy, angst, and anger in the room slowly dissipated, and most of the attendees who had a question had spoken, Hannah stood. Partly because she was so young and surrounded by a small group of young and attractive people, in a roomful of gray and subdued elderly folks, and partly because a number of the audience had heard her speak at past meetings, there was a hush in the room.

Amanda, Alice, and Aaron slunk down, never quite knowing whether Hannah might say something inflammatory. Alice, always so warm and caring, was sitting between Amanda and Aaron. As she often did, she quietly took Amanda's hand in hers. And as she had never done, she also took Aaron's hand in her right hand. Aaron was surprised, but welcomed the gesture, and enjoyed the shared camaraderie. After sitting through two hours of repeated reports of anti-Semitism, it felt comforting to see that there were also gentlepersons present who did welcome the company of a Jew.

Hannah spoke. "I am a Jew from Germany. Brought to this great country by the warmth and generosity of British people. Since 1934, I have had hatred for Jews thrown at me from every direction in my native Germany. My generation no longer knows what to believe. All this anti-Semitism. Everywhere. Is it because we people are Jews, or is it because we Jews are people?"

Otto Schiff seemed visibly struck by this question. He put his left hand to his jaw and looked down at the floor. The room fell silent. He wanted to provide an answer but he didn't have one.

Hannah then continued. "The Nazis tell us that the Jews are something less than people. Sub-human, they call us. The British and their Allies recognize that we are not subhuman people. But they treat us like Jews. They treat us like aliens. What are we to believe about ourselves? This criticism and abuse clearly affects what others think of us, but it also clearly affects what we think of ourselves. And it is so deeply painful.

Are we truly such dreadful creatures that so many people want us to be cleansed from France, from Germany, from Austria, from Poland? Can you help us? Can you please help us?"

Hannah sat back down. And no one knew what to say.

Since he was chairing the meeting, Otto Schiff felt that it was his obligation to respond.

"As painful as it is for you to ask that question, and for the question to torture you, it is equally painful to answer it. Or maybe I should say to address it. No one can answer it. We are certainly not dreadful creatures. We do not warrant or deserve all the terrible attention we are receiving right now. We are a nation of people with a unique culture, a unique religion, a unique heritage and a unique history. That is not so unusual on this planet. What is also unique for us is that the Jewish Diaspora dates back 2,500 years. First, the Assyrians exiled the ten Israelite tribes, then, one-hundred years later, the Babylonians destroyed the First Temple and took the remaining population to Babylon. Thousands of those people eventually made it back to Judea, but many remained in Babylon, and then our ancestors resettled in North Africa, Southern Europe, and elsewhere. Of those who had returned to Judea, many were then driven out by the Romans when they destroyed the Second Temple in 68 AD. As a result, these tribes from the Middle East were spread throughout Europe, taking their religion, and culture and heritage with them. Emigrants are always suspect and often unwelcome. When European cities, where these Jews lived, became largely Christian in about 1,000 AD, the Jews found themselves even further outside the mainstream. And so naturally they were frequently made convenient scapegoats by governments and others.

"Unless and until the Jewish Nation can establish, or perhaps re-establish, a homeland somewhere, they will continue to be a Nation of Outsiders. The current Fuhrer of Germany did not invent anti-Semitism, but he has taken it to an entirely new level. He and his band of wretched misfits now in power in Germany are literally mad. I have just seen you, Miss, and heard you speak so eloquently. I can assure you that the eminent Augustine Friar Gregor Mendel, were he to be so fortunate to study your genetics, would find you superior in every way to that clique of clowns who now cast aspersions on your heredity and mine. You and your offspring will prove them wrong for decades to come, long after these deviants from all accepted norms of society are dead and gone. I would be more than happy to confer with you and your young friends privately after this session is over."

Hannah responded quietly, solemnly. "Thank you, Chairman Schiff. Your thoughtful words are very comforting."

"This does lead us to my final point. A point which I hope to explore at much greater length in future meetings. I did promise our government friends here that I would not put them on the spot by asking them about the Palestine issue, and I am a man of my word. However, I want to echo the words of Arthur James Balfour, the former British Foreign Secretary, to Lionel Walter Rothschild. There does need to be, now more than ever, the establishment in Palestine of a National Home for the Jewish People. And I am well aware that the British Government has grave reservations about this, particularly in during wartime. But mark my words, if these often-unwelcome Jews are not particularly welcome in England and in the U.S., they must be made welcome in Palestine. If not by our generation, which is now failing to answer this urgent call, then most certainly by the new generation, including those here today asking this question. As Geoffrey Chaucer so aptly said in 1395, "Time and tide wait for no man." Young lady, our old generation has failed you. Now your young generation must make it happen or it will never happen."

It was getting late, and the audience dispersed fairly quickly. Hannah and her group headed up to the front of the Conference Room to have a few words with Chairman Schiff. They introduced themselves and he greeted them warmly.

"Miss Hanauer, may I call you Hannah? My tiny but active brain has been churning to find answers to address the grave concerns you have raised here today. Thank you for having the courage to speak out!"

Amanda, Alice and Aaron had a good laugh. Schiff picked up on it.

"You have a tendency to be outspoken. Good! There is so much to consider here, but it is particularly noteworthy that Jewish heritage places huge value on education for children. The widespread literacy of the Jewish people led them to a deeper understanding of the great value of numeric skills, the great value of networking skills and the great value of reliable legal systems and skills. They acquired these skills. And these skills, in turn, provided the Jewish people with expertise in trade, commerce, banking, finance, law, medicine and science, where they have had had enormous success for many centuries in many countries. It is a very long, very deep, very engaging history with many ups and downs."

Turning to Aaron he said, "It would be very interesting to hear the views of our Dr. Solomon here. I am making the assumption, based upon his legendary first and last names, and his chosen profession, that he shares our Jewish ancestry?"

Aaron smiled.

"Yes. I do. And I have been moved to hear your analysis. I have a thought, for your consideration. Hannah, who we all so admire, has openly shared her questions and concerns here today. But many other young Jews now living here have these very same questions and concerns. Perhaps we could establish, with your help and guidance, some classes, or discussion sessions, to focus on the story of the Jewish Diaspora over the past centuries. It seems to me that the only Jewish history taught today is the Old Testament."

"I fully agree, Doctor. An excellent suggestion. And I am absolutely sure that we will have plenty of volunteers to help us. It is shameful and disgusting to watch these Nazis pigs stuffed into their starched uniforms calling our people subhuman, when it is they themselves who are guilty of subhuman behavior."

They all agreed to pick up the threads of the discussion in the New Year.

As they were filing out of the room, Inspector Dunbar, who had been waiting patiently on the sidelines, walked up to greet them.

Aaron shook his hand and then took him aside because the young women wanted to talk among themselves for a few minutes.

"Good to see you, Inspector. Are you becoming involved in the plight of European refugees? That would be good news."

"I have to admit I have not paid much attention to the situation with all of these European refugees, nor the genocides going on in Germany and elsewhere. Not a good reflection on me. But you can be sure that I will now start paying attention. It is an awful situation. I really shouldn't share this, but I am here to check on this crowd, and get some feel for why Miss Hanauer is getting unwanted attention, and maybe from whom. Ironically, the Yard is wondering if this might be coming from some elements of the Polish Army in Exile. They have a history of vocal and active anti-Semitism. It is late. I promised my long-suffering wife that I would take her to a pub for a little pre-Christmas dinner date tonight. Keep an eye on that Miss Hanauer, I can see now that she is a very special young lady. Let's catch up next week."

Aaron returned to the three women and offered to take them out for their own little pre-Christmas dinner date. They readily accepted, and so they all headed off to a nearby tavern.

Once there, enjoying a warm meal, Aaron had to tolerate repeated verbal jabs and only half-joking digs from young Allied soldiers, sailors, and airmen, bemoaning the sight of Aaron basking in the attention of these three very attractive young women, when they had none. But like a small army of ants upon a sugar cube, these young males were not to be deterred. Before long, two strapping handsome and very tall New Zealand infantrymen struck up a conversation with Amanda and Alice, which the two ladies seemed to enjoy. And while their attention was seemingly diverted to these eager Kiwis, Alice did notice that Aaron and Hannah were holding hands, just under the table.

After finishing their late dinner, Aaron headed off to get some sleep because he had to report to the hospital at 7:00 a.m. Saturday morning. He paid the tab and left the tavern. By the time he walked out, there was a circle of hungry young ants in different uniforms gathering around the three women.

It was almost 11:00 p.m. when the girls themselves decided that they should also head home, which did precipitate some moans and groans from the Lonely Soldiers and Sailors Club. The plan was for Amanda and Alice to ride the bus with Hannah to see her safely home and then hail a cab from Hannah's house back to the Haythornwaite home.

58

A Cold, Dark and Misty Night

18 December 1942 Night, London

The London bus dropped off Hannah, Amanda and Alice at 11:30 pm. The night was dark and damp. The streets were a little slick, and sloppy, but their mood was cheery. The pre-Christmas season had a special glow. As the three women walked up Newcastle Street, they joked and teased each other about their soldier suitors, as young women always do everywhere. Amanda and Alice sort of liked the two big Kiwi infantrymen. Manly fellows, with funny accents, a little shy, and seemingly very impressed with the two blue-eyed blonde British 'birds' they had cornered. They were fun, and so the four of them had agreed they might meet up again in a couple of weeks, at the Tavern's regular Friday night Happy Hour. Although the sisters really preferred their RAF pilots.

Hannah found herself 'pigeonholed' by an over eager Free French Army officer, who seemed a little too stuck on both himself and Charles de Gaulle. Hannah was not feeling too kindly towards the French in view of their treatment of Jews in France. So, she did not agree to his four requests for a repeat get together at some future happy hour.

As the three young women approached Turner Drive, a Newcastle Street cross street, Alice noticed a small darting shadow, maybe ten feet ahead and on her right. She broke off from Hannah and Amanda, who were now discussing wounded pilots, and walked over by herself to check on what she thought she had seen. As they crossed Turner and continued up Newcastle, Hannah and Amanda noticed Alice break off from their group.

Amanda glanced back and saw her down on one knee with what appeared to be a small, black dog. Her suspicions were confirmed when she heard some puppy barks. She laughed.

"The only thing that my sister likes even better than big men who act like little puppy dogs are actual little puppy dogs. How she found one out here on the dark and deserted street in the middle of the night is beyond me."

The puppy was small, and seemingly lost from its mother, but very, very happy to have found Alice, who was holding and petting it enthusiastically. The puppy had no collar. Alice had picked it up, much to the puppy's delight, and started up the street to catch her sister and Hannah, both of whom were now about twenty-five feet ahead of her, all walking in the street because the sidewalks on that block were narrow and uneven.

When Alice and the puppy were still about to cross Turner Drive, a dark van pulled around the corner and drove up Newcastle at a rapid clip, headed straight for Amanda and Hannah.

Alice screamed, "Amanda! Hannah! Look out! Car coming up behind you!"

Amanda turned just in time to see the van. Without even thinking of her own safety, Amanda pushed Hannah hard to get her out of the way of the oncoming van. The hard push put Hannah up on the narrow sidewalk. The van swerved to avoid hitting Amanda and aimed in the direction of Hannah on the sidewalk, but it was now well past her. The van sped up Newcastle. Hannah fell down on the sidewalk.

Amanda was not so fortunate. For every action, there is an equal and opposite reaction. By pushing Hannah hard and fast to the right, she propelled herself hard and fast to the left. Because the van had moved to the right, towards Hannah, it did not strike Amanda, but the force of Amanda's move to the left resulted in her falling backwards and taking a very hard fall on the sidewalk curb on the left side of the street. She mostly landed on her left arm and left hip. The pain was sharp and deep. She knew it was not good.

The van stopped short a block ahead, did a very well-executed U-turn, turned on its bright lights, and headed back towards Hannah who was now on the sidewalk. A sitting duck. But Alice was running up the street, straight towards the oncoming van. Alice dropped the puppy and was now screaming and waving her arms, "Stop! Stop! Stop!"

The puppy was barking up a storm and running alongside Alice. There is nothing like a frantically barking dog and a woman screaming *Stop! Stop! Stop!* at midnight to awaken the neighbors. House lights went on. Three or four doors opened. The previously dark, dead and deserted street was suddenly full of light and life. The van had stopped dead in its tracks, as though the stunned driver was sizing up the scene before him. And just at that moment the little black puppy, with the biggest jump of its life, pounced up at the black front fender of the van and started barking its young lungs out at the dark van and its driver. It was quite a sight to see. And none of the eight or nine people who did see it on that dark night in December would ever forget it.

Leaving the van lights on bright to blind the onlookers, the driver slammed the van into reverse, backed rapidly and skillfully up the street to the next cross street, made a quick left turn onto Adams Street, turned off the van lights, and disappeared into the night.

Within minutes, Alice, Hannah, six neighbors, and a small black puppy were hovering over Amanda, who was cradling her left arm with her right hand and trying very hard to hold back tears.

"Amanda, you saved my life. You saved my life! But I am so sorry— you are *injured.* How bad is it?"

"It hurts plenty. It feels like a broken radius and ulna in my lower left arm. My hip is a little banged up, but I'm pretty sure it isn't broken. I did bump my head pretty hard. Someone should look at that, I guess."

One of the neighbors piped in. "I have a car, and petrol for a change! Let me take you to the hospital."

"Oh. Thank you. Queen Victoria Hospital. I am a nurse there."

It was almost one o'clock in the morning on Saturday when the three girls arrived at the hospital with a little black puppy with no name but plenty of heart.

When hospital admissions saw that Amanda, one of their own, was the principal patient, there was a scramble to treat her promptly. An elderly, but kindly doctor was working the night shift. He looked over at Amanda's arm, which was clearly broken, and her hip, which he said was probably okay. He checked on her possible concussion. He ordered x-rays and gave Amanda something to ease the pain. Then he returned to the RAF Pilot Severe Burn Unit.

As luck would have it, two exceptional service nurses were on duty since Friday and Saturday nights were busy. Senior Sister Helen Wilson

Cargill and Matron-in-Chief Gladys Taylor took charge. They ushered the girls and the dog to one large room. Each girl was assigned to a bed. The nurses bandaged Amanda's arm to stabilize it. The doctor said it could not be set and casted until the swelling was reduced. Amanda was soon in bed, propped up by several pillows as a precaution to prevent swelling in her cranial area. Because it had been a cold night, all three girls had been bundled up with woolen hats and coats, which had provided some cushion to Amanda's fall.

With morphine in her system, Amanda fell into a deep sleep. Sister Cargill awakened her every two hours to check for concussion symptoms. Alice was too excited to sleep, but her 'comfort puppy' helped her to relax, and soon she too was fast asleep. Sister Cargill very gently took the sleeping puppy out of Alice's arms and placed the dog into an enclosed area in the lawn behind the hospital.

Hannah was strung out. She felt very guilty about being responsible for serious injuries to Amanda. Her guilt was compounded by the realization that Amanda suffered these injuries while saving her life. Matron Taylor tried to comfort her, but wasn't making much progress. Then she offered Hannah a cup of hot tea, into which the Matron had discreetly placed a small morphine tablet. About fifteen minutes later, Hannah also fell asleep.

Matron Taylor instructed two of the young nurses to call the Haythornwaite and Hawkins families to inform them their girls had been involved in "an accident," describing the details. The messages also suggested that the families come take them home in the morning.

59

Saturday Morning – Queen Victoria Hospital

19 December 1942, London

Aaron walked into the hospital room at 6:45 am Saturday morning. All three young ladies were sleeping soundly. Sister Cargill and Matron Taylor filled him in on the details.

"From what we can see, Dr. Solomon, only Amanda Haythorn-waite seems to have suffered any significant injuries from the accident last night," said Matron Taylor. "Her younger sister, Alice, seems fine. Hannah Hanauer, who I believe you treated last July, fell to the ground, but does not appear to have any injuries. We saw no reason to check her closely, but you might want to do so. Amanda does not appear to have a concussion, but her lower arm is broken."

Aaron went first to Amanda. He gently probed her arm, which then woke her up.

"Good morning, Amanda. Looks like you succeeded in giving yourself a reason to be taken off duty for a month, yet hang out in the Queen Victoria Hospital ward with your handsome, young RAF Pilot Fan Club!" Aaron laughed.

Amanda did her best to smile.

"You have a simple fracture of both the radius and ulna bones. Very uncomplicated bones. Your wrist, which is a much more complicated structure, seems just fine. Matron Taylor and I want to check on your head and your hip, if that is all right with you?"

"Of course."

Aaron and Matron Taylor checked her head, neck, shoulders, both arms, her hips and her legs.

Aaron, with a big smile, reported, "The rest of you seems fine."

They gently awakened Hannah, who groggily gave her consent, and made a quick check of her. She did not appear to have any new injuries, and her injuries from last July seemed well healed.

Aaron and Matron Taylor left the room and proceeded on their Saturday morning rounds with the intention of returning a little later when the young ladies would be more alert.   Aaron stopped in his office and placed a call to Inspector Dunbar. Dunbar was away, but a junior constable took the report, promising that it would be delivered to Dunbar as soon as they could track him down. At 8:30, two young nurses walked into the room with breakfast and tea for Amanda, Alice and Hannah, and a little tray of some ham on a bone for the small black puppy with no name. All four of them were very hungry.

Aaron returned to their room around 9:30 a.m. All three ladies were awake and seemed upbeat. Captain Spencer and Pamela Haythornwaite were in the room, as were Ralph and Hazel Hawkins. The young ladies were getting lots of attention, but so too was the little black puppy sitting contentedly in Alice's lap. The room was buzzing with the lurid details of Friday night. Everyone was relieved to see that Aaron had returned to check up on them again and hung on his every word.

Shortly after 11:00 a.m., a young nurse came into the room.

"An Inspector Dunbar from Scotland Yard is here. May he come in?"

The Inspector immediately captivated the room. He conveyed an air of competence, confidence, good cheer, and professional purpose. Everyone was listening he spoke at length to each of the three patients to get a full report of the second incident. The Haythornwaites and the Hawkins were horrified to think that some lunatic was intentionally attempting to drive his van into Hannah. Dunbar made extensive notes of all the facts.

When Dunbar finished, he made some comments, and some suggestions. At this point, everyone was paying close attention.

"Before coming here today," he said, "I went back to the scene of the attack. This is now a serious situation. Someone is intent on doing severe bodily harm to Miss Hanauer. My job is to figure out who and why. We do know it is a man. We do not know his identity. But we do have some clues. We do not know why. But we do have some clues.

"As to his identity. He is not a professional killer, or professional hit man. Professional killers plan carefully. They do not miss. Both of these attacks were haphazard and amateurish. He is neither very bright, nor well equipped. No one with half a brain would sit on a street corner repeat-edly hoping to find an opportunity to run down his intended victim with a noisy old van. There was the same country mud at the scene. So, he has some connection to the countryside. But he is a highly skilled driver. It is interesting that he was extremely careful to avoid hitting Amanda. Twice. Notwithstanding the suspicions of MI5, it seems highly improbable that he is connected to the Polish Army in Exile. They are a hyper-macho group, and running over a helpless young woman, even if she were a Jewish woman, would be totally out of character. Also, the driver yelled, 'dump-kopf,' which is German for idiot. The Polish word would be 'gtupen.'

"I also think it highly unlikely that the man is upset with Miss Hanauer because she speaks in support of Jewish refugees. I have now seen her in action. British people who are anti-Semitic, and there are quite a few of them, do not become perturbed when people complain about the fact that they are anti-Semitic. In fact, they love to hear it. This man is pursuing some other agenda. Perhaps some deeply held vendetta. Since he spoke twice in German, I suggest that this relates to some situation in Germany. But we are a long way from figuring out the source. In the meantime, we do not want to create another opportunity for him to strike again. Third time lucky, as the saying goes.

"Miss Hanauer should not return to the Hawkins' home. She should be moved elsewhere. Continuing to reside with the Hawkins' places Miss Hanauer and the Hawkins at great risk. Is there somewhere to move her until we sort this out?"

Pamela Haythornwaite spoke immediately. "Hannah can stay with us. We would love to have her."

Captain Haythornwaite, Amanda, and Alice agreed right away.

Dunbar frowned. "Not a good idea, I'm afraid. Your two daughters are very closely connected to Miss Hanauer. And the driver has seen them together. It would not lessen the danger to Miss Hanauer, but it would put all of you at risk. There must be some better alternative."

Aaron spoke up. "Inspector, your analysis is frightening and comforting at the same time, if such a combination is possible. This country bumpkin could be capable of anything. Hannah, this entire discussion is focused on you. What are your thoughts on how this should be managed?"

Hannah chose her words carefully.

"I do not want to put anyone else in danger. I cannot refute Inspector Dunbar's wise counsel. But I do not know where I can go. It seems like anywhere I go I will be putting other people in jeopardy. I should probably get as far away from everyone here as possible!"

"We have some time to think about this," said Aaron. "Hannah is safe here in the hospital at the moment. I have spoken to Matron Taylor. Hannah, we both think you should spend the next several days here at the hospital. You are a bit shaken up, and that will give us some time to find some alternative living arrangement to you. Would that be agreeable?"

"Yes. Thank you, Doctor."

As the emotions in the room settled down, Inspector Dunbar walked over to Alice, and very gently but firmly picked up the black puppy with no name.

"Hello, little fellow. You seem to be The Hero of the Month. Did you find him all alone, so late at night?"

"Yes, I did. But the puppy seemed very appreciative at being found. Do you have any idea as to its breed and where it might have come from?"

"He is a male Kerry Blue terrier. Named for the Kerry county in Ireland where these dogs were first bred. They are the most beloved dog in Ireland, and the most beloved dog by my very red-haired and very Irish wife, Kayleigh. He is on the small side, but I would guess that he is about five or six months old. He looks like a purebred. I bet he somehow got out and wandered away from the Fernlee home on Boston Street, near the Hawkins' house. They breed these dogs. We know them at Scotland Yard because these terriers are our most popular police dogs. They are also wonderful family dogs. Kayleigh and I would love to have him, but after his performance last night I suspect that he is now Yours for Life, Miss Haythornwaite."

"I hope so! Mother, Father, could we keep him? Please!"

Pamela smiled. "Yes, of course, of course. But we will have to share him with Hannah. Alice, does he have a name?"

"I thought he was a shadow when he caught my attention, and now he follows me around like my shadow, so I was thinking I might call him 'Shadow.'"

Everyone laughed.

Inspector Dunbar took the puppy over to Hannah and placed him carefully on her lap. Whether from fatigue, or some injury, or too much excitement, or too much guilt, or too much morphine, we will never know. But Hannah held the dog very tightly and cried her eyes out. The crowd gathered around her to comfort her, but Aaron was discreet. He knew that he would be there to comfort her later, after the crowd disbursed.

Aaron returned to see just Hannah and Amanda around 4:00 p.m. The rest had gone home. He proposed a plan to get Hannah out of London. Maybe out of England altogether. Hannah just listened. She missed holding the frisky puppy, and sort of wished that Alice had not taken him home.

Amanda then said to Aaron, "You have been so kind and attentive to all of us, but please, don't let us keep you from your daily rounds. All these airmen are also anxious to get your attention!"

Aaron nodded, and headed back into the ward.

60

Four Requests from Sarah

20 December 1942, London

Sarah knocked on Robert's door on Sunday afternoon in December. She had not called to make a "date." Knowing his usual Sunday afternoon schedule, she assumed that he would be home reading the newspaper and the endless intelligence reports that piled up on the desk in his study. She was right.

She hoped he might be pleased to see her unannounced. She also hoped he might not have dinner plans. She wisely dressed well for the pop-in visit.

"Well, this is a pleasant surprise, and especially on this very dull and cold afternoon. Come in. Come in. Take off your coat! Can I get you tea, coffee, or a glass of wine?"

Sarah paused for a moment to hear the music from Robert's gramophone, making its way from his living room into the foyer. Vera Lynn was singing of *love and laughter, and peace ever after tomorrow, when the world is free.* The White Cliffs of Dover rendition gave Sarah pause as a barely audible sigh escaped from her which she brushed off before Robert had a chance to comment.

"Hello, Robert dear." She gave him a big hug. "I hate to impose on your precious day off. Four issues have arisen where I really need your help, and all these need some time for you to mull over. I thought it might be best to see you on a quiet Sunday afternoon when your office and your Wild Bill Donovan aren't hounding you. Am I forgiven?"

"No, you are not forgiven! Not unless you agree to have dinner with me tonight at a location of my choosing."

"Oh, I don't know about that. That is a very high price to pay for forgiveness. But I agree. And, thank you." She hugged him again.

The sun was beginning to set. So, Robert set out some tea and biscuits, and a bottle of white wine and cheese and crackers. As he sat down to listen, he took a long look at Sarah. A blue sweater and skirt nicely set off Sarah's light-brown hair and deep blue eyes. A pretty package.

Sarah paused for a few minutes to let Robert 'take in the view,' which pleased her.

"The first request—the French Resistance and my current and ongoing assignment for MI6 to establish a network of current and potential French Resistance persons who can help us with the eventual Allied landings in western France. Can you give me some American insight into the best ways MI6 can approach these individuals and groups working for the so-called Resistance? I know that your friend Donovan has also been looking into this group. Our reports say, whilst many of these people and groups are not supportive of de Gaulle and his Free French Movement based here in London, a number of them in France are supportive. To further complicate these questions, de Gaulle and the PM are often at odds with each other, and the U.S. Government wants to replace de Gaulle as head of Free France Movement. MI6 wants de Gaulle kept strictly in London, and MI6 is not enthusiastic about using his support and his people in establishing and arming these French resistance groups. I am told that Emmanuel d'Astier and Jean Moulin have deep ties to resistance groups who are on the ground, and active, yet they also seem to support de Gaulle."

Robert thought for a moment then responded.

"France has long been split into many factions. Too many factions. Left. Right. And Center. No one knows if these factions will ever come together. Probably not. But we need them to pull together long enough to support the Allied invasion. Moulin and d'Astier are left wing Republicans, but they are widely respected and can pull diverse groups together. The Communists do not like or trust de Gaulle, just like the Brits and the Yanks don't like him. De Gaulle is very arrogant and outrageously pompous. But he does speak for a lot of French people who oppose the Nazis, and unlike a lot of French, he does put his money where his mouth is. He is actually fighting to liberate France.

"My advice is simple. Since it is well known and notorious that French politics are hopeless, ignore the politics and seek out the people in whom you personally have trust and confidence. Jean Moulin and Emmanuel d'Astier are definitely 'worthies.' Moulin is one tough cookie—a true Resistance fighter. But you will be totally smitten with Emmanuel d'Astier. He was head of French Naval Intelligence before the French defeat. Get them both in your corner. When you meet Emmanuel d'Astier, you should be aware that his older brother, Henri, is also a major player in the French Resistance movement. Henri d'Astier has been operating in North Africa. In fact, his little band of fighters captured Admiral Darlan and General Alphonse Juive and turned them over to the Allies. Amazing! Expand from them and trust your instincts. But do not ignore de Gaulle. He is not going away, and right now he needs you a lot more than you need him."

Sarah was listening and taking notes.

"Understood. It would be hard to argue with that advice. It is interesting how all of these little puzzle pieces eventually fit together. Menzies mentioned Henri d'Astier to me a couple of weeks ago. He regards Henri very highly. There is also a third brother, Francois d'Astier, the youngest French general ever, here in London. He, too, is active in the Resistance."

"I hope that the next request is an easier one!" teased Robert.

"It isn't. Second request—Gunther. Menzies brought him up to me on Friday. As is so often the case, Menzies thinks Donovan is wrong. Menzies is a big believer in the German Resistance. He gets his own 'signals' from someplace in Germany. He agrees with Donovan that eventually German senior military line officers will start reaching out to Allied military commanders in the field in an effort to negotiate limited area surrenders, but he sees that coming sooner, rather than later as Donovan expects.

"Menzies believes that every rational Wehrmacht general and field marshal now has as his greatest fear the onslaught and retribution of the Soviet armies, which are a gathering storm on the entire Eastern Front. Menzies wants to send strong signals up the chain of military command in the Wehrmacht that the Allies are open to reasonable area specific negotiations. He 'instructed' me to set up more meetings with Gunther, and hopefully with you, early next year, in London or North Africa, since that is where Gunther is stationed. And then Menzies told me he himself would be in North Africa this coming week and wanted to talk to Gunther, but acknowledged that any contact would put Gunther in grave danger. Menzies said, 'I will be closely watched by our fickle 'Frenchies,' who could and would be happy to score points with the Fritz by betraying this very brave, but probably very foolish, young German officer.'"

"That's interesting," said Robert.

"Menzies never leaves London, so his visit to North Africa must have significance. Will you please facilitate another meeting with Gunther for me?"

"Can we meet again in Margate at the Walpole Bay? On a Sunday? After a Saturday Night Dinner date?"

"You drive a hard bargain. But I will always Do My Duty for God and My Country, no matter how high the price. So, yes. I agree to your onerous terms!"

Sarah delivered another warm hug, and Robert opened the bottle of chilled white wine.

"Oh, the wine is so good. Thank you! You are always the best host. And a glass of wine or two will hopefully soften you up a bit for my next two requests!"

"Uh, oh. Should I have my guard up?"

"Maybe. My third request entails a personal favor. But probably not too painful. But *be warned,* my fourth and final request raises some potentially significant military, political, and intelligence sensitivities and conflicts. It is perfectly fine if you wish to say 'No' to either or both."

Sarah smiled, and paused for a few minutes to have another cheese and cracker, and a few sips of wine. Then she continued.

"Here goes. Number three. I need a U.S. Entry Visa for a young German-Jewish refugee, a Miss Hanauer. You might recall that back on 5 August I mentioned that, at the request of Dr. Aaron Solomon, the young flight surgeon who you met with Professor Lindemann, MI5 asked Scotland Yard to investigate a very suspicious car accident, which may have been intentional, in which a young German Jewish woman brought to London in the Kindertransport was injured. You asked to be kept updated because of the anti-Semitic overtones."

"I do remember. The lady's name sounds familiar. Has she recovered?"

"She has, under the very attentive care of Dr. Solomon. But last Friday night the woman was attacked again by the same car at the same spot and in the same manner. It is now clear that someone is very intent on killing her. No one seems to know why or who. I received a call from Dr. Solomon on Sunday afternoon, and then I spoke with an Inspector Dunbar from Scotland Yard. Everyone thinks we should get the young woman out of London. Somewhere safe. We are well aware that the US authorities are adamant about not accepting any more German-Jewish refugees, but this is a unique case. It would be very embarrassing to the British Government if the woman were to be killed here in London by some raving British anti-Semite. I myself have not met her, but I'm told that she is a very impressive young woman from a professional family with deep ties to Dresden. I am also told that she has been very outspoken in seeking assistance for Jewish refugees. Do you think we could do something for her?"

"Candidly, I do not know. But we must try to help her. I've been very impressed by Dr. Solomon. And I think that there are a couple of channels that might be useful. One channel is Donovan, of course, but he has his hands very full these days, and this is not really 'up his alley.' One other possible channel, an influential Jewish gentleman in New York City who I know very well. He might be induced to take a personal interest in this. If I am going to pursue it, I will first have to meet Miss Hanauer in order to vouch for her. Analogous to your need to meet Gunther face to face. Could such a meeting with Miss Hanauer be arranged quickly? As you have described her, she sounds like a young Jewish lady—a girl, really—I met a couple of years ago. But there are many Jewish refugees in London these days."

"Yes," Sarah said, "I am sure that it can be. I will work on that in the morning. Thank you, Robert! You open so many doors!"

"Do you know how old she is, and her full name?"

"Hannah Hanauer. Age twenty this month, I think. No relatives in the UK or the US. The status of her family in Germany is unknown. She had a mother, father, and one younger brother, his current age is around eighteen. Strong suspicion that they all ended up in concentration camps in Poland. But we really do not know."

"Maybe Dr. Solomon or Inspector Dunbar should join us when I meet her. What about her UK host family? Are they close to her?"

"Very close. But they trust us to manage this situation. Do you want me there, too?"

"Probably not. My guess is that we are better off if the US State Department regards this as a one-off Humanitarian Visa. If they sniff heavy MI5 involvement, that will kick the request 'upstairs' in Washington bureaucracy, and it will take a year to clear, if ever."

"Makes sense. I'm sure I can find an opportunity to meet her myself before she leaves for the US. I'll let you boys handle it. Thank you! Now, my Final Request. Straight out of left field. This wine is warming me up. Do you mind if I get comfortable, before we address my final request? Maybe you might want to get comfortable, too."

Sarah took off her woolen sweater and kicked off her shoes and helped Robert "unwind" as well, by taking off his heavy Cardigan sweater.

Sarah asked, "Are we going out to dinner somewhere?"

"Why don't I just pull out some leftover pasta? If we go out, we'd have to climb back into all the heavy coats and sweaters, which you have so carefully draped on the furniture."

"There's a fine idea. Let's just stay here."

They sat together on the sofa, warming up.

"This warm-up for the Final Request is beginning to make me nervous. I feel like a fly caught in a web. Or worse still, poor Samson among the evil Philistines!"

Sarah ran her fingers through his hair, which she knew from experience would arouse him. And she smiled.

"Oh, Robert. Your hair is so fine! I hope that old busybody Bill Donovan didn't tell you my MI6 Code Name. It really is most unflattering. And I do think the that 'Delilah' was wrongly condemned by those stuffy old Hebrew scholars who redacted the Old Testament. They just never approved of perfectly nice gentile women pursuing one of their precious Jewish men. And anyway, Samson was having plenty of fun along the way. Delilah was a beauty of Biblical proportions, and Samson was just a circus strongman. If I am really making you nervous it is not evident! You appear to be more 'aroused' than frightened!"

She gently patted the front of his trousers and laughed.

Robert smiled. "I'll try to restrain my manly desires for one more request. It better be a good one. I sense that I am about to be asked to Sell My Soul to the Devil. Will this be painful?"

"Either not painful at all, or way too painful. The request is very short. The request might be unfathomable. Here's the story. Little Bill, that is Bill Stevenson, from the MI6 New York office, sent me a coded message last week. Two of his MI6 agents in New York City were grabbing lunch at the Colombia University cafeteria, where one of the agents had gone to college. At the table next to them, two older gentlemen were seated. They both looked like somewhat frumpy professors from one of the university science departments. The agents overheard the younger of the two professors say these exact words to the other, 'A fellow professor told me in strict confidence that Enrico's experimental pile of graphite bricks and enriched uranium, or some similar material, went critical on 2 December. The fellow who told me said I could tell you, but no one else.' The older Professor stared at the younger professor with a very surprised look on his face, and said, 'Oh my God!' When the two left the table to head back to their offices, the agents followed them to see who they might be. As the agents suspected, the two professors returned to Columbia's Graduate School of Physics."

Robert smiled. "You really are 'Delilah.' Menzies named you well. Even though you have me where you want me, or should I say, where I want you, I cannot tell you what your people do not know, even though we are allies. I can maybe confirm what your people do know, or what they certainly should know.

"I am sure the "Enrico" they named is Enrico Fermi, who was a member of Colombia's physics department for years. He has been working with Leo Szilard and other physicists for years to develop nuclear power. This is well-known. Fermi was awarded the Nobel Prize five years ago for his work using neutrons to bombard uranium to create new elements. If he and his colleagues are making headway towards developing a new source of power, such as nuclear power, that is great news indeed for the Allied cause. And Ultra-Secret. But that is really all I know about this very complex scientific field. Tell Little Bill to check with your British physicists. People such as Patrick Blackett from Operations Research. This is way out of my field. But these two agents are really good. This is a very big deal, if it is true."

"Robert, that was very helpful. You are amazing."

"Please tell Little Bill that it would be a disaster if this information were to leak to the Germans. As I said, it *must* be treated as Ultra-Secret. And you should burn the little piece of paper on which those words are written." Robert smiled, took a deep breath, and said, "Please may I now have some dinner and some Delilah?"

"Yes, you can! Which do you want first?"

"You can perfectly well see which I want first!"

"Stevenson does have a sense of humor. He teased me a little. He said he could put the question to Donovan, but he knew that Donovan wouldn't tell him anything. Then he said, 'You seem to have a way to get Johnston to talk!'"

Robert stood up with a smile. "Is this true? Do you have a way to get me to talk?"

"Yes, I do. But I haven't found a way to get you to stop talking! Now, it is time to focus on Delilah!"

Sarah stood up and took off her blouse, skirt and slip. She helped Robert remove his shirt, trousers, shoes and socks. Then she took his hand and guided him into the bedroom. Knowing that Robert had 'a thing' for her legs, she stretched out on the top of the bed, lying flat on her back, wearing just her undergarments, and looked up at Robert. Then she said, "Robert, may I call you "Enrico" tonight? Such a sexy Italian name!"

Robert smiled. "Yes, of course. If that will turn you on. May I call you "Bruschetta?""

"Bruschetta? Why?"

"Because I plan to have you before the tortellini entrée!"

Robert got the message. He stretched out next to her in bed, and began to stroke her legs. She held her legs tightly together to tease him, but he could easily insert his right hand between her thighs, and so he did. Stroking up, and then down, and then up, and then down, taking care to never touch her crotch. Just coming close. Finally, Sarah took his hand and placed it firmly on her crotch. She held it there, while hugging him tightly. After a few minutes, he heard her sigh, and felt her relax.

Then it was Robert's turn.

61

The Second Meeting with Hannah

21 December 1942 Afternoon, London

On Monday morning, Robert received a phone call from Sarah on his office line.

"Thank you for tolerating me yesterday. And for the bottle of wine. I have made the arrangements with Hannah Hanauer. She can meet you at 4:30 today. Dr. Solomon and Inspector Dunbar will bring her. Do you want to meet at your office?"

"I would prefer to have them meet me for a drink and a light supper at The Old Bell Tavern. I am holding the little table you and I use back in the corner. This will give me more insight into her. It's more relaxing, with some other people present so she won't feel so intimidated, and also a little more social. I want to see how she handles herself. It's a little like a job interview. I want her to open up. What do you think?"

"It's a good plan. I will send them there. Good luck! Talk later? Maybe tomorrow?"

"You bet, Sarah. Call me tomorrow."

Hannah, Aaron, and Inspector Dunbar walked into the tavern shortly after 4:30. Robert was waiting for them at the table. He stood up, and they all shook hands. Robert sat opposite to Hannah.

"This is very exciting for me, Mr. Johnston," said Hannah. "Meeting you for the second time. You probably won't remember, but you and I met over two years ago during the Blitz, September 1940. You were kind enough to assist me and a small group of German-Jewish refugees when we were ordered to leave a London Underground station during a bomb raid, 'because we were taking space reserved for English people.' Does this ring any bells?"

"Hannah, yes, of course. You underestimate your charisma. It was you who took command of that awful encounter. Like a young Lady Moses, you led your people out of that quagmire. I was just fortunate to be around to assist. When I first heard about you yesterday, from Sarah Leach, I did wonder if it could be the same young woman I met two years ago. So very nice to cross paths again. We have an urgent matter to address concerning your personal safety. Shall we order something to eat and drink, and put our heads together to address this situation?"

After they all ordered, Robert continued probing for information.

"Hannah, would you be comfortable telling me a little about yourself, where you were born, your family background, how you came to be in England, and the current whereabouts of your family, if you know?"

Hannah related her background, and Aaron occasionally chipped in with comments about Hannah's activities in London, the strong bonds she had built in London, the facts surrounding her two near misses, and the current state of her injuries.

The food was served and they all began to eat. Robert and Inspector Dunbar had some wine, but Hannah and Aaron declined. Robert watched Hannah carefully. He was impressed by her, but also by Inspector Dunbar and Aaron. He thought it would be very pleasant to have dinner with this small group every week. And adding Sarah would provide her usual spice and dash.

Towards the end of dinner, Robert said to Hannah, "I am prepared to seek a Visa for you to travel to the U.S. for your own protection. I can see the wisdom of doing that. But I must inquire, do you want to leave England, or even London? You do seem embedded here."

Hannah looked down at her now empty plate. Very empty. She had been hungrier than she realized. Robert noticed and quickly ordered two plates of cheese and crackers, and more tea and wine, for the table.

"No. I do not want to leave London at all. My life here has been interesting and my friends are very warm. If I stay here, I might get news about my family. I do not know a soul in America, and it is thousands of miles away, but everyone is telling me that I have to put a great deal of space between me and this bizarre person who is trying to kill me."

"Give me a day or two to mull this over," said. Robert. "I will start the process to obtain a U.S. Visa for you. I do have some channels for that— I think I do. In the meantime, we four can think about whether there might be some other possible solution to your problem. One thing is crystal clear, we must give high priority to protecting you. You are a unique person, who we can ill afford to lose. Where are you currently staying?"

"I have made arrangements with Queen Victoria Hospital for Hannah to stay there for a few more days," said Aaron. "We have a little time. But the hospital is pretty confining."

"And no one can long survive on hospital food," added Dunbar. "As you may have seen for yourself during this dinner meeting, this is a hungry lass! I must say it was a stroke of genius for you to invite her, and the rest of us, to a meal. Thank you! You now have a well-fed friend in Scotland Yard. Permit me to add one suggestion. Whenever someone is seeking out another person, as this perpetrator is currently looking for our Miss Hanauer, the seeker relies ninety percent on the target's recognizable articles of clothing. Miss Hanauer is now very recognizable by her attire, and her attire is very typical of the attire of refugees in London. She does have a couple of well-dressed young friends. Perhaps they could take her shopping. It would help to disguise her a bit by changing her appearance."

"Excellent point, Inspector. I think we can make that happen. Hannah, I am heading back to my office to make some calls to the US. Would you please come to my office tomorrow afternoon around 4:30?"

"Yes. I'd be happy to."

"I will bring her," Aaron added.

"Great! Thank you!"

Robert knew exactly what he had to do.

62

A Call to Ellen

21 December 1942 Late evening, London

As soon as Robert arrived back at his office, he called Ellen. She was at her house, as were his son and daughter, home for Christmas. Ellen was a little surprised to hear from him during the workday.

"Ellen, I need your advice on an awkward but interesting situation here in London, involving a very young and impressive German-Jewish woman, whose life seems to be in danger."

"Of course, Robert. How can I help?"

He spent the next forty minutes describing the situation.

"You are absolutely right, Robert. We should help her, and I'm quite sure we can. But this endeavor is so far out of your usual target range of ships, planes, tanks, bombs, troop movements and clandestine spy machinations. I am curious. Have you now opened lines of communication with the Jewish Refugee Committee, or did this intriguing saga reach your ears from that young WREN officer from British Military Intelligence who seems to have caught your ear—-and your eye?"

"I have never communicated with the JRC, although perhaps I should. They are a powerful group. Yes. This situation came to me through that WREN officer Lt. Sarah Leach. But really through her father, British Royal Navy Captain Benjamin Leach. Captain Leach is very close to the father of the two young British women who've spent much time with Miss Hannah Hanauer. In fact, it was one of these daughters who pushed Hannah out of the way during the second van attack and suffered a broken arm. The WREN officer has never met Hannah."

"Hannah's story is compelling. I do remember you telling me two years ago about a dynamic, young Jewish woman who helped all of her fellow unfortunate refugees make a fast exit from the London Underground bomb shelter. Incredible that she should reappear two years later. But then, exceptional people do get noticed."

"Ellen, what would you think about calling your father about this? He could be very helpful if so inclined."

"I intend to call him as soon as we get off. Could you possibly arrange for my father and me to talk with Hannah tomorrow? We should act fast. Everything shuts down soon for the Christmas holiday."

"She will be in my office tomorrow at 4:30 London time. I will place a call to you then. And thank you. I count you among the impressive women in my life!"

"Thank you, Robert. The U.S. and U.K. are very lucky to have you there. Maybe someday when all this insanity ends, we will get you both back *here*. Your children miss you very much. And so do I."

63

An All-American Father-Daughter Team

22- 23 December 1942, London

Robert met with Hannah and Aaron for fifteen minutes before the call to the States. Robert explained to them that he had enlisted the assistance of his wife, Ellen, from whom he is now separated, and her father, Dr. Daniel Finerman, both of whom live in New York City. He told them he and Ellen had agreed to a formal separation because he felt it was his duty to remain in London to assist the war effort, in view of his experience living and working in Berlin in the early days of the Third Reich. He had no intention of bailing out of the impending global crisis. For the sake of the children, they had agreed to stay married, but enter into a formal separation.

"My wife's father is a distinguished Jewish physician with many friends and connections in US Jewish Refugee organizations. We could use their connections to get a Visa for Hannah. Both Ellen and her father want to talk to you, Hannah."

"I am happy to," Hannah replied.

Robert put through the radio telephone call to Ellen and her father on the secure line, and made the introductions, including Aaron. Ellen and her father had asked that Aaron join the call to take some pressure off of Hannah.

The four of them spoke for more than an hour, providing Ellen and Dr. Finerman with all of the relevant background, and much more. Hannah gave them painful and very personal details about the European refugee problems in general, and the excruciating situation for Jewish refugees in particular. She did not pull punches on the very sensitive topic of the US lackluster response to admitting Jewish refugees. Ellen and her father were absolutely blown away by Hannah's detailed knowledge of the situation and her eloquent facility with English, German, Hebrew, Yiddish, and some French; her charm, good manners, and deference to these people who have shared a keen interest in her case were all equally impressive.

Dr. Finerman started asking questions about Hannah's family and her father. After listening for ten minutes, Dr. Finerman said, "I just realized that I have actually heard of your father through his Jewish medical circles. Dr. Hanauer was a distinguished psychiatrist in Dresden prior to the advent of the Third Reich. I seem to recall that the doctor's wife, your mother, had been a teacher of mathematics and physics."

Hannah was very moved and brought to tears to hear that her parents were so widely known. The discussion continued with Dr. Solomon explaining his background.

When the call finally ended, it was well after 6:00 pm. Robert asked Hannah and Aaron to wait for him in the guest office, while he signed off with Ellen and her father.

Alone, back in his office, he picked up the phone.

"Well, Ellen? What do you think?"

"Robert, my father and I agree. Hannah is an extraordinary young woman. Lt. Leach was wise to bring this matter to your attention. We absolutely want to help. We will work on the US Visa, but it will take some time, and then there will be all of the travel arrangements. At the end of the day, it is really terrible that she should have to leave London, giving up her new life and her new freedom, and of course being even farther away from her family somewhere in Germany. And what a family! Until you can find a safe home for her, father and I were wondering if you could move her into the housekeeper quarters of your London house, where we put the children while all four of us were staying together in London. It has a bedroom and small kitchen and bathroom, and a separate entrance from the street. Is it still empty? Would your law firm care? It seems well hidden and safe, and no one would ever think to look for her there. Would that be uncomfortable for you?"

"That is a great idea. There is an interior entry door of course, but it locks from both sides. I will check with her and Dr. Solomon, who seems to be keeping a close eye on her. He too is a special person. A Jewish flight surgeon who has been very active in protecting their young RAF Pilots. Thank you, Ellen and Daniel. Thank you so much. I will look into this and call you back tomorrow."

Robert invited Aaron and Hannah out for dinner to talk things over. Over a hot meal, he broached the subject of a move in with him until a safe home could be found. They both agreed it was a terrific and very generous idea.

The next morning, 23 December, the eve of Christmas Eve, with the happy assistance of Aaron and Alice and the little black puppy, Hannah moved into the housekeeper's quarters of Robert's home. Amanda was still in the Hospital, and due to have her arm casted, now that the swelling had gone down. She was anxious to return home.

After they stopped at the Hawkins' house to pick up Hannah's things, Alice, Hannah, and Aaron walked over to the Fernlee's home on Boston Street just three blocks away.

A knock at the door, and Mrs. Edith Fernlee appeared with a black puppy under each arm. Upon seeing the small, black puppy clutched tightly by Alice, Mrs. Fernlee shouted in joy, "Little Number Seven! Where have you been, my clever little fellow?"

She dropped the other two somewhat larger puppies, and gently took the smaller puppy from Alice, who was clearly reluctant to surrender custody. Mrs. Fernlee fawned over him for few minutes, and then put him down, so that the puppy could reunite with his mother and six siblings. All of the litter family members seemed very happy to have him back.

Alice then related to Mrs. Fernlee the story of how she found the puppy out on the street at midnight. She did not relate the full story of the van attack on Hannah.

"Mrs. Fernlee, this puppy is now very dear to me. I do want to purchase him."

"Number Seven is the smallest of the litter, but he is definitely *not* the 'runt of the litter.' Because he is a bit smaller, he was able to get through a small hole in our fence, and then have a walk about. I am sorry to say that we did not notice that he was gone until Saturday morning. And then we couldn't find him. Thank heavens you found him before he got hit by a car!"

Hannah, Aaron, and Alice all looked at each other. Mrs. Fernlee picked up on it.

"Was he hit by a car? Did you find him injured? He looks fine, but I did not check him closely."

"He was not injured. He is perfect. Hannah and my sister and I were walking on Newcastle Street on Friday night. A van was driving too fast and recklessly. It almost ran into us. The puppy jumped on to the fender of the van and barked bravely at the driver. It clearly startled or frightened the driver, who then turned tail and disappeared into the night. My sister was injured in all the turmoil, but we are all right. And so, we must have him! Please. I am very happy to pay for him."

"Oh, what a terrible night. Of course, you must have him. He is yours and you may not pay for him. He is a present. A Christmas present! But I must tell you, puppy number seven has been a gift almost from the moment he was born. He is exceptionally bright and quick. Very affectionate and attentive. And all heart. The biggest puppies in the litter do not dare to challenge him. Or maybe once. But never a second time. I will give you a set of printed instructions which I give to all my customers listing his pedigree, the very best, and his care and feeding."

The puppy ran back to Alice and practically jumped back into her arms.

"Alice, it is obvious that he is now your dog. Forever. He is now four months old. We have not named him, because the owners usually name the puppies themselves when they pick them up. Do you have a name in mind?"

"I do. 'Shadow.' I thought he was a shadow when I first caught a glimpse of him last Friday night, and now he follows me around, like my shadow. And, of course, he is dark and grey like a shadow."

"'Shadow' it shall be. I will note it on his record. I do have one request. We ask that our customers try to bring all our dogs back here every four months for the first two or three years, so that we can reconnect with them and check on them. They are like our children, and especially Shadow!"

"Not a problem at all. We live in London and welcome the opportunity to reconnect with you!"

Alice knew that Amanda was healing. And she knew that her big sister was depressed. But she also knew how to cheer her up. As soon as Alice arrived back home, she and Shadow cornered Mrs. Haythornwaite for a sort of "girl-to-girl" talk. Alice related her Cheer Up Amanda Plan. Mrs. Haythornwaite agreed one hundred percent and added a few new twists of her own to make a good plan even better.

About fifteen minutes later, Mrs. Haythornwaite and Alice called Captain Haythornwaite in his office. He, too, agreed with the plan.

No more than ten minutes later Captain Haythornwaite called Air Commander Donald Bennet, the soon to be named Group Commander of No. 8 Group, the new Pathfinder Force at Bomber Command, and extended a Christmas Day dinner Invitation to two particular young *Mosquito* pilots under Bennett's Command. Commander Bennet assured Captain Haythornwaite that he would take care of it.

A Hannah Update for Sarah

23 December 1942 Afternoon, London

After Hannah was settled into the housekeeper's quarters in Robert's house, he told the threesome that he was heading off to a meeting. He suggested that maybe they could all go to lunch. He handed Hannah a twenty pound note with a big smile. They loved the suggestion.

Robert knew that he had promised Sarah a full report on the Hannah situation, and that his report might not be entirely well received. But Sarah had put the matter in his lap, and he handled it as best he could, taking into consideration the best result for Hannah. So, he went off to her office at MI5. She was sitting there, in uniform, reading reports. She did seem happy to see him.

"I had been hoping to hear from you. Please sit down and tell all!"

"Yes, Ma'am. Retired US Navy Lt. Johnston ready to Report to his Superior Officer!"

Sarah laughed. "Only slightly superior!"

"Before I relate the current news on Hannah, I do want to confirm that you and I have a dinner date for tomorrow night, a Christmas Eve dinner and concert."

"We do indeed. But it promises to be a cold night. You may be forced to warm me up. Care and feeding of your superior officer!"

"Yes. I think I can provide that for you. Here is the story on Hannah. It is pretty complicated, so bear with me. The meeting on Monday afternoon went very well. As reported, by everyone, she is quite impressive. Thoughtful, refined, elegant, charming, well turned out, as they say, and exceedingly intelligent and well informed. Deeply and emotionally buried up to her eyeballs in the European refugee problems. Incredibly, she is the young woman I met two years ago in the London Underground bomb shelter.

"I expect that you will meet her yourself very soon. But I will get back to that. As an aside, it did occur to me that she could be a valuable asset for MI6 or for our US Intelligence group. In order to pursue the US Visa for her, I contacted Ellen in New York City, and Ellen's father, who is not personally involved in the refugee situation but has numerous contacts who are involved. They have many Jewish connections. They both spoke with Hannah at great length two days ago by radio telephone. They were plenty impressed, too. Ellen's father is chasing the US Visa, but we three would also prefer to find some safe way to keep her here in London. Her life here is now all that she has in the world. Ellen insisted that I move Hannah temporarily into the housekeeper's quarters in my house—the law firm's house where I stay. Hannah liked the idea, as did Dr. Solomon, Inspector Dunbar and the Hawkins and Haythornwaite families. So, we moved her in today."

Sarah looked at him and her jaw literally fell open. She did not say anything for a few moments, and then she spoke deliberately.

"Robert, I am trying to connect the dots here. And there are lots of dots to connect. You enlisted Ellen, your separated wife? And her father? They have Jewish connections? And Hannah has moved in with you? For a man who is always so focused on problems having global repercussions, it appears that you have taken a relatively small very local problem, that you never even heard of until last Sunday, and suddenly clutched it, and Hannah, too, I guess, quite firmly to your breast. I am very surprised. Perhaps I need a little background?"

"I certainly have not, and never would, "clutch Hannah" to my anything. She is two-hundred percent safe with me."

"Oh, Robert. I am so sorry. I did not mean it that way, at all. Sorry. Sorry. Sorry. You are the finest man around. And everyone knows this. I just mean that you have taken on someone else's problem, and made it your own, when you have your plate full already."

"Background, Sarah. You do need background. My wife's father is Doctor Daniel Finerman, a very distinguished New York City neurologist. He is Jewish by background. I don't think he actively practices his faith. He has been somewhat involved in the Jewish refugee problem in the States. He himself is not a big player, but he has some friends who are. Ellen's mother is a Methodist, born and bred. And Ellen was raised in the Methodist Church, as were our children.

"But, because of her father's Jewish background, and the fact that she is half-Jewish, and the way the Nazis have been treating the Jews in Berlin, she came absolutely unglued. She insisted that we leave Berlin and move to London. Which we did. Then a few months later she announced that the four of us were returning to New York City.

"I recoiled as well, and as much, at the Nazi nightmare, but each of us chose an entirely different course of action in response. Ellen chose flight. She resolved to get as far away as possible. She even talked about moving our family to Australia. Her father talked her out of that. I, on the other hand, chose to fight. I resolved to stay as close to the action as I can, and as involved in the action as I can be, in all manners and ways to destroy those Nazis butchers.

"My views and my stance were not well received. Ellen had a fit, and to punish me she insisted that we separate. She said, 'I do not approve of what you are doing, but it is your life. If you want to devote your life and your soul to this horrible war, then go ahead. But I am out. For the sake of our children, we will not divorce. Maybe we can reconcile after the war, if you, Robert, survive the war.'

"The issue of rescuing Hannah from some British anti-Semite pushed all of Ellen's buttons. It was a perfect storm. And so, too, it pushed all her father's buttons. It is they who have 'adopted' Hannah, not me, although I do admire Hannah. And just to make things more entangled, our daughter is almost the same age as Hannah, and in college, and many of her college friends are Jewish, and involved in the refugee problem. So now my daughter is also involved. I am most definitely tangled in a web. But that's really okay. If Hannah has lost her parents, and her younger brother, as I suspect in this case, she now has some replacements. And she would be a very welcome addition to our family, be she Jewish, a Methodist, or Hindu, or Buddhist. But being Jewish does make for a better fit in this case."

Sarah's mood was now much lighter.

"A fascinating story, Robert. I have known from the beginning of our relationship that you and Ellen are formally separated, but I never had the full picture. Does she know of our relationship? And of our intimacy?"

"Yes, and no. She knows that you and I work together, and she knows that you and I are very close. She also knows that you brought the Hannah situation to me. She does *not* know of our intimacy, as you put it. She has never asked. And she never will. If she were to ask, of course I would tell her. We don't keep secrets from each other. Ellen and I did agree that we would both 'date' and all that entails. I am very proud of my relationship with you, Sarah. Who knows? Our relationship might help both of us survive this war."

Sarah smiled. "This has been our best conversation ever. And I now have a lot of respect for your separated wife. I can see from that photograph you have of her that she is what you Americans call 'a fox.' And she has clearly outfoxed you and me, my dear. With Hannah 'safely ensconced' in your home, you and I no longer have our getaway place. A very cleverly well-placed 'little fox to guard the hen house!'

"Hmm. Never even thought about that. Maybe you are right. Sarah, you and I have grown very close. We're a good team. You have the brains and the body, and I have the food and the wine. But Hannah will never keep us apart. If something is going to pull we two apart, it will be the winds of war, or James, or Ellen—not Little Brown Fox Hannah. Not ever. Anyway, no worries for Christmas Eve—you and I have a swell room booked at The Savoy!"

"Oh, Robert. My hero!"

"Ellen might have been trying to slip a hook to me. Bill might have told Ellen your code name, and that might have raised her hackles. But that would be out of character for her. Bill wants to meet you, of course. No way! But the hook I gave Ellen is a lot bigger. The Saga of Hannah now has her hooked. The desperate plight of Hannah and all those refugees, having now been brought vividly to her attention, and personalized by Hannah, will force Ellen to stop ignoring this war, and all of its terrible consequences. Now Ellen will have to engage. And when Ellen engages, she is all in!"

65

Christmas Eve 1942

24 December 1942, London

At 9:30 a.m. on Christmas Eve day, Hannah came upstairs, at Robert's request, to join him for a hardy English breakfast of eggs, bread, processed meat products, cheese, coffee and tea. They discussed the events of the past several days. Hannah talked about her long phone call with Ellen, Dr. Finerman, and Aaron. They had all bonded, which was a real emotional lift for a fairly depressed Hannah. She needed some cheering up. Robert asked about her plans for the day.

"Hannah, not to intrude on your privacy, but I have an invitation for your consideration. It may seem odd. I do not know you very well. Feel free to say 'no.' Christmas Eve is special to me. A time when everybody gets a warm feeling of good cheer and fellowship. And I also have a great love of classical Christmas music. I have invited my good friend Lt. Sarah Leach to join me for an early dinner, and then we plan to go on to a Christmas Eve caroling and music service at St. Paul's Cathedral. It's mostly just beautiful music, not really much of a religious service. We would very much like you to join us tonight, if that would not be uncomfortable for you? I can definitely promise a good meal!"

Hannah did not miss a beat, and her delighted smile was a very clear signal that she hoped to accept, perhaps with a slight reservation. "That is a wonderful invitation, but are you sure I would not be imposing on your private dinner with your lady friend?"

"No, no. Not at all. She is very excited to meet you. In fact, it was she who brought your situation to my attention, with a request for help."

"Really, I wonder why she came to you?"

"It is a circuitous tale. Sarah's father is a decorated Royal Navy Captain, very involved in military intelligence. His very close friend is Royal Navy Captain Spencer Haythornwaite. Amanda and Alice Haythornwaite were very concerned about your situation, and so their father called Captain Leach, knowing that Captain Leach's daughter, my friend Sarah, an MI5 agent, has good connections with Scotland Yard. Ergo Inspector Dunbar. She then came to me as a possible channel to a US Visa for you. Anyway, it is a long story. The short version is that she is absolutely dying to have dinner with you, and I am absolutely dying to hear some classical Christmas music. So, will you accept?"

"I will. And, thank you so much. Although my family is Jewish, and attended regular services at our synagogue in Dresden, I have on occasion gone to church services with Christian friends, both here and in Dresden. And Christmas music does fill the air in both Dresden and in London during Christmas season, so it has seeped into my bone marrow, as well. May I ask, as you are now my 'Host Family,' would you mind if I were to head out shortly just for a few hours this afternoon to meet some friends?"

"Not at all. Let's reconnect here at 5:00 pm, and then go together for dinner. Would you like to invite Dr. Solomon to join us tonight? A very impressive young fellow, who seems keen to keep an eye on you!"

"Yes, he does, doesn't he? It probably seems odd to you but having him around is pretty comforting to me. He keeps watch on my medical recovery, but now he seems to have taken an interest in my Jewish history education. Maybe that's not a bad idea. My education has been sidelined for the past few years and I can learn a lot from him. I do like him. I will call on him at the hospital today, as I plan to check up on poor Amanda. Thank you!"

When Hannah and Robert met up again at 5:00 p.m., Hannah had some good news.

"Dr. Solomon was able to put a cast on Amanda's arm today, and she is relieved to go home at last. It is a little ironic, I guess, because she and the Haythornwaite family, including Amanda and Alice, intend to visit that very hospital tomorrow, as it is their custom, to bring Christmas gifts and cheer to the wounded servicemen. They are such nice people. And they invited me to join them, if that is all right with you. Dr. Solomon finishes his rounds today at 4:00 p.m., and he happily accepted your invitation. He will meet us at dinner."

At 5:30 pm, Robert headed out the door into the cold night, with his new charming houseguest following closely behind him, he could not avoid the memory of those days in 1938, before Ellen and the children returned to New York City, of the pleasure he felt at walking out that same door, on the way to some restaurant or somewhere with his then sixteen-year-old daughter Nancy following closely behind. That mystical bond between a father and a daughter. Hard to define. Hard to replace. Hard to forget.

They arrived at the small, private restaurant that Robert often used for his mostly business dinners. As he was one of their best long-term customers, this restaurant always took good care of him. They followed all the rationing rules, but they did have a few good items squirreled away for their best customers. Although those items were also pricey. As this was a Christmas Eve dinner and noting that Robert was squiring the very attractive young WREN officer who frequently comes to dinner with him, they did their best to lay a nice table. They also particularly liked this young WREN officer because, unlike some of the British well born, she did not look down her nose on the wait staff. On the contrary, she always inquired as to the health of their families. And it was very evident that her kindness and consideration of others was second nature to her.

Aaron was the third to arrive. He was wearing his RAF uniform, and looked very dapper. He thanked Robert for the kind invitation, and sat down next to Hannah, opposite from Robert. A few moments later, Sarah arrived, also in uniform. Robert realized that in this time of global war, with Britain fighting for its very survival, they were very proud of their military service, and anxious to show off their uniforms. Robert felt almost ashamed to be in civvies, like he was ducking his patriotic duty. He was now giving more thought to Bill Donovan's persistent request that Robert rejoin the US Navy, with a promotion in rank to Commander. He would outrank Sarah!

Sarah gave a big hello to Aaron. "I have heard so much about you from Robert. He calls you, 'The Inspector General of RAF Pilot Training.' Good for you! And, Hannah, what a great honor to meet you. So very sorry about your terrible encounters with some mysterious mad man, but you should be safer staying with Robert."

Before she sat down at the table, Sarah walked over to the owner and the wait staff, as she always did. She asked about their families. She wished them Merry Christmas. They really appreciated the attention. Robert sat watching her. He adored her good manners and good breeding. But it gave him mixed emotions. It brought back powerful memories of Ellen. Her good manners. Her good breeding. Her gracious consideration always for the feelings of others. In that regard they were carbon copies. Class shows. It always shows! Yet, when they both came face-to-face with this all-engulfing war, Sarah went nose-to-nose with it, just like little Shadow, while Ellen turned tail, literally fled back home to New York City and figuratively hid under her bed, waiting until it all just went away. Like a childhood nightmare.

And in that fleeting moment of scrambled thoughts, he looked at Hannah and Aaron, and somehow knew that, because of them, and most particularly because of Hannah, the increasingly desperate plight of the Jewish refugees would give immediacy and a very human face to the grim horrors that Ellen had witnessed in her days in the Third Reich, and she, too, would become involved. But it would take some time. People do change their minds about things, all kinds of things. But change does take time.

Sarah sat down, and asked Hannah about her experiences in London. A lively discussion ensued. After the meal, the foursome bundled up and headed out into the night. It was cold and dark, but it was Christmas Eve, so there were plenty of folks out for socializing, eating, drinking, and celebrating. Everyone just sort of assumed that the Germans would not dare bomb London on Christmas Eve.

They made their way to St. Paul's, found seats together, and sat down. Lots of people there hoping to hear some uplifting music. And they did. The program included:

Profofie by Troika

A Festive Sleigh-ride by Mendelsson

Hark the Herald Angels Sing, Whitacre, Little Tree, to a Poem by E.E. Cummings, Britten

A Ceremony of Carols by Bach

Christmas Oratorio, ironically celebrating about the circumcision of Jesus, by Tchaikovsky

Nutcracker, ironically about toy soldiers, by Holy Hutchinson

Symphony of Carols and *The Holly and the Ivy*, including old favorites, and *L'Enfance du Christ* by Berlioz.

Robert was enjoying Sarah's company immensely, but he was particularly focused on the reactions of Hannah and Aaron. Especially Hannah. And he was not disappointed. She was clearly engrossed in the beautiful music. As was Aaron. They both sat quietly. Listening closely. Enchanted. Robert noticed that Hannah had taken Aaron's hand. So, he took Sarah's hand. After all, it was Christmas Eve 1942.

After the concert, Aaron took Hannah to the Haythornwaite home, where Hannah had been invited to spend the night. Robert took Sarah to a charming and elegant room at The Savoy Hotel for a special Christmas treat.

Maybe Ellen wasn't so clever after all.

Queen Victoria Hospital Christmas Day

25 December 1942, London

In keeping with its annual Christmas tribute, Princess Mary's Royal Air Force Nursing Service (PMRAFNS) had arranged a small Christmas celebration for the sick and wounded RAF Pilots stuck in the hospital. Wandering around the wards were a number of the nurses in civilian attire and quite a few very well-dressed London families. As usual, there were plenty of cookies, small gifts and cider. A great deal of good cheer all around.

The newly wounded Amanda was there, her arm in a new cast and a new sling, plus both of her parents, Alice and Hannah. And Shadow, which was clearly a violation of strict hospital rules. But all agreed that Shadow was above the law. The Haythornwaite group made the rounds, spreading lots of smiles and laughs. Alice was becoming a little annoyed that a number of the handsome young pilots were showing a lot more attention to the puppy than to the three lovely ladies. But the little dog reminded them of home and family. So, she just bit her lip.

Todd and Ben, the two wounded pilots who had spent the previous Christmas talking to Captain Haythornwaite, were long ago healed and returned to flying. But there were many newly wounded RAF pilots in their place.

Amanda noticed that this Christmas, in addition to all the civilians, there was a small group of hale and hearty young RAF Pilots in crisp uniforms, none of whom appeared to be sick or wounded, also spreading out and talking with the pilots who were patients. She thought that was a nice gesture by the brass at Bomber Command. Then someone tapped on her shoulder. She turned around, and there was Lt. Charles "Chad" Clarke.

"Hello Amanda. I did not realize that, in addition to being the best nurse ever, you are also a wounded combat veteran! Good for you! I hope you took down a few Jerries before they got you!"

"Chad! What a wonderful surprise. I was not expecting to see you here today. Has your beloved Butcher Harris now become Mother Harris?"

Amanda was well aware of Bomber Harris' fearsome reputation.

That got a big laugh.

"I wish! It was a kind and generous call from your father that "sprang" Harry and me from a night raid so that he and I could join your family for a Christmas dinner tonight. A very welcome treat for us. In fact, Commander Bennett thought it such a good idea to have some 'fit-for-service' pilots stop in here today to spread some cheer that he asked an additional ten pilots to join us, and he himself is here. I have to tell you, Amanda, Bennett is not the most popular of Group Commanders among the RAF brass because he always seems so aloof, but he is one of the most revered Group Commander by all the Air Crews. He is the straightest of straight shooters. It would be an honor for me to introduce you to him."

Amanda and Chad headed over to meet Group Commander Bennett. On the way, Amanda looked around for Alice. She saw her across the ward, talking to one of the non-patient pilots, who was holding Shadow. It was Harry! Chad followed her gaze.

"My young friend Harry has rediscovered your sister. Harry is not a womanizer. He regards himself as the consummate gentleman, in the image of Superman, I guess, straight out of Action Comic Book Number One! Sometimes we even call him Kal-El, Superman's Krypton name, or Clark Kent. But, unfortunately for Harry, your sister arrived today with Kryptonite. Harry loves, loves, loves dogs. Alice plus a puppy is like ham and cheese, ice cream and cake, or steak and potatoes. I have never seen Harry make such a beeline to a woman."

Amanda laughed. "Good for Alice. She's no dummy. Maybe she will catch an RAF Pilot Glamour Boy of her very own!"

"Harry is more of a Gremlin than a Glamour Boy. But he is an exceptional pilot and a true gentleman. That counts for something these days."

At the opposite end of the ward, the four on-call doctors moved quietly into the room. Once again, Dr. Archibald McIndoe, Dr. Conegy, Dr. Smith and Dr. Solomon were present. All in their signature white coats. They separated and began making rounds. Shortly thereafter, Dr. Solomon found himself standing next to Hannah, and Hannah lit up like a candle to see him. She knew that it would be inappropriate to betray their personal relationship in the medical setting. Aaron quietly guided Hannah over to a corner of the ward that was ten or twelve feet away from the others who were milling about, where they could talk.

"Hannah, thank you for last night. A wonderful Christmas Eve, even for two people who do not celebrate Christmas. And how nice of you to come again this Christmas Day to cheer up our wounded pilots."

"Thank you for being my escort last night. That was wonderful. The music was inspiring. And here we find ourselves together again today. Probably the only two Jews in this crowd of happy Christians celebrating their most cherished day."

"Actually, Hannah, that is not entirely true. I do know for a fact that there are at least seven other members of our faith here today in hospital beds suffering from air combat injuries in the RAF. I'm sure there are more, because some Jewish RAF, and Allied Air Forces Pilots, tend to keep their faith to themselves. These RAF and Allied Air Forces started out in 1939 and 1940 as an elitist middle- and upper-class British clubs, with only a small number of Jews and other outsiders allowed. But that number grows each year, as the war grinds on.

"Seeing you here today reminds me that we first met one year ago, here, on Christmas Day 1941. As I look at you one year later, and think back to my memories of that day, I can see you have changed. I know that this was a very difficult year for you, in many ways, but you seem so much stronger and more confident. Forgive me, please, for saying but I am so proud of you, and what you stand for, and what you have been through. You inspire me to stand tall beside you. Thank you!"

Crowd be damned. Hannah hugged Aaron. And held the hug for several minutes. People hug at Christmas. No one noticed, or even cared.

Hannah suggested that they meet some of the wounded Jewish pilots. On the way, they passed three pilots from the Caribbean Islands in beds next to each other. Aaron stopped to greet them.

"Hannah, meet Lt. Weeks of Barbados, a *Spitfire* pilot, Lt. Kelsick of Montserrat, a *Typhoon* pilot, and Lt. Dowdy of Montserrat, a bomber pilot. The RAF has almost 500 Caribbean pilots and crewmen. And unlike the US, our crews are integrated."

Several hours later, the Haythornwaite family, plus Shadow, now a part of the family, plus Hannah, Lt. Charles "Chad" Clarke, and Lt. Harry Noble, all arrived together at the Haythornwaite home at promptly 4:00 pm on Christmas afternoon. The house was bright with lights, decorations, and a large Christmas tree. The tree was a gift from their good friends, Sir Reginald Bullock and Lady Sandra Bullock, from the Bullock Estate garden. The couple that Hannah had met at the Haythornwaite house back in October 1941, shortly after the waning days and nights of the Blitz.

There were also several large tables with plentiful food and drink. Quite a spread for a Christmas buffet. The always very hungry *Mosquito* pilots, Chad and Harry, headed straight for the food and drink. It was their culture as well as their biology. The three young ladies noticed right away and had a good laugh about it.

Alice commented, "Glamour Boys' Priority List: Drink, Food, Dogs, then *maybe* Female Companions." They all laughed.

The ladies chatted together, waiting somewhat impatiently for the fly boys to return to their female company. Eventually, they did. Even Hannah was amazed to hear their stories of *Spitfire* and *Hurricane* derring do, shooting down those overconfident Luftwaffe bullies. But to their mild annoyance, "the boys" then began to gravitate from the drink and the food and the ladies, over to British Royal Navy Captain Haythornwaite, and they were talking with him about airplanes and combat aerial maneuvers. And Shadow was nestled happily into Harry's left arm. Fickle dog!

The Captain was regaling "the boys" with tales of Supermarine Seafire *Spitfires*, Hawker Sea *Hurricanes*, the U.S. *Corsairs*, and the new U.S. experimental *Hellcats*. "The boys" were spellbound. The Captain was impressed by these two seasoned and polished gentlemen pilots. He thought that Chad was a Wise Owl, and Harry was a Fearless Bulldog. His daughters had chosen well!

But the girls were now annoyed.

Amanda looked at her sister. "Alice, my wonderful young sister, your Glamour Boys' Priority List has been amended. It is now 'Drink, Food, Dogs, Airplanes and Aerial Tactics, and—maybe never—Female Companions!' This is ridiculous. Let's go and butt in. It's bad enough to bring fellows home or watch them fall for your mother. But these big dopes have fallen for our father! They love dogs and fighter planes. So, the one thing they absolutely cannot and will not ignore, is a Dog Fight. We must move in like a Female Fighter Squadron. Hannah, you take on Father. I'll go for Chad. Alice, you close in on Harry and Shadow.

"Form up F Squadron. Attack!"

67

Two Telex Messages from NYC

28 December 1942, London

When Robert arrived at his Office on 28 December, there were two Telex messages waiting for him. The first was from Dr. Finerman, Ellen's father.

"Happy Holidays from New York! I hope you had a nice Christmas with your British friends. It is clear that you have formed strong bonds there, but we do very much look forward to your return home. I have been giving a great deal of thought to the late-night attacks on Hannah Hanauer. The story does not add up. There are too many facts that just don't fit into the British anti-Semitic scenario. If the attacker is a British anti-Semite, as has been postulated, going after Hannah because she has been speaking out in support of admitting more Jews in Britain, then why her? There are quite a number of senior Jewish superstars in Britain advocating those views. With all due respect, in that crowd, Hannah would be an afterthought. And for that attacker, or that group, to kill her, Heaven Forbid! That would be highly counterproductive. Then too, this pattern of 'lying in wait' for her to come home, and then trying to run her down with a muddy delivery van, is highly irrational behavior, so poorly designed to accomplish its purpose.

In both attacks, the driver delivered an expletive in German. It was postulated that he said, 'Gottverdamant Judin' to hurt her feelings in her native tongue. But he spoke in German the second time, as well, to the young English woman, when he called her 'dummkopf!' This strongly suggests that he was speaking in his native tongue—German. All these factors suggest to me that her attacker is actually a German, and that the reason for his attacks is rooted in Germany, and not in England. I am now very suspicious. Some of the Jews now in New York City who emigrated here from Germany before the war do have roots in Dresden. I will do some digging and revert. And thank you again for placing her under your protective wing. Best regards, David."

The second Telex message was from Ellen:

"Merry Christmas again, Robert. We all miss you! Father has become very intrigued with the Hannah Hanauer saga. I think he plans to Telex you. I am also intrigued. I hope that you didn't leave her home alone on Christmas Eve and Christmas Day. They can be lonely occasions for Jewish people. I'm sure you did not. Don't know why I even asked. The more I think about it, she is a Prize Catch. Your British Spy Lady Friend was shrewd to bring Hannah to you. She must be one sharp lady. Thank her for me. Can your spy network track down Hannah's family in Dresden? Is she comfortable staying with you? Is that nice Jewish doctor becoming more than a friend to her? I bet so. I am dying for some more news. And your daughter Nancy wants to make Hannah her Official Pen Pal. I assume that is all right. Nancy is also jealous that Hannah spends time with you, and she does not. I sense some vicarious motive in the Pen Pal Endeavor. As you know, Nancy does worship you. News please! With affection, Ellen."

68

New Year's Eve 1942

31 December 1942, London

Robert received an invitation to join Lt. General Ira Eaker and his wife and other US and UK Military big wigs for a private dinner party. Eaker's new best friend, Bomber Harris, and his wife were coming. Robert knew two things. He obviously had to go, and he obviously could not take Sarah. It would not have been his first choice for a New Year's Eve party, but it was an honor for him to be invited.

Maybe it was just as well. New Year's Eve had turned out to be a disjointed affair.

Hannah was heading off with all the girls to join the party scene up in Essex. There Hannah would find plenty of dashing US and RAF pilots, beautiful 'Essex Girls,' ample and tasty libations and canapes, lively Big Band Music and energetic dancing. Hannah said she would "probably be home late tonight and sleep late in the morning." Hannah mentioned to Robert that Aaron was on duty at the hospital that night, leaving Hannah free as the proverbial "British bird".

Sarah was not happy to be abandoned by Robert on New Year's Eve, but all her Spook and Duke buddies were gathering at The Old Bell Tavern, so she would not be alone. Far from it. And Robert did promise to join her later.

The dinner party given by the Eakers was one of those fancy military black tie affairs. Most men were in their senior military officer formal attire. And there would be many young Air Force enlisted personnel, mostly male, "catering" the affair. The wives, all seasoned veterans of the Senior Military Wives Clubs on the bases, would have great fun visiting with each other, each sipping a cocktail.

The men hobnobbed amongst themselves, each having a cocktail also provided by the enlisted man bartender, Dirk. Dirk had learned from experience that senior US officers like their drinks "hard." A mark of their manhood. And he had also learned that the senior British officers like their drinks Hard and Fast, "keep 'em coming."

After a long cocktail hour, they all sat down at a long table at 9 pm to start the dinner service. During the appetizer course, mostly hearty bean soup and a salad, there were a few short speeches. Then, as the wait staff was serving the entrée, Dover sole with vegetables, Ira Eaker, called for everyone's attention.

"This has been a very difficult year. Perhaps a year of transition from an end to a lot of losing to the beginning of a fair amount of winning. I suggest we go around the table to ask each man, and any woman who wishes to chip in, for a toast to anyone or anything during the year who deserves a 'Thank You!'"

Everyone thought that was a super idea. They were all anxious for their turns to toast.

As usual, Arthur 'Bomber' Harris, certainly the "Biggest Personality in the Room," spoke first.

"I for one want to toast the growing role of technology. Our good friends at Operations Research have helped us immensely to carry out our critical bombing assignments over Germany. Hats off to Director Patrick Blackett, sitting here with us tonight with his charming wife, for his scientific and mathematical achievements. 'Technology is the future of Warfare!'"

Tooey Spaatz, was next.

"RAF Fighter Command was first in my mind. A toast to them! Against all odds, they held the line for us. For all of us. The first major defeat suffered by the Third Reich! Those beautiful *Spitfires* are now legendary. But we all know that the burly *Hurricanes* did a lot of the dirty work!"

Next up was Patrick Blackett.

"Perhaps it is a bit self-serving for me, but I would like to toast the British Admiralty. The best in the world. Other military units have had their great flashes of brilliance, of course, for which they richly deserve enormous praise. But the Admiralty, our Royal Navy Battle Fleet, is there for us every moment of every day in every way."

Robert Lovett, the US Assistant Secretary of War for Air, was next in the line-up. A Navy combat pilot from WWI, he was instrumental in setting up the US Army Air Forces, and in choosing Hap Arnold as Chief of US Army Air Forces. Lovett was visiting London, and so of course, Eaker invited him to dinner.

"I want to offer a special toast to the British Government and the British people. They fought on for the rest of Europe, and for the entire world, really, until others, like the recalcitrant US, finally got their act together. We can see the world order and the British Empire changing and evolving before our eyes, but this tough little Island stood very tall and defended us all. Hail Britannia!"

Big Cheers for that one, all around.

David Bennet stood next.

"A toast to the USA. It did take them a while to awaken, too long really. Nobody is perfect! But when the USA did *finally* 'spring to life,' thanks to a stiff kick in the butt by Emperor Hirohito and a not-too-subtle push over the proverbial cliff from Adolf Hitler, spring to life they did! Here come the Yanks! And thank God for them!"

Many roaring cheers around the table.

Robert Johnston then rose.

"A toast to the British Intelligence Agencies. They usually do not wear the flashy uniforms always adorning our dazzling RAF and Royal Navy Comrades, and our very dapper US Army Air Force fliers, because the military intelligence job description requires that they be low key, out of the spotlight. Still and all, our ever-vigilant dear friends and allies in MI5 and MI6 also deserve a big thank you. I have repeatedly seen them in action, and they are awesome. MI5 is ably represented here tonight by no less than the Boss, Sir David Petrie, DG of MI5. His counterpart at MI6, Sir Stewart Menzies, is no doubt off somewhere on a very Secret and very Critical Mission, or else at Chequers with the prime minister."

"More likely enjoying a very ample dinner at Chequers with our very ample prime minister!" interrupted the irrepressible, sometimes inappropriate, Bomber Harris with a big laugh.

Robert continued, "So I propose my toast this evening to your British Secret Service. Stealthy stoics, who ply their trade so very ably in dark and shadowy inner sanctums, with dark and sinister saboteurs, all throughout this messy and murky war. And with my toast, I offer a promise. When this war is finally over, and the true tales of MI5 and MI6 are finally revealed, you will be *dazzled*."

The dinner guests shouted, "Hear! Hear!" with many quiet smiles and knowing glances.

David Petrie, one of those stealthy stoics himself, then took the floor.

"Thank you, Robert, for those flattering words. Your own US Military Intelligence operations, now called the OSS, are coming along brilliantly. Aided, I hope, by your very close liaison with our agents." He cast a subtle glance in Robert's direction. "You may regard my toast today as a bit odd, or perhaps over the line, in this setting here tonight. If it offends you, I ask for forgiveness. I want to toast the Soviet Union."

Silence settled in the dining room.

"At enormous cost in human life, and human sacrifice beyond comprehension, the Russians have thrown us a much-needed lifeline. For the past eighteen months, they have been pinning down, chewing up and spitting out the cream of the German Army and Air Forces. Saving us from that grizzly task and saving us from that excruciating sacrifice. So, to our fearsome Allies. The Soviet Union and her long-suffering people!"

All stood up to toast.

The honor of having the final word fell to the Host, Lieutenant General Ira Clarence Eaker, from Field Creek, Texas, just named Commander of the US Eighth Air Force.

"The last seven toasts are a tough act to follow. But I will try. My toast is to RAF Bomber Command. They are taking the war into the heart of Germany. Every day. And paying a very high cost for doing it. But someone does have to do it. To Bomber Harris and his fine wife, who we are honored to have with us tonight, and to the brave pilots and crews of Bomber Command. Thank you, and God bless you!"

Again, a standing toast from the entire table.

General Eaker then asked if any of the wives present would offer a toast. Three did.

Mrs. Spaatz, Ruth, offered a toast to Winston Churchill.

Mrs. Blackett, Constanza Bayon, toasted to FDR.

Mrs. Harris, Jillie, his second wife, lifted her glass to Lord Beaverbrook and Baronet Freeman.

"To Lord Beaverbrook, William Maxwell Aitken, Former Minister of Aircraft Production, and then Minister of Supply, and also to Air Chief Marshall Sir Wilfred Rhodes Freeman, Vice Chief of the Air Ministry. Without our own crusty and grumpy 1st Lord Beaverbrook, and our very eloquent and elegant Baronet Freeman, we would surely have run out of RAF fighter planes and bombers long ago."

It was a rousing dinner party.

At 11 pm, Robert thanked the host and hostess, said his good nights and Happy New Years, and quietly slipped out.

He made a beeline for The Old Bell Tower and arrived just in time to give a New Year's kiss to Sarah.

At 1 am, as previously planned, they headed out together for a private celebration at Robert's house. When they got comfortable, Robert asked, "Were your ears burning around 10 pm?"

Sarah thought a minute, and said, "Yes. The left ear."

"That's odd. I wonder if that was because I was only half talking about you?"

Sarah thought, and said, "No. It was because RAF Captain Guilfoyle was only nibbling on my left ear!"

She laughed.

Robert wasn't quite sure if she was joking. He said, "You are *so* Delilah!"

The End of the Beginning … and to be Continued

Author's Note

Some Long-Forgotten Truths About WWII:

- In 1940 and '41, the US State Department advised the White House that the US should not provide significant assistance to Great Britain because they believed that Great Britain could not survive.
- Threats of a German invasion of England were highly exaggerated.
- Deputy Fuhrer Rudolf Hess really did fly to Scotland in an ME 110 hoping to strike a peace deal with King George VI.
- The US had virtually no significant air force at the beginning of the War.
- The US had very limited intelligence gathering and interpretation capability in the beginning of the War.
- RAF Bomber Command was consuming 65% of the total British War budget, but for many years was totally unable to make a meaningful impact on the Axis war effort.
- Pilot and fight crew young age and limited training were huge problems for RAF Bomber Command, particularly during the early years of the War, contributing to the losses of one-sixth of aircraft and crews on every mission.
- Churchill Advisor Frederick Lindemann did commission young David Butt to study the effectiveness of Bomber Command, and his study did find that Bomber Command was largely ineffectual in the early years of the war.
- British code breaking successes were an overwhelming factor in virtually all aspects of the War.
- Both President Roosevelt and Prime Minister Churchill did send warnings to Stalin about the impending German invasion of Russia, which were apparently totally ignored by the Kremlin.
- The British government was highly conflicted about allowing Jews to emigrate to Palestine because of overwhelming Arab-state objections (when the United Nations voted to establish the state of Israel in 1947, Great Britain abstained).
- There was significant anti-Semitism in Great Britain and other allied countries.

- In a number of reported instances, German Jews were actually thrown out of British underground bomb shelters during air raids.
- The damage caused by the Luftwaffe bombing of Great Britain was relatively minor when compared to the devastating damage to Germany caused by the combined forces of RAF Bomber Command and the US 8th Air Force.
- As part of the Top-Secret Manhattan Project, a team led by Enrico Fermi, a physics professor at Columbia University, did design and build Chicago Pile-1, which became critical (meaning that each fission event releases a sufficient number of neutrons to sustain an ongoing series of reactions) on December 2, 1942. It was the world's first artificial nuclear reactor. This was a vital first step to developing the Atomic Bomb, which was achieved by the Manhattan Project two years later. So ironic. Hitler was desperately seeking a new all-powerful weapon to stave off the Allies. By driving off so many Jewish and other physicists from Axis countries, he effectively gave that weapon to the Allies, even though the discovery of nuclear fission was made by German chemists Otto Hahn and Fritz Strassmann in 1938.